THE ADMIRABLE
COMPANY

THE
ADMIRABLE
COMPANY

Why corporate reputation matters so
much and what it takes to be ranked
among the **BEST**

MICHAEL BROWN AND PAUL TURNER

P

PROFILE BOOKS

First published in Great Britain in 2008 by
Profile Books Ltd
3a Exmouth House
Pine Street
Exmouth Market
London EC1R 0JH
www.profilebooks.com

A CIP catalogue record for this book is available from the British Library.

ISBN 978 1 84668 086 1

Typeset in Stone Serif by MacGuru Ltd
info@macguru.org.uk

Printed and bound in Great Britain by Clays, Bungay, Suffolk

The paper this book is printed on is certified by the © 1996 Forest Stewardship
Council A.C. (FSC). It is ancient-forest friendly. The printer holds FSC chain of custody
SGS-COC-2061

Contents

Authors' note and acknowledgements

The pitfalls of corporate storytelling

There's a challenge in corporate storytelling. Tom Peters and Robert Waterman found this when in their seminal book *In Search of Excellence*[1] they used as examples Atari and Wang, which subsequently failed to demonstrate the authors' eight key learning points. The success of some of the companies in their case studies failed to endure. On several occasions it seemed that no sooner had the company been analysed and often praised than things began to go wrong. We had a similar experience as the fortunes of companies that had been featured in the most admired company surveys changed dramatically from one year to the next.

- Many companies in the banking and financial services sector will have seen their reputations for such things as financial soundness and quality of management plummet as a result of the credit crunch that began in 2007 and the global financial crisis that erupted in 2008 following huge write-offs of sub-prime debt.

- Before the ink had dried on the comments about the success of Cadbury Schweppes, its ratings fell dramatically.

- BP, winner of most admired companies surveys in a wide range of categories, including overall top spot in Britain, revealed that its CEO had been less than forthcoming about his personal affairs. He too resigned.

- BP's arch rival, Shell, which had fluctuated wildly in most admired company surveys and had largely dropped out of the running in recent years, declared record profits in 2008.

- In the months before this book went to press Marks & Spencer, which in 2007 had recovered the ground it had lost since 1997, was experiencing a reverse in its fortunes and its chief executive,

Sir Stuart Rose, was under fire. After its return to the number one position as Britain's most admired company in 2007, Marks & Spencer fell out of the top 20 in 2008 but still scored highly within its industry and in some individual categories.

- As for Enron, rated as the most innovative company in America's most admired company survey by business executives over a number of years and widely praised for its approach to strategy by leading academics ... well, no more needs to be said on this subject.

So we had to decide whether to include specific case studies or simply draw out general trends from appropriate statistical analysis. We chose the former. This was because although the business environment is increasingly complex and all companies experience ups and downs in their fortunes and reputation, it is always instructive to learn from the lessons of the past.

Acknowledgements

The authors would like to thank Stephen Brough for his overall editorial guidance and Penny Williams for her professionalism in getting us through the final stages. We would also like to thank all those who have contributed to the most admired companies surveys over the years, without whom this book would not have been possible.

1

Introduction

Sir Stuart Rose and Steve Jobs had a great deal to be proud of in early 2008. Rose's company Marks & Spencer had been voted as Britain's most admired company in *Management Today*'s annual survey. Across the Atlantic, Jobs's Apple had become America's most admired company in the survey conducted by *Fortune*. Both leaders recognized the business benefits of a good corporate reputation, something that Sir Stuart will have been even more mindful of when Marks & Spencer's fortunes declined in 2008 and the company didn't make the top 20 in Britain's most admired company survey. Sir Clive Thompson, when chief executive of Rentokil, which was Britain's most admired company in 1994, summarized these benefits:

- Customers 'may gain reassurance from the knowledge that they are in good hands'.

- Employees 'can derive great pride from being part of the very best'.

- Shareholders 'can feel reassured that their company has been judged to be the best by a group of highly credible judges'.

- Standing within the local community, 'from whom we want to attract good employees', increases.

- Suppliers 'will potentially enhance their own reputations by such a prestigious award'.[1]

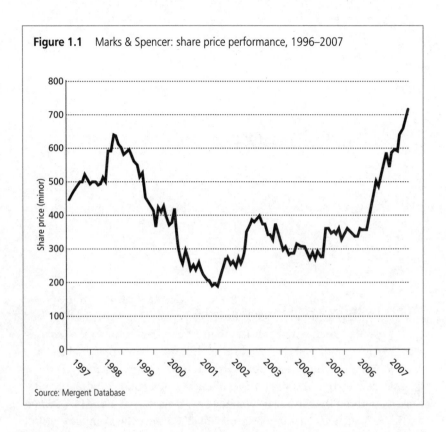

Figure 1.1   Marks & Spencer: share price performance, 1996–2007

Source: Mergent Database

For many companies, according to Charles Fombrun and Cees van Riel, 'a good reputation can act like a magnet. It attracts us to those who have it.'[2]

Fombrun, Professor Emeritus of Management at Stern School of Business, New York University and co-founder of *Corporate Reputation Review,* defines corporate reputation as 'the overall estimation of a firm by its stakeholders'.[3] In some cases, corporate reputation is based on hard facts such as profit and shareholder returns. In others, it is based on perception. 'Ultimately, a good reputation matters because it is a key source of distinctiveness that produces support for the company and differentiates it from rivals.'[4]

Reputation and results

Fortune said in March 1998:

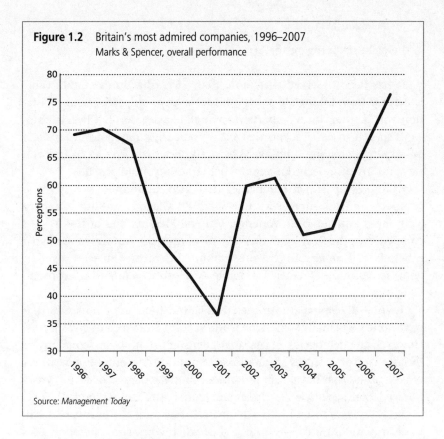

Figure 1.2   Britain's most admired companies, 1996–2007
Marks & Spencer, overall performance

Source: *Management Today*

[In America] a ten year investment in most admired companies from
1987 to 1997 across industrial winners and high growth services
would have returned almost three times the shareholder value of the
Standard & Poor's 500 stocks.

In Britain, companies with better reputations often achieve better
financial results. The close relationship between company performance
and reputation is shown in figures 1.1 and 1.2. British retailer Marks &
Spencer's share price is mirrored in its results in the most admired survey
(its reputational score).

Research has also shown that a good reputation:[5]

• can lead to superior financial performance;

• encourages shareholders to invest in a company;

- attracts good staff;

- helps in retaining customers.

It has been observed that more than 75% of a firm's market value is derived from intangible assets[6] and for many companies their reputation will be their most important intangible asset. As Sir Clive Thompson's speech in 1997 acknowledged, a company's reputation can affect purchasing decisions, employee decisions about whether to engage and stay and investor decisions about whether to buy, hold or sell.[7]

Examples of British companies that have performed well in most admired company surveys include Shell, BP, GlaxoSmithKline, Cadbury Schweppes and Tesco. In America, General Electric, one of the first 12 companies in the Dow Jones Index in 1896, regularly features in the upper echelons of *Fortune*'s annual most admired company surveys together with, for example, Procter & Gamble, Microsoft, Wal-Mart, Exxon and Citigroup.

Toyota, BP, Singapore Airlines, Nokia and BASF are companies that have done particularly well in the world's most admired company surveys. However, the democracy of the surveys ensures that no one company or business sector achieves an unassailable position. Among the diverse set of companies that have been prominent in the surveys are Steve Wynn's Mirage Hotels, the *New York Times* and Manchester United football club.

It takes years to build up a reputation but only the events of a day to destroy it, and it can be a steep slide when corporate reputation goes wrong. Some companies whose corporate reputations fell in most admired company surveys, such as International Harvester, Pan Am and Lonrho, also experienced poor business performance. Sustaining reputation is extremely hard to do.

The information we have on corporate reputation

To answer the question of how companies achieve good reputations, we have looked at the track record of over 1,000 companies which over the past 20 years or so have participated in surveys of the most admired companies in the world conducted by *Management Today*, *Fortune* and *The Economist*. These surveys provide an annual pulse check on corporate reputation and are based on the views, opinions and votes of thousands of business executives. There is probably no better guide to corporate reputation than the views of others in the business world – a peer group that consists of chairmen, chief executives and board members who have offered frank opinions about other companies in their own sector. Industry analysts, management consultants and business commentators are also included in the survey. The result is a unique 360-degree view of how a company is doing from year to year through the eyes of those who should know.

The British survey of most admired companies started in 1990. Over the years more than 600 British companies have participated, first in *The Economist* survey until 1992 and then in *Management Today* from 1994. This survey was regarded as a 'consistent, stable core of world class companies' that seemed always to be on top and the correlation between 'financial performance and admiration is indisputable'.[8] As the years went by, the scope of reputation became broader – innovation was recognized, along with clarity of strategy, quality of management and quality of goods and services.[9]

In America, *Fortune* has run the most admired company awards since 1983. In the early 1980s the American surveys covered around 250 companies. By 1992 the number had increased to 307 and in later years to over 500. By 2007 thousands of managers were responding to the surveys with their views about American companies, the emphasis of which changed from year to year. In 2007 *Fortune* said that 'having fresh ideas and being green were among the qualities that distinguish the year's winners'. In 2006 it said companies that took the long view received a boost and in 2005 that it was the companies that 'avoided commodity hell'. The results of America's most admired company survey reflect a deep and wide view of American economic success over the past two decades.

Since 1997 Hay Group, on behalf of *Fortune*, added a further survey of the world's most admired companies.

These three sources, together with other studies and the views of financial journalists, company reports and accounts, business journals and academic papers provide a foundation on which to base a picture of how corporate reputation is derived, how it is maintained and how it is lost.

In the surveys companies are assessed against a basket of criteria including, in order of importance: the quality of management; financial soundness; quality of products; people and talent management; value as a long-term investment; innovation; marketing; community and environmental responsibility; and the use of corporate assets. In Britain all of these nine categories are surveyed. In America there are eight categories, quality of marketing being subsumed within quality of products. In the world survey, an extra factor – globalness – is added.

By tracking the performance of individual companies against these criteria and over time, it is possible to build up a picture of what works and what doesn't in building and maintaining reputation.

The structure of this book

This book shows how companies achieve a strong corporate reputation through an analysis of the strategies and tactics that have led to them being voted among the most admired companies.

Chapter 2 reviews the results of the three national and international surveys, outlining the winners of the various categories, the sectors that seemed to be strongest over time and the key learning messages from the performance leading companies.

Chapters 3–11 offer a comparative review of Britain, America and the world, showing how the top companies in each category achieved their positions. The order of the chapters roughly equates to the importance of the category, and each chapter includes case studies of companies that have been much admired in that category. Each chapter also highlights the lessons that appear to be the most dominant in terms of the strategy and execution of a particular category.

Detailed appendices describe the methodology used in the most admired company surveys and list the winners from the three surveys over time, showing correlations between categories and company/sector analyses.

2

The most admired companies in the world

G iven the importance of corporate reputation, it should be no surprise that the competition to become a most admired company is intense. But how companies achieve this status is by no means certain. Writer Abrahm Lustgarten says:[1]

> Corporate reputation is the product of alchemy – a mixture of everything from the way a company nurtures homegrown talent to how it manages its balance sheet. Throw in one part customer satisfaction, another part shareholder return, add a splash of community citizenship – and voila! – you have a measure of that company's station in the hierarchy of American business.

Clearly, to do well in the most admired company survey, as *Fortune* said in 1999, requires 'managers of genius, innovative products, financial stamina, global reach and a fanatical devotion to shareholders'.

America's most admired companies

Between 1983 and 2008 there have been eight overall winners of the American survey: IBM, Merck, Rubbermaid, Coca-Cola, General Electric (GE), Dell, Apple and Wal-Mart. Some companies have been able to win year after year. GE had remarkable run in which it was America's most admired company for five consecutive years between 1998 and 2002, and it won the overall award again in 2006 and 2007.

As well as the overall winners, more than 45 companies have won one of the individual categories in the survey. In recent years, the rise of newer entrants such as Google, Whole Foods Markets and Kinder Morgan has kept the competition to be a most admired company in America fresh and dynamic.

Merck has won most individual awards over the past 20 years. In 1988 it swept the board, winning in seven out of the eight categories and losing out only to arch rivals Johnson & Johnson in social responsibility. In total Merck won on more than 30 occasions, but it hasn't won in any category since 1993. Maybe chief executive Dick Clarke's 'Plan to Win' will return Merck to the industry-leading position it once enjoyed.

IBM had a similar experience. Big Blue was the overall winner of the first four surveys run by *Fortune* from 1983 to 1986, and during most of the 1980s it finished in the top spot in various categories on 16 separate occasions. In 1984, John R. Opel, IBM's CEO, said: 'I think this is the finest industrial enterprise in the world. I've thought so for a long time.'[2] But by 1991 IBM had fallen to 32nd in the overall rankings. A year later it was 118th. By 1994 it was down to 354th position. It took a dramatic turnaround strategy by Lou Gerstner for the company to regain some of its former prowess and by 1999 it was once more top of its business sector, ahead of Hewlett-Packard, Dell, Sun Microsystems and Apple. In 2007, IBM was top in its industry sector for quality of management, use of corporate assets, financial soundness and value as a long-term investment.

IBM's performance is proof of two things:

- A reputation, hard won over decades, can fall like a stone. Keeping that reputation is something that is a constant challenge to even the best companies.

- A company can claw its reputation back if it is damaged. This sometimes calls for radical thinking. IBM was fortunate to have a couple of inspirational chiefs who were able to do this.

Over the period of the survey, IBM, Merck and Microsoft have finished top in the categories more than any other companies. But Coca-Cola and Rubbermaid, together with Berkshire Hathaway, Johnson & Johnson and UPS, have each won on more than six occasions. And before its unacceptably innovative accounting practices were discovered, Enron won the capacity to innovate category every year between 1996 and 2001.

Berkshire Hathaway, Warren Buffett's company, finished top in five out of eight years for use of corporate assets between 1996 and 2003. By 2006, a

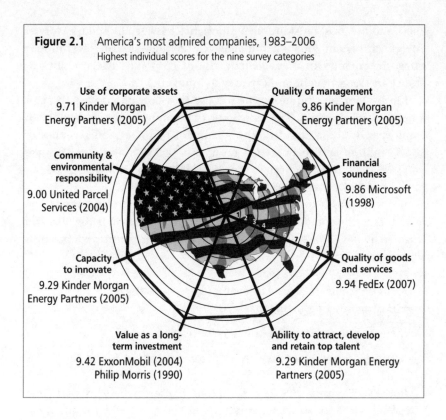

Figure 2.1 America's most admired companies, 1983–2006
Highest individual scores for the nine survey categories

Use of corporate assets
9.71 Kinder Morgan
Energy Partners (2005)

Quality of management
9.86 Kinder Morgan
Energy Partners (2005)

Community & environmental responsibility
9.00 United Parcel
Services (2004)

Financial soundness
9.86 Microsoft
(1998)

Capacity to innovate
9.29 Kinder Morgan
Energy Partners (2005)

Quality of goods and services
9.94 FedEx (2007)

Value as a long-term investment
9.42 ExxonMobil (2004)
Philip Morris (1990)

Ability to attract, develop and retain top talent
9.29 Kinder Morgan Energy
Partners (2005)

single Berkshire Hathaway share was worth $100,000. So legendary is Buffett and his company that some 27,000 shareholders attended the 2007 annual shareholders' meeting at the Qwest centre in Omaha, Nebraska. Buffett's formula for success is covered in later chapters. At the forefront of his ideas is that the directors invest in the company. As Buffett puts it, 'we eat our own cooking'. And there is a commitment to long-term investment:[3]

> Regardless of price, we have no interest at all in selling any good
> businesses that Berkshire owns. We are also very reluctant to sell
> sub-par businesses as long as we expect them to generate at least
> some cash and as long as we feel good about their managers and labor
> relations.

Figure 2.1 shows that the highest scores achieved for the eight categories in the surveys up to 2007 are spread among six companies: Kinder Morgan Energy Partners, UPS, Microsoft, Philip Morris FedEx and ExxonMobil. Only two of the highest scores of all time occurred before

2000, and the most outstanding performance has been by Kinder Morgan Energy Partners in 2005 when it achieved the highest scores ever in four categories: quality of management, use of corporate assets, ability to attract and retain talent and capacity to innovate.

Kinder Morgan's prime business is the transport of gasoline through a network of pipelines. The Houston-based company has around 9,000 employees. In 2006, according to its annual report, it had revenues of $8,955 million and its operating profit was $1,256 million, an increase of 23.9% over 2005. Net profit was $972 million in fiscal year 2006, an increase of 19.7% over 2005.

But what was it in this particular year that made it so admired? The maxim that 'the company's management team focused on being lean and frugal' may have something to do with it, as may the company's business strategy to:[4]

- focus on stable, fee-based assets that are core to the energy infrastructure of growing markets,

- increase utilization of assets while controlling costs,

- leverage economies of scale from incremental acquisitions.

Both FedEx and UPS have achieved highest scores in particular categories – UPS for social responsibility (2004) and FedEx for quality of products (2007).

Mike Eskew, chairman and CEO of UPS, has said: 'If you are not a socially responsible company, you are not truly a customer-focused company … let alone a shareholder-focused company.'[5] UPS has a big commitment to social responsibility. Through its programmes for the environment (such as expanding its green fleet), sustainability (commitment to United Way) and education, and its commitment to the community through the UPS Foundation and to diversity, UPS has demonstrated that it earned its all-time high score.

FedEx, which according to its annual report had revenues of £32.2 billion in 2006 (up 10% on 2005) and income of $1.8 billion (up 25% on 2005), was clearly seen as having created and delivered a product that satisfied the needs and aspirations of the customer.

In recent years there has been a greater spread of companies winning most admired company awards. Between 2000 and 2007, there were 29 companies on the list that had won at least one of the categories, compared with 19 in the 1990s and 11 in the 1980s.

Britain's most admired companies

There have been eight winners of Britain's most admired company award since 1990: Shell, Marks & Spencer, Glaxo, Rentokil, Cadbury Schweppes, Tesco, Reuters and BP. Unlike their American counterparts, British companies tend to have shorter stays at the top. However, four of the winners were still in the overall most admired top 20 in 2007. Figures 2.2 and 2.3 show the fluctuating fortunes of eight of the leading British companies.

Between 1994 and 2007 around 100 companies secured a top 20 slot in the overall most admired rankings. Some, such as Unilever and Cadbury Schweppes, have been in the top 20 since 1994 and Tesco since 1995. GlaxoSmithKline (or its earlier forms) has been in the top 20 in every year except one and BP since 1996. Marks & Spencer finished in the top five in 1994, 1996 and 1997, but fell steadily in subsequent years and out of the top 20 completely until its revival under Stuart Rose which got the company back to the top in 2007.

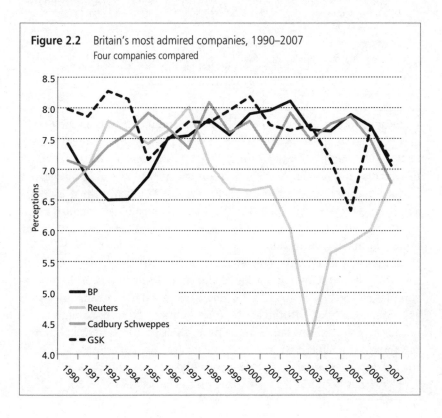

Figure 2.2 Britain's most admired companies, 1990–2007
Four companies compared

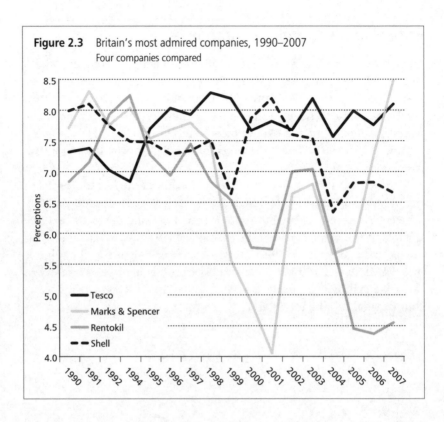

Figure 2.3 Britain's most admired companies, 1990–2007
Four companies compared

Other companies had more variable performances, making the top 20 lists but unable to sustain a presence there. J Sainsbury featured at 16th in the 1994 survey, rising to ninth in 1995, but failed to capitalize on this success and fell out of the top 20 for the next ten years, only making a reappearance in 2006 at 18th, under a new CEO, Justin King. By 2007 Sainsbury was seventh. Shell has also had its ups and downs: top 10 in 1994 and 1995, 15th in 1996, 17th in 1997, first in 2000 and out of the top 20 completely after 2004.

Similarly, Lloyds TSB, created by a merger in 1995, rose to ninth spot in 1998 in the overall rankings and then dropped out of the top 20 completely. By 2007 it was 133rd in the overall rankings. Companies such as Reuters, Rentokil, Whitbread, Next and Burford all reached high levels in the early surveys but failed to maintain their positions in the rankings. In subsequent chapters we look at how some companies are able to sustain their corporate reputations – and how others are not able to do so.

BSkyB has been a category winner on seven occasions: in 2001, 2004,

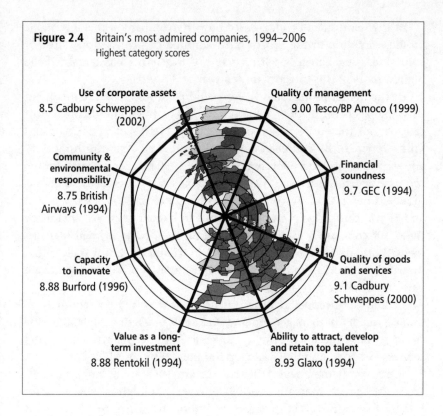

Figure 2.4 Britain's most admired companies, 1994–2006
Highest category scores

Use of corporate assets
8.5 Cadbury Schweppes (2002)

Quality of management
9.00 Tesco/BP Amoco (1999)

Community & environmental responsibility
8.75 British Airways (1994)

Financial soundness
9.7 GEC (1994)

Capacity to innovate
8.88 Burford (1996)

Quality of goods and services
9.1 Cadbury Schweppes (2000)

Value as a long-term investment
8.88 Rentokil (1994)

Ability to attract, develop and retain top talent
8.93 Glaxo (1994)

2005 it came top in quality of marketing; in 1999, 2000, 2001 and 2003 it was top in innovation. In 2007 it reached third in the overall charts.

GlaxoSmithKline has finished top in five categories as has Cadbury Schweppes. Tesco has finished top in eight categories, community and environmental responsibility being the only one in which it has missed out. BP and Shell have both finished top in three categories.

What these charts also show is that corporate reputation is fragile. Today's winners have to work hard at maintaining their reputation, which is built up over a long period of time, but can take a hammering as a result of a year's poor financial results or a strategy that is misunderstood or poorly explained.

Figure 2.4 shows the highest score for each of the nine categories in the British survey and the company that achieved the score. Only Cadbury Schweppes and Burford have been able to achieve the highest scores in more than one category. This reflects both the intensity of competition and the challenge of excelling in more than one area in a business.

In 1996 Burford, a London-based property company with a low public profile, came top in the British most admired company survey's use of corporate assets category with a score of 8.29. This has remained the highest score in this category for ten years.

Of the higher-profile brands, Tesco and BP scored 9 for the quality of their management in 1999, which proved to be the highest score in this category for the entire period of the surveys. Terry Leahy of Tesco and John Browne of BP had been close in the previous year, finishing third and second respectively, but their success in 1999 preceded a battle for the top spot which was to continue for the next seven years. In 2000 BP was number one, in 2002 Tesco hit the top spot, and in 2003 Tesco was first and BP was third. This position was also maintained in 2006. What made these two companies so highly admired for the quality of their management? Both are featured as case studies in Chapter 3, but it is clear that Browne's shrewdness and Leahy's high-but-unflashy profile had resonated with those taking part in the surveys.

Cadbury Schweppes achieved its first victories in 1995, coming top in both quality of management and quality of marketing. Since then the company has collected the highest scores ever for the quality of goods and services and for community and environmental responsibility.

Some companies have failed to sustain their high rankings. GEC (before it became Marconi in 1999) achieved the highest ever score for financial soundness. The company's performance since this high point shows just how difficult it is to sustain admirability and how easy it is to squander long-term reputational gains through strategic decisions that do not work out. In 1994 the company had a £1.7 billion cash mountain built on the watch of Lord Weinstock. He retired in 1996, handing over the reins to George Simpson, who set about a massive reorganization of the company. Various bits were sold off, an American defence contractor was acquired for over $1 billion just a year before the whole defence arm of GEC was sold to BAe Systems to allow the company to focus on telecommunications under the new name of Marconi. A rush of acquisitions followed, fuelled by the excitement of the dotcom boom. When boom turned to bust Marconi was in deep trouble. What was left of this once greatly admired company was acquired by Ericsson in 2005.

BA, which achieved the highest ever score for marketing in 1994, is another company that has not been able to sustain its position, lying 91st in the 2007 overall rankings, 64 places lower than easyJet.

Of the eight companies that have achieved the highest ever scores in

Britain's most admired company surveys, three were still in the overall top 20 in 2007: BP, GlaxoSmithKline and Tesco. But the majority of companies in the surveys have just one victory in one category, often reflecting a much admired strategic initiative. For example, Orange's 1998 top spot in the quality of marketing category came after its strategy to expand the brand globally, and Enterprise Inns' 2004 success in use of corporate assets came after it agreed to buy the Unique Pub Company for £609 million, thereby creating a combined chain of 9,000 pubs.

The world's most admired companies

In the relatively short period of the survey to 2007 there have been only two companies that have won the overall award in the world's most admired company survey, General Electric and Wal-Mart – although Apple pipped both to the post in 2008. But there has been a wide range of national champions: Alcatel and Carrefour from France, RWE, EON and Siemens from Germany, Nestlé from Switzerland, Edison from Italy, Shanghai Baosteel from China and Singapore Airlines, among others.

GE was transformed under Jack Welch. Its current CEO, Jeffrey Immelt, recognizes that:[6]

> In today's dynamic business environment, standing still is not an option. No matter how large or small, organizations must continue to grow in order to survive let alone succeed, particularly in light of the recent globalization phenomenon. Just to maintain recent growth, GE must expand by approximately the size of Federal Express this year.

With $172 billion in revenues and $22.2 billion in earnings in 2007, GE certainly has the financial clout to do well globally. And we know that GE is a pioneer of six sigma techniques that ensure operational efficiency worldwide with top management support and an organizational infrastructure to make it work.[7]

GE's success is undoubtedly a result of a complex mixture of competences that combine brilliantly to produce a business that is greater than the total if its individual parts. Outstanding leadership, integrated processes, a global view and the ability to respond to external forces are just a few of these. But tougher trading conditions will stretch these competencies to the limit.

In 2007 Wal-Mart had sales of $349 billion (up from $309 billion in 2006), producing a net income of over $11 billion. According to its website, the company has an employee base of 1.3 million 'associates' as it calls them and it is estimated that its stores attract over 7 billion customer visits per year. More than half of all Americans live within 5 miles of a Wal-Mart store and around 90% within 15 miles. Wal-Mart is also the largest retailer in Mexico and Canada and one of the largest grocers in Britain, where it owns Asda.[8]

Of the 19 companies that have had multiple entries in the charts since the world's most admired company survey started in 1998, 14 had revenues or profit from outside their home base of more than 50% and six have more than 80%.

Five British companies stand out as national champions in the world list. The one with the most entries is BP, which has made every list since the survey began, followed closely by Shell, Tesco, HSBC and Glaxo-SmithKline. Both Sainsbury's and Unilever have multiple entries, and BA, Rio Tinto, Pearson and Reuters have all featured. France has an equally dominant company in L'Oréal, which has appeared in the top three in every survey so far. Other French companies that have done well include Total, Carrefour and Group Danone. Vinci (engineering,) Areva (energy), Alcatel (telecommunications) and Suez (Finance) have all made multiple appearances.

BASF (chemicals) is the German company that has done best in the survey but BMW, Volkswagen and Siemens have also featured. Japan's national champion to date has been Toyota, which rose to prominence in 2000 and has stayed at the top of the list; it was second behind GE in the 2007 overall rankings of the world's most admired companies. Canon, Honda, Sony and Takenaka (engineering) have also performed well. Other notable national performers include Nestlé (Switzerland), Nokia (Finland), Ericsson (Sweden), South Korea's Samsung and Singapore Airlines.

In 2006, there were enough Chinese companies achieving high scores to justify a separate section. Of the eight Chinese companies in the 2007 list, China Mobile Telecommunications stood out. Only one Indian company, Oil and Natural Gas, made the list in 2007.

Strategic focus is a feature of those companies that do well globally. When Samsung wanted to ensure that it continued to derive over 80% of its business from outside South Korea, it narrowed its strategic approach to four key messages. HSBC has also refined its strategy in this way with an objective of 'coordinated services on a worldwide scale', according to

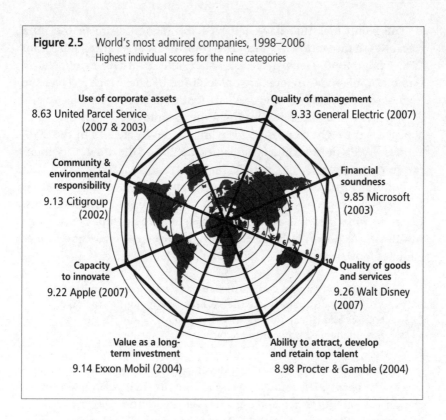

Figure 2.5 World's most admired companies, 1998–2006
Highest individual scores for the nine categories

Use of corporate assets
8.63 United Parcel Service
(2007 & 2003)

Quality of management
9.33 General Electric (2007)

Community & environmental responsibility
9.13 Citigroup
(2002)

Financial soundness
9.85 Microsoft
(2003)

Capacity to innovate
9.22 Apple (2007)

Quality of goods and services
9.26 Walt Disney
(2007)

Value as a long-term investment
9.14 Exxon Mobil (2004)

Ability to attract, develop and retain top talent
8.98 Procter & Gamble (2004)

its 2006 annual report. If companies can achieve economies of scale and scope on a global basis, this puts them in an extremely strong position. In HSBC's case, its commitment to transferring best practice around the world will give it 'both cost efficiency and speed to market'. (In 2006 HSBC was the fourth largest bank in the world by market capitalization at $98 billion just behind Citigroup, JP Morgan Chase and Bank of America.[9])

Carrefour has a strategy in pursuit of 'gaining volume and winning market share' in which 'low prices and strong promotions are non-negotiable and basic customer requirements'.[10] BP has '4 Steps to the Future: Getting the essentials right; Executing more effectively; Investing for the long term; Contributing to the future of energy.'[11] Of course, such statements are all very well. What matters lies in whether the company can deliver and how it will.

National champions in the world survey are companies that not only have clear strategic focus but also are able to execute their strategy effectively.

The companies that have achieved the highest score in the nine categories in the world's most admired company surveys are all American: UPS, ExxonMobil, General Electric, Microsoft, Walt Disney, Procter & Gamble, Apple and Citigroup. ExxonMobil and UPS have each received the highest score ever in two categories (see figure 2.5 on the previous page).

What is it that separates out the leading companies? First is sustainability. Of the eight companies in figure 2.5, seven are still in the 2007 *Fortune* world's most admired companies top 20 and the other (Citigroup) was just outside at 21.

Second is a spread of risk. GE has operations in over 100 countries and because of this has an extremely diverse choice among its managers. It has also invested in people who can deliver the company's strategy worldwide. As Robert Heller, a writer on management issues and former editor of *Management Today*, said of GE:[12]

> The better everything is going, the harder you must strive to improve everything – by initiatives like the Six Sigma programme. You take weaknesses and threats so seriously that you act before they even appear. Challenge and change are built into GE's values.

GE does one more big thing: it develops people, evaluates them and acts on the results. The result is an extraordinarily high-performing organization. 'The ability to demand high performance without being heartless', says Immelt, 'has been a part of GE for a long time.'[13] It is acknowledged that GE has a wealth of human capital. The company trains 10,000 new managers each year and evaluates 5,000 senior-most managers on detailed performance/values criteria each year.[14]

Microsoft's highest ever score for financial soundness came in 2003 and it was still top in its sector in this category in 2007. In 2006 Microsoft had revenues of $44 billion and operating income of $16 billion. Like GE, it has a solid global base with operations in over 100 countries. This allows it not only to take advantage of economies of scale but also to spread financial risk should any one territory suffer a worse economic performance than another. The company's mission 'to enable people and businesses throughout the world to realize their full potential' reflects its global perspective. Furthermore, Microsoft's integrated business structure allows investments made in one of its segments to benefit other segments, which in turn 'motivates shared effort'. This highly effective financial structure has been recognized by the company's peers as a characteristic that each year is rated highly. In this respect, ExxonMobil, like Microsoft, is able to spread its risk. The company's organization structure, according to its website, is 'built on a concept of global businesses and is designed to allow ExxonMobil to compete most effectively in the ever-changing and challenging worldwide energy industry'. Its return on average capital employed increased from 13.5% in 2002 to 31.5% in 2005, and in 2004 its score of 9.14 was the highest on record for value as a long-term investment. In 2007 the company was still in the top three in this category with another former winner, Berkshire Hathaway.

Walt Disney achieved the highest ever score for quality of goods and services in 2007; this was the second time it had won the global award in this category. The company was founded in 1923, and with the creation of such famous cartoon characters as Mickey Mouse and films like *Snow White and the Seven Dwarfs* the Disney name became synonymous with entertainment for the whole family. The company has since diversified into a much broader corporation with four major business segments: studio entertainment, parks and resorts, consumer products and media networks. Under the leadership of Robert A. Iger, and with such luminaries as Steve Jobs (Apple) and Orin C. Smith (Starbucks) on the board, the company achieved revenues of $34 billion in 2006, up from $32 billion in 2005. Net income was over $3 billion, a 33% increase on the previous year. The largest business segment was media networks at over $14 billion, but parks and resorts at nearly $10 billion also made a healthy contribution. Studios and consumer products produced combined revenues of around $10 billion.

Disney strives for service standards that begin with the attitude of employees and extend to every part of the customer experience. What's more, the processes should be aligned to support the continuous delivery of quality service.[15] These beliefs form the basis of Disney's service proposition.

Another world achiever was Procter & Gamble, which hit the headlines in 2004 when it registered the highest ever score for quality of people management – no mean feat for a company with over 135,000 employees in 80 countries. It went on to win the award in three out of four years from 2004, only being beaten by GE in 2005. The company's people managerial philosophy is to 'build-from-within', and to foster 'an inclusive culture' in the belief that 'a fully engaged diverse workforce is a competitive advantage'. According to its website, some of the ways in which the company seeks to attract the best talent from around the world are to:

- focus on the talents of each individual through 'effective assignment- and promotion-planning processes';
- make excellence in performance management and its retention and employee support systems and processes a priority – such systems include 'effective first-year orientation/join-up programmes, ensuring a good match with the first boss, developing coaching/mentoring/advocacy relationships and high-quality challenging work/career plans';
- use a global online candidate-recruiting system;
- operate intern programmes, 'participating in recruiting conferences and increased outreach to high-school students'.

In his 2006 letter to shareholders, A.G. Lafley, CEO of Procter & Gamble, stated that the company's unique organizational structure – global business unit profit centres, a global market development organization and global shared business services – allows it to deliver its strategies and leverage its strengths. He said that this structure allowed 'a number of highly focused companies that share common go-to-market operations and business services'.

When Steve Jobs urged his team to innovate at a party celebrating the 20th anniversary of Apple's trade show at the Musée d'Orsay in Paris in 2003, he was ushering in a new era for the company.[16] This led in 2006 to the company coming top in the innovation category, only to achieve the highest ever score the following year.

Citigroup is the world's biggest bank and since it achieved the highest score ever for globalness, it has been seeking to become even more global. Getting on for one-third of its income of over $21 billion came from outside America and it stated in its 2006 annual report that 'approximately 70% of our new branches are in the emerging markets'.

The most admired companies

Taking all the results from the three surveys, around 50 companies have come top in more than one category or come top for more than one year. These winners are from a broad range of sectors and include such companies as Dow Jones, Philip Morris, Cisco, Procter & Gamble, Astra-Zeneca, Smiths Industries and Vodaphone.

In America, companies such as IBM, Merck and Rubbermaid dominated the most admired company surveys for long periods during the 1980s and 1990s, but these companies have not won outside their industry sectors since before 2000. Others, such as Procter & Gamble, FedEx, UPS and Kinder Morgan, have risen to prominence in the surveys since 2000 and Google has become a new much-admired star. Interestingly, 14 companies have been able to sustain their pre-2000 success and come top in categories in the past few years as well. They have demonstrated that they have staying power in sustaining their corporate reputation over time. The companies are listed in figure 2.6.

Figure 2.6 The most admired companies in the world

Berkshire Hathaway	15 times individual category winner	1996–2005
BP	8 times individual category and overall winner	1999–2004
BSkyB	9 times individual category winner	1999–2003
Cadbury Schweppes	13 times individual category and overall winner	1995–2006
Citigroup	9 times individual category winner	1984–2002
ExxonMobil	16 times individual category winner	1989–2006
General Electric	24 times, including both America's and the world's most admired company overall 7 times	1999–2007
GlaxoSmithKline (or Glaxo)	12 times individual category and overall winner	1994–2004
Marks & Spencer	8 times individual category winners and overall winner	1991–2007
Microsoft	16 times individual category winner	1995–2003
Shell	8 times individual category and overall winner	1991–2002
Tesco	33 times individual category or overall winner	1996–2006
Wal-Mart	10 times, including both America's and the world's most admired company overall twice	1993–2003

As we have shown, past success is no guarantee for future performance and the question for all the companies is how to sustain their corporate reputation which requires prescience, vigilance, skill and application.

Subsequent chapters show how the most admired companies in the world achieved their status in each of the categories and draw lessons from those that were successful.

3

Quality of management

Three key factors influence the perception of a company's management in most admired company surveys. The first is the profile of the chief executive and how well he or she manages stakeholders. The second is how clearly the CEO or chairman articulates the company's strategy. The third is how the CEO or chairman is perceived as delivering against this strategy, that is, the business results. So when Indra Nooyi, chief executive of PepsiCo, stated that delivering superior financial performance can improve the world,[1] and Bill Gates said that Microsoft had to innovate to come up with the breakthrough that would ensure his company stayed ahead of the competition,[2] they were setting the agenda against which both performance and perception would be judged.

But other factors are also important. Perceptions of a company's management are influenced by the company's financial soundness, ability to attract and retain talent and value as a long-term investment, and whether it uses the company's assets wisely. To achieve a high quality of management rating, therefore, acts as a bellwether of other factors. Not only is the quality of a company's management a beacon of company performance – 'good management enhances firm value: well managed firms have higher profitability, are able to sustain operating perform-ance for longer and are rewarded by higher market valuations'[3] – it also improves the quality of corporate reputation.

High-profile managers in the mould of Jack Welch, former chief executive of GE, and Bill Gates get the point. They say and do the right things, catch the mood of their 'electorate' and state their company's position clearly to stakeholders. As Jeffrey Immelt, CEO of GE, puts it:

> I always use Jack [Welch] as my example here. Every leader needs to
> clearly explain the top three things the organization is working on. If
> you can't, then you're not leading well.

There is value in making sure that all the company's stakeholders
have a positive impression and it is normally the CEO or the chairman to
whom this task falls.[4] Those who have been highly regarded in the surveys
include Britain's John Browne and Stuart Rose and America's Bill Gates,
Warren Buffett, Jeffrey Immelt, A.G. Lafley, Meg Whitman and further
back Lou Gerstner, Katherine Graham and Jack Welch.

It should be no surprise that if a company is ranked highly for quality
of management, there is a good chance that it will do well overall. In
Britain, for example, eight of the past ten winners of this category between
1998 and 2007 finished in the top three overall, with Tesco being the best
performer. Only Royal Bank of Scotland (2004) and Persimmon (2007)
failed to convert their winning quality of management scores into top 10
overall positions.

Britain's best-managed companies between 1994 and 2007 were Tesco,
BP, GlaxoSmithKline, Next, Unilever, Cadbury Schweppes and Smiths
Group, followed closely by GKN, Serco Group, Marks & Spencer, Lloyds
TSB and Wolseley. During this period, 109 different companies made the
top 20 for the quality of their management. Of these a few were able to
sustain their positions over time: 28 appeared three times or more; 12
appeared five times or more; and seven appeared six times or more.

In America, 15 companies have been recognized for the quality of their
management from the start of the *Fortune* surveys. In recent years these
included GE, Procter & Gamble and Kinder Morgan. Previously Wal-Mart,
Merck and Rubbermaid took the top or one of the top positions for several
consecutive years. Berkshire Hathaway's success in financial measures –
value as a long-term investment and use of corporate assets – was complemented by recognition of the quality of its management.

The best-managed companies in the world survey in 2007 included
leading US companies Procter & Gamble, GE and Walgreen. In Europe,
L'Oréal, BMW and Nestlé were notable, and on the world stage the
management of companies such as Toyota was much admired.

How did the leaders of these companies demonstrate their quality of
management?

The highly visible but not flashy leadership style

When Terry Leahy joined Tesco in 1979 the company was a shadow of the business it is today. As head of marketing in the 1990s he worked with chief executive Ian MacLaurin to move Tesco's strategy away from the 'pile it high, sell it cheap' philosophy. There was more focus on new ideas. One of these was the one-stop-shop approach which led to the company buying sites on the edge of British towns, allowing it to build larger superstores with a greater range of products. Also, as head of marketing, Leahy introduced and kept faith with Club Card, the company loyalty card, while other retailers stumbled in competitive confusion.

Tesco had already been admired for its quality of management, goods and services and people management under MacLaurin's leadership in 1996. It fell to Leahy as MacLaurin's successor in 1997 to ensure that this continued. Under Leahy's stewardship, Tesco topped the overall most admired companies list in 2005 and 2006 and it was top for quality of management in 2002, 2003 and 2006.

Tesco's performance has been outstanding and there is clearly a strong link between quality of management and financial soundness. In 2006, according to its annual report, Tesco's sales were £42 billion, its profit before tax was £2.2 billion and its market capitalization was £31.2 billion. In that year the company operated in the UK, the Czech Republic, Hungary, Poland, the Republic of Ireland, Slovakia, Turkey, China, Japan, Malaysia, South Korea, Taiwan and Thailand. *Management Today* described Tesco as 'an immensely powerful organization and ... probably the country's best managed company'.

In March 2007 in an interview on CNN Leahy was asked about his leadership style and that of his team. He commented:

> Working in Tesco and working with people has taught me that of course the important thing is what you cause other people to do rather than what you do yourself. And so over time you learn that it's much more about motivating and inspiring other people and challenging other people to do more, to do things differently ... people have got to want to follow you and ... that has a lot to do with not what you say but really your value system and people actually watch what you do more than what you say. If you can be consistent over time, and what you say is what you then go out and do ... people see that and they start to trust you.

Authenticity, consistency, doing what you say you are going to do, trust and causing others to be successful are leadership qualities that have been crucial to Tesco's achievements.

Leahy has demonstrated it is possible to be a successful leader without being flashy, to be visible when necessary but to shun the limelight at other times. He has been remarkably astute in representing the company but has not sought to be the company.

The dominant leadership style

Chris Gent provided outstanding leadership during the growth of Vodafone. In 2000 BBC News commented:

Invariably described as confident and unflappable, Mr Gent has not missed a trick in launching Vodafone into the very top flight.

This was the CEO who had allegedly instigated the acquisition of Airtouch for £36 billion by a mobile phone call from a cricket match he was watching in Australia. *Business Week* called Gent the 'mobile phone king of the world'. It is hard to see how much more visible it was possible to be than Gent at Vodafone. Under his leadership the company's customer base grew from 4 million to 120 million – a remarkable feat. Gent's – and Vodafone's – reputation was one of the strongest in British business.

But such a high profile also carries risk. In 2000 Vodafone fell behind its rivals, Orange and BT Cellnet (now O_2) in the most admired overall category. As *Management Today* noted in December 2001:

Vodafone's modest ranking may betray the fact that it is not as good as it thinks it is ... The fallout from the sale of 3G licences, which Vodafone estimated would cost £10 billion to roll out, clearly dented the faith of business leaders in how effective it was as a company. And it didn't help when the chief executive, Chris Gent, admitted later that he didn't know when the company would get a return on its expenditure on the licences. Some observers thought that the profile of its chief executive was too high; that the company was associated with one individual and that there may not be depth in management.

Nonetheless, Gent still emerged as the second most admired leader, but faith in the company to deliver its promise was dented. Vodafone's position in the overall most admired list fell to 52nd from 15th and it languished at mid levels. At a press conference in Düsseldorf as he launched his hostile bid for Mannesmann Gent tried to persuade his critics that he was 'not a ruthless shark' when putting together the $183 billion deal.

In December 2003 *Management Today* suggested that there was an inference that the company was promising more than it could deliver and asked: 'Is it just a coincidence that the share price is still a third of the level seen in the go-go days?' When Vodafone was doing well it was a combination of the right strategy, excellent performance and its high-profile CEO, who was rated highly for the quality of his management over a long period. But was the profile of the CEO too dominant? And was there a perception of a lack of depth in the management? To be truly admired, a company's leadership should emphasize its management bench-strength.

Gent retired in July 2003 but remained life president until 2006 when he severed links with the company. It is hard to get the balance right as CEO. The new team at Vodafone wanted to consolidate and build on past successes but also to put blue water between itself and aspects of the previous management style. In an interview with *International Herald Tribune* in December 2004, Arun Sarin, the CEO who took over from Gent in July 2003, spoke of focus and cost-cutting. 'We're in the integration phase of our life,' he said, and talked of partnerships rather than the adrenalin of acquisition. In 2004 Vodafone made it back into the top 20 most admired companies. In 2005 it finished eighth overall but by 2007 had fallen back 86th in the overall chart, proving the fragility of reputation.

Figure 3.1 illustrates the changing fortunes of Tesco, Royal Bank of Scotland and Vodafone.

The determined leadership style

Shrewd and visionary are two adjectives that have been applied to the quality of management at Royal Bank of Scotland (RBS), which has been led since 2000 by Sir Fred Goodwin, a strategically aggressive CEO, who has transformed the bank from an efficient regional player to a global financial powerhouse.

In 2004 RBS headed the list as the most admired company for quality of management. Its success in the acquisition of NatWest bank in Britain, ground-breaking investments in China and a buying spree in America through the £5.7 billion acquisition of Charter One had made RBS one of

Figure 3.1 Britain's most admired companies: quality of management, 1992–2006
Three companies compared

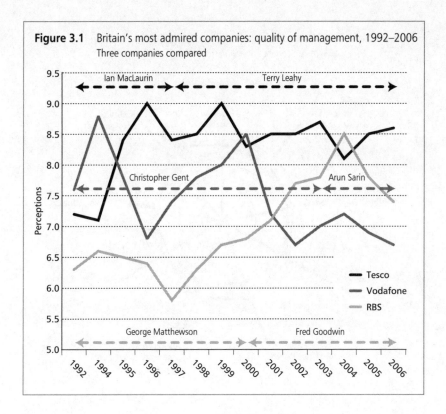

the world's ten biggest banks. The top rating for quality of management seemed to be a just reward for the outstanding business performance of the company and took RBS to 12th position overall in 2004, up from 20th the year before. The CEO was high profile and it was inevitable that market watchers would be interested in his management style. Since taking the helm, he had made the bank a global player and had seen his company's assets quadruple and profits increase significantly to over £9 billion.

But views of RBS's senior management changed in subsequent years. Its quality of management rating in Britain fell to fifth in 2005 and to 20th in 2006, and its overall position fell from 12th in 2004, to 19th in 2005 and 41st in 2006. In 2007, the year it threw its hat into the ring to acquire ABN AMRO, RBS was rated top for quality of management within the banking sector for a sixth consecutive year; but once again this was not reflected in the overall survey where the company was rated 20th. Why did this happen when the bank's financial performance continued to be outstanding?

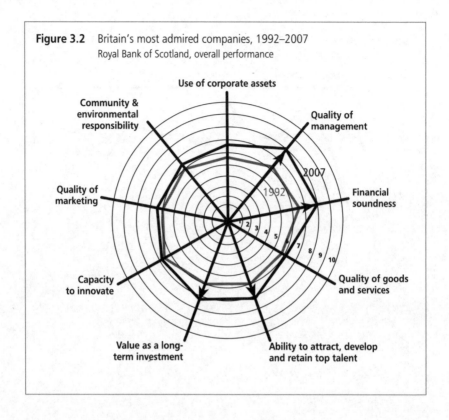

Figure 3.2 Britain's most admired companies, 1992–2007
Royal Bank of Scotland, overall performance

There is a view that 'people didn't take to Sir Fred'[5] but this is belied by much of the data as RBS's chief continued to garner the respect of many of his peers. Before the announcement of its rights issue in 2008 following the credit crunch and its acquisition of ABN AMRO, RBS's quality of management ratings were still very respectable, and better than they had been a decade earlier. But such improvements did not take place across all the categories, and for innovation, marketing, product quality and community, social and environmental responsibility there had been little movement. The company has to rate highly across the board if it is to be among most admired companies overall. RBS has fallen short in this respect. Figure 3.2 illustrates how RBS was rated in 1992 and 2007. The two circles show increases in ratings for quality of management, financial soundness, value as a long-term investment, the ability to attract, develop and retain talent and the use of corporate assets; but also illustrated are the lower levels of improvement in innovation, marketing, quality of goods and services and community and environmental responsibility.

However, improvements in all of the most admired survey categories would not have been sufficient to prevent Sir Fred's departure from RBS in November 2008 and his replacement by Stephen Hester of British Land. The paroxysms that had struck Britain's banks and forced them to seek extra capital from their own shareholders or a lifeline from government reserves hit RBS particularly hard, especially because of the perceived over-payment for ABN AMRO. As the architect of the deal, Sir Fred found his position had become untenable.

Rising and falling (and rising again)

In 1994 Marks & Spencer was Britain's third most admired company, narrowly behind Rentokil (the winner) and Glaxo and just ahead of Unilever. In that year it was ahead of all of its retailing competitors and the headline in *Management Today* in December was: 'Triumphant Marks & Spencer stands in a class of its own.' Then something dramatic happened: Marks & Spencer fell out of the top 20 completely.

For nearly a decade Marks & Spencer lost its pre-eminent position in British retailing. In 1998 the company announced a fall in profits and in 1999 the share price fell dramatically after a disastrous Christmas season which cost the company £150 million and led to a profits warning. It was pretty much downhill for a long period after that. Inevitably, perhaps, the CEO at the time, Peter Salsbury, appointed to succeed Richard Greenbury, after a difficult boardroom battle, announced a shake-up of management staff and possible redundancies. The reasons given were over-optimistic sales forecasts and ordering, excessive stock and poor ranges.[6] This was perceived as a failure of management and it was no surprise when Marks & Spencer's ratings in Britain's most admired company survey began to tumble (see figure 3.3 overleaf).

A new chairman, Luc Vandevelde, was appointed and a boardroom cull of three executive directors took place. But the company's perform-ance continued to be lacklustre and in 2000 Salsbury resigned as CEO, Vandevelde became both CEO and chairman and Roger Holmes was appointed as head of UK retail. The perception of the company was that of a continuing series of poor management decisions that had unravelled decades of success.

Things seemed to be turning around in 2001 (see figure 3.4 overleaf). George Davies launched the highly successful Per Una range and in May 2002 profits rose sharply. Holmes became CEO and Vandevelde

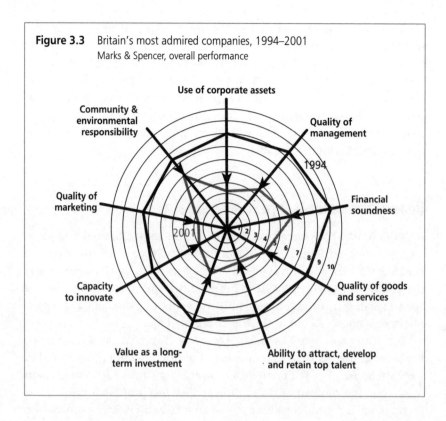

Figure 3.3 Britain's most admired companies, 1994–2001
Marks & Spencer, overall performance

non-executive chairman. But things didn't stay on course and by 2004, sales were disappointing, Vandevelde decided to step down and the first bid approach came from retail entrepreneur Philip Green's acquisition vehicle, Revival Acquisitions.[7]

In 2004 Stuart Rose, who first joined Marks & Spencer in 1972 but later left to pursue his career in a variety of retail positions, was appointed CEO to thwart Green's takeover attempt. It took a year to steady the ship and a further year to introduce the world to Plan A: the company's five-year strategy giving clarity and direction to the ailing organization. A new emphasis on TV and advertising (something the old M&S felt it didn't need to engage in), new clothing ranges, better sourcing and ordering and a major refit of the stores turned things around.

After these changes Rose was able to announce sales up by 10%, operating profit up 22% to over £1 billion and a dividend up 30%. Rose had achieved incredible results in a fairly short time. He got rid of the 'gross overstocking, the lack of focus, too many product lines and

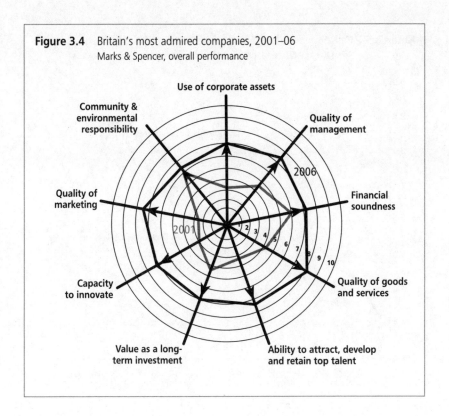

Figure 3.4 Britain's most admired companies, 2001–06
Marks & Spencer, overall performance

a tediously long and winding decision-making path', banned the word strategy 'insisting that focus, drive and broaden was nothing fancier than a plan' and created success that had not seemed possible only a year or so before.[8] In 2007, Marks & Spencer returned as the most admired company in Britain. Figures 3.3 and 3.4 chart the company's rise and fall and rise again. However, in July 2008, falling sales as a result of the credit crunch forced Marks & Spencer to issue a profits warning, and there was also strong criticism by institutional shareholders over the plan to make Rose both executive chairman and chief executive.

A comparison of the Royal Bank of Scotland and Marks & Spencer allows us to investigate the difference between a company that is perceived as relying too much on its CEO and one where the CEO is perceived as successful in taking all parts of the business forward. Figure 3.5 overleaf illustrates RBS's average total admirability scores. The trend is generally a rising one. The thick line indicates the quality of management score is significantly higher than the company's average overall score.

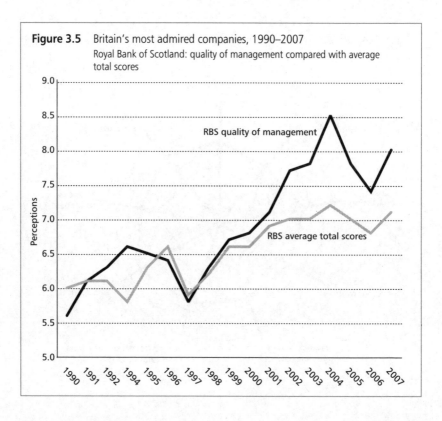

Figure 3.5 Britain's most admired companies, 1990–2007
Royal Bank of Scotland: quality of management compared with average total scores

In contrast, for Marks & Spencer (figure 3.6) the quality of management perception is very much in keeping with the average for the company each year. In the early years the same problem that faced RBS is evident, where the average is significantly higher as a result of the high perceptions given to quality of management. It is not enough for a company to have a well-regarded CEO if the rest of the company's activity is poorly viewed. The one will rarely be powerful enough to counter the other. The point is – reinforced in both RBS and Marks & Spencer – that a good deal of care needs to be given to perception of, for example, a company's quality of service or talent management as well as perceptions of those factors that we believe dominate the running of a business: the quality of management and financial soundness.

There are other lessons to be learned from Marks & Spencer's dramatic fall and rise. First, it was perceived that the company had become complacent and had taken its eye of the ball, notably with regard to customers but also employees. This is a perception that affected another great icon

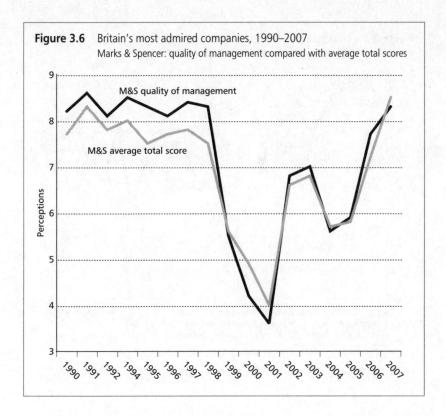

Figure 3.6 Britain's most admired companies, 1990–2007

Marks & Spencer: quality of management compared with average total scores

of global business, IBM, which had been 'the' most admired company in America every year between 1983 and 1986. Yet it seemed to let competitors assume the risky role of innovation. In 1986 the company had recorded the highest scores for any attribute, 9.4 for financial soundness and 9.1 for the quality of management. But the perception of IBM's ability to innovate began to fall and this had a knock-on effect on its overall position, such that by 1994 the company had gone from top to close to bottom (see figure 3.7 overleaf).

The turnaround was begun by Lou Gerstner, who was appointed CEO in 1993 and was chairman of the board of IBM from 1993 to 2002.

The performances of Gerstner and Rose have a lot in common, even though they were ten years apart. As figure 3.7 shows, there was remarkable similarity between the experiences of Marks & Spencer and IBM. Complacency, taking the company's eyes off the consumer, a lack of innovation, poor marketing and an extremely conservative culture are all reasons Marks & Spencer and IBM lost their lustre.

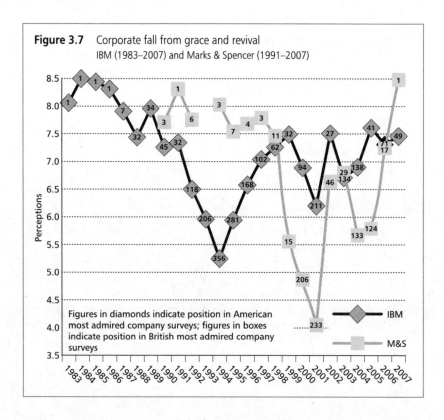

Figure 3.7 Corporate fall from grace and revival
IBM (1983–2007) and Marks & Spencer (1991–2007)

In both cases new managers managed transformations through an energetic focus on the consumer and on the problem areas. Rose identified where Marks & Spencer had been going wrong and the challenges that needed to be met. He then took the tough decisions that were necessary in both strategy and quality of management to meet those challenges. Presenting a strong and capable face to stakeholders, not backing down under intense pressure and a determination to succeed have contributed to the turnaround in Marks & Spencer's fortunes. That things turned sour in 2008 for the firm was as much to do with a more difficult retailing environment as Rose's strategy.

Be shrewd and wily

BP was in the top three for quality of management in Britain's most admired company survey from 1998 to 2006. It has also been in the top three overall in most years between 2000 to 2006, finishing top in 2002.

Some of these qualities were captured in *Management Today*'s assessment of the role of BP's CEO, John Browne (later Lord Browne). In December 1999 it noted: 'The vision comes from the top and it trickles downwards like an upended can of motor oil.' By 2002 BP had become Britain's largest company and one of the largest in the world overall. It was also Britain's most admired company and was rated second for quality of management, behind Tesco. The CEO, who joined BP after graduating from university in 1969 (Tesco's Leahy was also a long-term company man), was hailed as a 'dual paragon' of corporate reputation and for his achievements in turning around the former state-owned company, masterminding huge international mergers and acquisitions and providing a clear, forward-thinking strategy. He was also accessible, 'well tapped into government', and was thought 'wily' enough to, for example, talk down the potential for a fall in crude oil prices to minimize future risk. As Browne said himself: 'We came from the middle of the pack and we knew what it felt like to taste failure.'[9]

In addition to his accessibility and shrewdness, others noted Browne's visionary aptitudes, taking the company further internationally towards higher-risk frontier-type exploration.

Browne's departure in 2007, after 12 years in the job, has brought changes in management style and strategy and it remains to be seen whether BP under Tony Hayward will be as highly rated for the quality of its management in the future as it has been in the past.

BP's success over an extended period can perhaps best be seen when compared to Britain's other oil giant, Shell. In 1991, Shell ranked second in the most admired company overall ratings and was top for quality of management. *The Economist* noted in January 1991:

> Managers often view a job at Shell, where they are given plenty of decisions to make early on in their career, as an alternative to taking an MBA.

At the time, Shell's visionary claim to fame was that it didn't get involved in bid battles. But by 1994, the company was down to tenth and then fell out of the top 20 for quality of management for five years before reappearing in 2000 (and 2001) in fifth position before falling out of the top 20 again. This roller-coaster rating was reflected in Shell's overall rankings: between 1994 and 1997 from ninth to 17th, eighth in 1998, out in 1999, third in 2000, top in 2001, and out of the top 20 from 2004 to 2006. How could a company that finished top of the overall

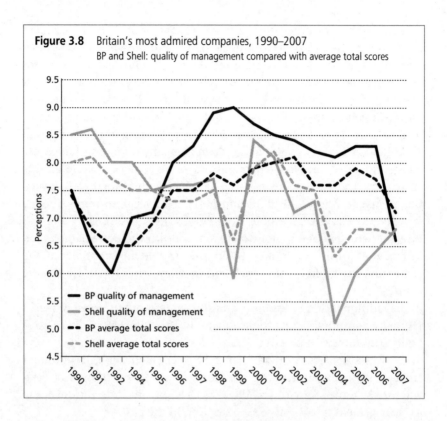

Figure 3.8 Britain's most admired companies, 1990–2007
BP and Shell: quality of management compared with average total scores

league in 2001, whose chairman, Philip Watts, had 30 years' experience in the business and closed the deal with Texaco that made Shell the largest retailer in America, fall to 64th position by 2004?

Figure 3.8 shows the quality of management rating for the two companies over the last 17 years.

The superior esteem in which BP and Browne were held is clearly evident as is the noticeable dips in admirability at Shell for one of the number of reasons we have mentioned. The final value for BP on the right shows the significant drop in the quality of management perception left by Browne's departure.

There was a difference in approach between the two companies that led to these variable scores. Shell, initially a paragon of disciplined conservative management, tried to break out of the mould and, maybe through ill luck, things did not go well. Strategically, its response to difficult trading conditions was uncertain, which affected performance. Bernard Taylor, in his article 'Shell shock: why do good companies do bad things', attempts to highlight some of these issues.[10] These include the criticism Shell has faced over the disposal of its Brent Spar North Sea oil platform and its operations in Nigeria. In 2003 Shell failed to meet its stated production target, and in 2004 it overstated its proven oil reserves. As a result it was forced to cut its estimate of proven reserves by one-third. Within days the company's share price had fallen by 8%. In July 2004 it had to pay £83 million in fines to settle disputes with America's Securities and Exchange Commission (SEC) and Britain's Financial Services Authority over its incorrect reporting of oil reserves. Between 2000 and 2005 Shell's share price fell by 40%. To get back on track it has merged the two companies Shell Transport and Trading and Royal Dutch into Royal Dutch Shell, reduced duplication and made operations simpler, but still the company has not regained the reputation it once had. Its announcement of record profits in 2008 may change perceptions once more.

Personal commitment matters more than glory

With earnings of $22.2 billion in 2007 on revenues of $172 billion, GE has finished high in America's quality of management ratings for some years. Not surprisingly, there is a good correlation between the financial performance of a company and how its management is rated, but exactly how this is communicated is important too. GE's chairman and chief executive, Jeffrey Immelt, who succeeded Jack Welch, noted in the company's 2006 annual report:

> Your GE team is better than ever. They are more innovative ... more global ... more technical ... than at any other time in our history. Most importantly, they are committed to work on your behalf. It is this desire to win that defines your team, one that will 'Invest and Deliver' for the future.

And more than that, he emphasized his personal commitment to the company:

> Just like after September 11, I am still buying GE stock. Our earnings have almost doubled, our portfolio strategy is complete and our initiatives are in place. We have worked hard to improve this Company. We have built a better GE. I know that our best days are ahead. Invest and deliver. Courage and discipline.

It was clear that Immelt was committed to the company in ways that matter: doing the things that are right for the company first; being seen to do the right things for the company; and most importantly emphasizing this point at every opportunity. Immelt told *Fast Company* in 2004:

> Enron and 9/11 marked the end of an era of individual freedom and the beginning of personal responsibility. You lead today by building teams and placing others first. It's not about you and it does take time to get there. But again, one of the things I learned from Jack is that when you're running GE, it's your job to pick ideas, pick people and spread those ideas across the company. It's not as much a question of confidence as much as it is a combination of confidence and actually seeing the pathway you want to follow – not just for a year or two but for a long period of time.

Personal commitment to the company has to be publicly demonstrated, genuine and most of all has to transcend personal gain or glory.

The long drive to sustained quality of management

Toyota is one of those companies that has sustained its position as one of the most admired companies in the world, having clambered into the charts and stayed there for a long time. Toyota was the 16th most admired company in the world in 1999, had risen to 11th by 2003 and was second, behind GE, in 2006. It was consistently the leading company in Japan during this period, staying ahead of Canon, Honda and Sony. Clearly there was something about this company's management that was special. As one observer noted: 'They have delivered strong performance when many other companies in their sector have struggled.'[11]

In 2006, having sold nearly 8 million vehicles, Toyota's president, Katsuaki Watanabe, highlighted the management approach as pursuing strategies of 'stepping up strategic measures targeting growth and steadily consolidating foundations for growth'.[12] Organizations like Toyota, Procter & Gamble, Tesco and GE that are repeatedly rated highly for quality of management focus their management attention on growth but also seek to consolidate and continuously improve existing operations. A key feature of quality of management is the ability to grow and consolidate simultaneously and not flip-flop between the two. Furthermore, high-quality management will identify and deal with issues whether they are of strategic or tactical importance. In the company's 2006 annual report, Watanabe noted:

'Consolidating foundations for growth' means making 'visible' issues
that have been hidden by growth, sharing these issues, and steadily
working toward their resolution. I do not feel that identifying numerous
issues is necessarily a bad thing. The emergence of a large number of
issues shows that opportunity for growth remains. Rather, I would be
anxious if we became a company that could not identify any issues.

Among the issues he identified were the need to enhance quality
continuously, strengthening cost competitiveness, and, most relevant to
the quality of management, developing the quality of Toyota's managers
by encouraging and developing self-supporting business organizations
worldwide, i.e. strengthening the depth of the company's management
– a perceived failure we saw in earlier examples. As the president wrote in
the 2006 annual report:

We want to heighten the quality of our management and operations.
If we can advance quality, quantity will follow naturally.

External analysis backs up Watanabe's internal views, since Toyota
is one of the most 'storied' companies in the world. Stephen Spear's
excellent analysis of learning to lead at Toyota, for example, gave some
of the management principles by which Toyota remained pre-eminent,
including managers as coaches to other managers and the encouragement
of experimentation as a method of continuous improvement.[13]

As noted earlier, quality in depth of management in most admired
companies is achieved by ensuring that managers, whether internally
developed or externally recruited, have the company's fundamental principles as the DNA of their management style. It should inform the actions
of all managers from the chief executive downwards. But this is not easy
and it has been noted that:[14]

[Toyota's senior executives] take great pleasure in explaining that
other companies find it difficult to emulate Toyota because its
management tools matter less than its mindset.

In Toyota's case, the mindset is one of growth and consolidation, of
identifying issues and dealing with them by paying attention to detail
through observation and experiment, of developing self-supporting
managers at all levels and in all businesses, and of instilling a company-
wide mindset – a 'way we do things round here' – which ensures a high-
quality management.

Beware of hubris

We have highlighted how driven, high-profile leaders and their companies achieve corporate reputations. Sometimes this power or reputation becomes too much and the same leaders, who may have done a great job, are overcome by a bout of hubris that leads to their undoing. We define hubris as exaggerated pride, over-optimism, overconfidence or arrogance.[15]

It is possible to plot hubris through the most admired company surveys. When senior executives are asked to give their views on the performance of their own company we are able to compare this with the views of others from outside the company. The results are enlightening.

We measured the self-perception of a group of executives and external perceptions of their companies and then plotted the data against the cumulative share price returns of these companies. The findings could be grouped into four clusters:

- **Consensus cluster (20/20 vision).** Senior executives' overall perceptions are accurate in representing reality.

- **Confident cluster (rose-tinted glasses).** Senior executives see only the good things within their company. There may be evidence that they misjudge reality in some of the categories and as a result are over-optimistic. Their self-perception may match that of their peers in some of the categories. In others, however, they over-optimistically consider themselves to be good, when their peers are suggesting that they are not.

- **Very confident cluster (tunnel vision).** Senior executives do not see the whole picture of their company. They may feel that they know their company better than anybody else and they may be right, but they ignore what others, such as their peers, think about their company. As a result they are so wrapped up in themselves that they can see only their own viewpoint.

- **Super-confident cluster (delusions of grandeur).** Companies in which the gap between senior executives' self-perception and peer perception is the widest experience the poorest performing shares. Senior executives' views are out of touch with reality. They see themselves much better than they really are. Unlike the tunnel vision group, who did not see other stakeholders' views, these

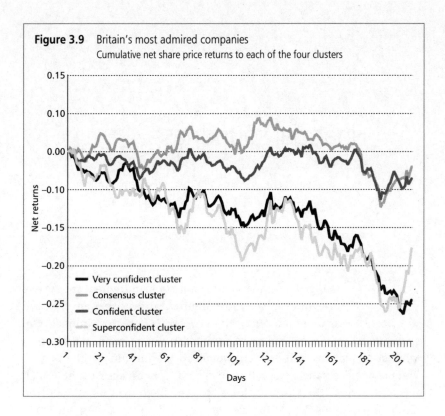

Figure 3.9   Britain's most admired companies
Cumulative net share price returns to each of the four clusters

managers may be aware of their peers' and other stakeholders' perceptions but choose to ignore them. Without hesitation or explanation they think they are alone in knowing how well their company is performing.

There is a noticeable inverse relationship between overconfidence and share price returns: the wider the overconfidence the lower the cumulative share price returns. Indeed, the largest returns are to companies in the consensus group, where peer perception is similar to self-perception (see figure 3.9).

When we looked further we found that of our original sample of companies, 27% of the super-confident, with delusions of grandeur, were no longer listed on the London Stock Exchange (since we did the research), whereas 70% of the confident remained.

The moral of the story is to beware of hubris.

4

Financial soundness

Financial soundness and quality of management are the two categories in the most admired surveys that are regarded as more important than others. Like success in quality of management, success in financial soundness gives a good indication of whether a company will do well overall. In Britain, nine of the past 13 winners of the financial soundness category have finished in the top 20 overall. Of these, three companies stand out: Tesco (winner in 2006 and 2007), HSBC (2004 and 2005) and Shell (1997, 1998, 2001 and 2002). When a company wins in both financial soundness and quality of management, it always finishes in the top spot overall.

In America, Microsoft has been top on six occasions, most recently in 2003; ExxonMobil has won six times, first in 1987 and last in 2007. Merck (five times) and IBM (three times) were also multiple winners in the earlier American surveys, although the last time either of them was in top position was in 1993. However, in 2007 IBM was the leader in its industry category for financial soundness, reflecting the fight-back that has returned it to the forefront of its sector. Only two American banks have ever achieved the top three places in this category: JP Morgan and Citigroup (although Berkshire Hathaway's financial services prowess has been recognised).

There have been five winners of the world's most admired company survey for financial soundness: ExxonMobil, Microsoft, UPS, Fuji and Intel.

It is not surprising that strong profitability underpins those that do well in financial soundness. In 1984 *Fortune* noted that 'profits provide the surest path to respect'. It was a year when the top 10's median return on shareholders' equity was 20%, compared with 13.5% for the *Fortune* 500, and none of the top 10 had had an annual loss in over 35 years. Nearly 20 years later in 2003, *Management Today* reported that British retailer Morrisons had an 'amazing track record – 35 years of rising profits, which allowed the Bradford-based company led by Sir Kenneth Morrison to bid successfully for Safeway, the UK's fourth-largest supermarket.' Indeed, profitability would have influenced Coca-Cola's chairman Roberto Goizueta's vote in 1990 when he shifted the focus of the company from boosting sales to maximizing shareholder returns. Goizueta stated that he wrestled over:[1]

> ... how to improve value and financial stability from the time I get up in the morning to the time I go to bed. I even think about it when I'm shaving. But I use an electric razor, so I think I'm safe.

But profitability alone is not enough to persuade observers that a company is financially sound and other indicators are taken into account.[2]

Marks & Spencer found this out in 1991, when, even though the company's pre-tax profits had tripled over the previous ten years to £604 million and the balance sheet was 'rock solid',[3] the company finished only third in the financial soundness category. The head office restructure (often a sign that things might be going awry) or the perceived lack of innovation in bringing through products that were future financial winners possibly influenced those who took part in the survey. For a long time Marks & Spencer was not regarded highly for financial soundness, but in 2007 it came second as a result of Stuart Rose's recovery programme, increased group profits, share price and the promise of global revenues.[4]

The best performing sectors for financial soundness

The catastrophic events that led to the crisis in confidence in the world's banks towards the end of 2008 came after a long period during which financial services was considered to be the most financially sound sector. In Britain, for example, banks had grown in strength and by 2005–06 led the field in the category. Before the sub-prime crisis and credit crunch, the sector had increased its bench-strength for financial soundness since the start of the surveys in 1994, with HSBC leading the pack and Royal Bank of Scotland, Barclays and Schroders (back in the FTSE100 in 2007 and achieving notable growth) all high in the rankings. A few insurance companies, including CGNU (now Aviva) and Legal & General, have also made fleeting appearances.

It wasn't always the case that financial services companies were seen as the most financially sound though. Indeed, in earlier periods, engineering, property and media companies were seen as financially sounder than banks. But from 1997 this changed. It is possible that the stock market 'mini' crash of October of that year (stemming from the economic crisis in Asia and causing over $600 billion to be wiped off market capitalization on American stock markets) had a 'correction' effect on perceptions of financial services companies, which thereafter were seen as sound bets. But the sub-prime write-offs and the dramatic events at Britain's Northern Rock and America's Bear Sterns have changed perceptions of banks' financial soundness.

The property sector has performed consistently since the mid-1990s, with companies operating in this sector attracting around 8% of votes in the financial soundness category. Land Securities has been the leading property company in this category. Oil companies BP and Shell have regularly featured in the top 20 for financial soundness. Other companies that have done well are Unilever, Cadbury Schweppes and GlaxoSmithKline.

As in other categories of most admired company surveys, the media have fallen from favour. From being one of the leading sectors for financial soundness in the mid-1990s, when companies such as Reuters, Pearson and Reed were regularly in the top 20 most admired companies, the media sector has fallen back dramatically, with votes cast in most admired surveys dropping from 16% to less than 1%. Between 2000 and 2006 only BSkyB and the *Daily Mail* group made the top 20 for financial soundness. But in 2007 WPP (18th in the overall chart compared with 45th in 2006) and Pearson (26th compared with 100th in 2006) were gaining respect for their financial soundness.

For the past ten years the American survey for financial soundness has been dominated by the energy sector (with ExxonMobil coming top in four out of eight years since 2000 and Kinder Morgan Energy Partners surprising everyone in 2005 when it won in six out of eight categories). The technology sector representation was boosted by Microsoft, which has won the financial soundness category three times since the turn of the millennium. In earlier years, Merck won the category several times and JP Morgan and Coca-Cola each won during the 1990s. But no American financial services company has been most admired for its financial soundness since 2000, whereas in the British survey HSBC has won twice (2004 and 2005).

This analysis suggests three things. First, there is a benefit to individual companies from the overall warmth of feeling towards a particular business sector. Hence a bank can make the top 20 for financial soundness in one year (Lloyds TSB and Prudential were placed in the top 20 in Britain's most admired survey in 1999) and this can, though not always, have a pull-through effect on what people think of other companies in the sector in subsequent years (in 2000 five from the financial services sector made it into the top 20 for financial soundness and in the following year seven did). The lesson is that a company may benefit from the reputation of the sector in which it operates. In contrast, even if financially robust it may suffer if the sector is seen as a poor performer.

Companies should spend time 'reputation watching' not only their own reputational performance but also that of the sector as a whole. This will allow them to anticipate how to take advantage of sector trends or take steps to protect themselves from them.

Bucking a downward or unfavourable sector trend is difficult but not impossible. Rolls-Royce's financial reputation goes against that of the engineering sector trend, which has been downwards for some time; BSkyB has done a similar thing in the media sector.

Profits finance growth

When Intel posted its 2006 financial report, the company knew that it had been a tough year. Revenues and profits were down. For a company that had been voted America's most admired company for financial soundness in 2005 this was a potential disaster. CEO Paul Otellini put his hands up and said 'yes this is a bad year, and this is what we're going to do about it'. In his 2006 letter to shareholders he wrote:

> We faced increasing competition, and our revenue declined due to greater than normal pricing pressure. Although we ended the year on a strong note and reported our 20th consecutive year of profitability, our 2006 revenue of $35.4 billion was down 9% and our operating profit of $5.7 billion was down 53% compared to 2005.

The company took action:

> We responded during the year by launching a comprehensive structure and efficiency review, and by implementing a broad restructuring effort aimed at cutting costs and creating a more nimble, customer-oriented Intel. We also accelerated the introduction of new products, leading the industry into an era of energy-efficient, multi-core computing and ending the year with one of the strongest product line-ups in our history.

The CEO was open, explaining why the financials had changed and what the company was going to do to put them right. The solutions covered all aspects of the company's operating performance: costs, revenues and profits. The management was perceived to have its hands on the key levers of company performance.

Otellini then went on to announce actions that were being taken for the long term including restructuring, cutting non-essential programmes and 'improving organizational breadth and depth'. Headcount took a hammering and 8,400 staff were cut from mid-2006 to the end of the year. Furthermore, divesting non-core businesses also featured, including 'certain assets of our communications and application processor business'.

But here's where Intel excelled in its management of what could have been a crisis of confidence. Not only was a cost reduction and divestment programme announced but the company also reassured stakeholders about its prospects for future growth by making public new processes for 'sustained technology leadership in microprocessors wherein we plan to introduce a new micro-architecture approximately every two years and ramp the next generation of silicon process technology in the intervening years'.[5] These actions gave anticipated savings of $2 billion in 2007 and $3 billion in 2008.

There was a pattern here. In 2002, when Intel's revenues were $26 billion down from the heady days of 2000 when they were over $33 billion, it adopted the same holistic approach to presenting its financial situation. In the 2002 annual report, chief financial officer Andy Bryant gave details of actions that had been taken to ensure continuing financial health:

- A 6% reduction in the workforce, accomplished without major lay-offs, reducing the workforce by 13% since peak employment in March 2001.

- Savings of hundreds of millions of dollars as resources are redeployed to areas of higher productivity and strategic importance. In 2001, these efforts took an estimated $1 billion out of the cost structure, followed by additional savings in 2002 of more than $300 million.

- Outstanding credit controls. The quarterly DSO (days' sales outstanding) ranged from 34 to 37 days. A lower DSO is an indicator that the company will be able to turn receivables into cash faster.

- Capital spending of $4.7 billion and research and development investments of $4 billion, primarily directed to advanced technologies and processes.

Intel was able to balance cost reductions against investments for future revenues in the long term, dealing with the immediate crisis while trying to persuade stakeholders of a bright future. By 2007 Intel was able to announce an increase in its dividend of 13%, making its five-year dividend growth rate higher than the industry as a whole. In the volatile world of chip manufacturing, Intel appears to have held its own and most importantly persuaded stakeholders that there was a firm hand on the financial tiller. And it was noted that Intel was able to respond quickly to technological developments, which reinforced belief in its strategic plan.

In *Good to Great*, published in 2001, Jim Collins gave a ringing endorsement when he wrote: 'Intel have always been great.'[6]

Intel has a good track record for financial soundness: second overall in 1998, 1999 and 2000, third in 2002 and still leader in its industry sector in 2008. The company's reputation for financial soundness was based on 16 consecutive years and 64 consecutive quarters of profitability. But Intel has gone beyond focusing on the single measure of profitability when presenting the financial case. If things are going well the management says why and if things are going badly they say what they are going to do about it. Perhaps most important is that the company came clean when things went wrong; investors were told the score and were reassured that the company knew how to deal with the problems.

Things were hotting up in the early years of the new millennium. The fight between Intel and its arch-rival Advanced Micro Devices forced price reductions and speeded up the pace of innovation and launch. Gross margins were down to 46.9% in 2007 compared with over 53% previously, and Intel has lost some market share. But the feeling is that the company's manufacturing prowess and new product innovations are an advantage.[7] The future is, as always, unpredictable in this most competitive of markets. But Intel has demonstrated over a long period that it understands the importance of financial soundness and has in place mechanisms for ensuring its continuity. The company has been here before. In 1980 it was voted one of the five best companies in America but in the stock market crash in October 1987 its stock price plummeted. Then the story was about the battle between Intel and National Semiconductor. Intel prevailed and has continued to do so.[8]

Expertise, skills and focus bring competitive advantage

In Britain's 1991 most admired survey, Land Securities took the top spot for financial soundness ahead of Shell, BT and Glaxo, among others, and has remained ahead for most of the period since. Figure 4.1 illustrates the consistency of Land Securities' financial soundness.

Land Securities has been in the property market for over 50 years and has ridden economic peaks and troughs without expanding outside Britain (apart from a brief flurry in Canada). Its business is therefore

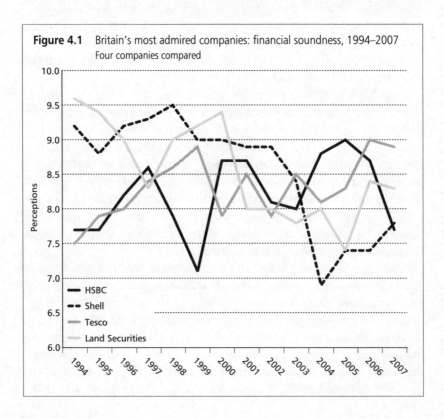

Figure 4.1 Britain's most admired companies: financial soundness, 1994–2007
Four companies compared

highly focused. The company's priority is to be recognized as Britain's leading property company, the success of which will be measured by returns generated to shareholders. To achieve this objective the company has, according to its website, a strategy 'to invest in commercial property in sectors where we have expertise and operational skills which gives competitive advantage. In these sectors we will apply our risk management skills and we will actively re-cycle capital with a view to delivering total returns in excess of our cost of equity.'

In 2007 Land Securities had a property portfolio worth £14.8 billion comprising nearly 140,000 developmental lettings. Its earnings per share were 753.59 pence, up 110% on 2006.[9] At its AGM in July 2007, the company's chairman, Paul Myners, in explaining how the company could generate returns in excess of the weighted average cost of capital, said:

> For property investment, this means adding value by actively
> managing our assets and judging the right moment to buy or sell.
> For development, it means creating the right product and delivering
> it on time and on budget, at the right moment in the market cycle.
> For property outsourcing it means accessing new markets and new
> income streams profitably.

He further noted that:

> In 2006/07 we had considerable success across all these areas.
> Highlights include:
>
> • Total return on capital employed for the 2006/7 year at 16.6%
>   substantially exceeded our weighted average cost of capital of
>   6.75%.
>
> • Our developments delivered a valuation surplus of 21.9%.

Land Securities' financial strategy is based on performance against multiple measures. As well as short-term profitability, it pays attention to other measures such as ROCE and valuation surpluses on property owned over their book value, while looking at new markets and revenue streams (which it does through its subsidiary, Trillium).

Figure 4.2 overleaf compares the company's performance in Britain's most admired company survey in 1994 and 2007. Although the 2007 figure indicates a lower perception of its financial soundness, this remains the core strength of the organization in others' eyes.

Both shapes, however, also illustrate those areas where the company's

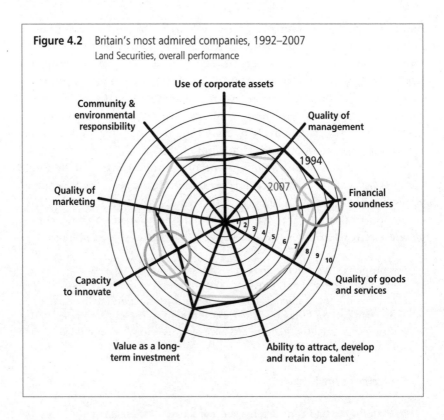

Figure 4.2 Britain's most admired companies, 1992–2007
Land Securities, overall performance

performance is less well regarded, in particular the use of corporate assets category. John Waples, business editor of the *Sunday Times*, highlighted that Land Securities stood for financial strength and stability but that alone was not enough:[10]

> It [financial soundness] is something the company prides itself on, but that in itself is insufficient reason to exist. It also has to innovate in a way that is visible to the outside world. On that count it has failed. The group is clearly frustrated that after converting to a tax-efficient real estate investment trust (REIT), the shares stand at a discount to net assets of nearly 25% ... Land Securities needs to justify why it exists, but to try and buck a cycle would be foolhardy.

But innovation usually comes at a price. When the company launched its redesigned corporate identity in 2007 (created by Hat Trick Design Consultants), it was aiming to reposition itself as a real estate investment trust (REIT), a type of company 'that invests money (obtained through the sale of its shares to investors) in mortgages and various types of invest-ment in real estate' so that 'shareholders receive income from the rents received from the properties and receive capital gains as properties are sold at a profit'.[11] The company pays no corporation tax but has to distribute 90% of its income to its investors, who may be taxed on it. The rebrand was a reflection of this new entity:

> [and] of how the nature and structure of the business has changed over the past five years ... Its previous identity, which uses building blocks, is based on an old idea of the company being focused on bricks and mortar. There has since been a big increase in service delivery, including building sourcing, refurbishment and maintenance, as well as construction.[12]

With this change in profile, Land Securities has been perceived as becoming more innovative. For some, this is a positive step forward; for others this innovation carried with it a risk of becoming less financially sound and this is reflected in the most admired survey results shown in figure 4.2.

Growth assets underpin financial soundness

Rupert Murdoch is not a man to shirk a challenge. So when he took the News Corporation's Fox Business Network into battle with CNBC, 'the entrenched leader in cable business news', it was fascinating to media watchers around the world. As Bill Carter wrote in the *New York Times* on 15 October 2007:

> [The company] made no secret that it intends to do in the realm of business news exactly what the Fox News Channel did in general news. As in: conquer ... there are already indications of just how fiercely the battle will be waged. In a pep talk to his troops Friday afternoon, Roger Ailes, the chairman of both networks, said, 'I'm not interested in anything short of a revolution.' That is what Rupert Murdoch, the chairman of the channel's parent, the News Corporation, expects from his latest media property – and, as Mr. Ailes put it in a telephone interview, 'When Mr Murdoch wants something, you try to deliver it.'

This wasn't the only new venture grabbing the attention of Murdoch and News Corporation in 2007. The $5 billion acquisition of Dow Jones, publisher of the *Wall Street Journal*, created a good deal of speculation about how being a member of the News Corporation empire would affect this bastion of American business news and information. As one commentator noted:[13]

> You can count on one hand the number of media moguls you
> bet against at your own risk. Atop the list is doubtless News Corp
> chairman Rupert Murdoch ... Whatever happens, you can bet
> Murdoch will use his far-flung resources to cross-promote the *Journal*
> and FBN, hoping to graft the blue-chip newspaper brand on his
> newbie network.

In 2007 News Corporation came second after Disney as the most admired entertainment company in the world survey. The company had revenues of over $28 billion in 2007 (compared with $17 billion in 2003) and income of $4.4 billion (up from $3.8 billion in 2006, $3.5 billion in 2005 and nearly double that of 2003). Its double-digit growth in 2007 was the company's fourth consecutive year of record results.[14] In the company's eyes, a 'compelling combination' of information and entertainment meant that 'few media companies' were able to match the sheer breadth of offerings. So why should News Corporation be considered among the candidates for most admired company votes? Murdoch revealed an important indicator when he stated:[15]

> We maintain what we believe is the ideal mixture of established,
> developing, and new businesses with significant potential. This
> balance serves an important purpose: it guarantees that we always
> have at least one generation of assets that can be considered our
> growth assets.

News Corporation has a strategy that appears to be consistent with three characteristics that have been identified in successful companies:[16] taking market share from other worthy competitors; having a huge open-ended market opportunity; knowing exactly how to lock in customers and work closely with them.

To ensure that there are enough assets to deliver financial soundness in the future as well as the present, News Corporation has built a portfolio of companies in vertical and horizontal markets that includes:

- 20th Century Fox and associated companies (such as 20th Century Fox television);

- MyNetwork and Star TV;

- Cable TV channels including national geographic;

- Satellite channels Sky and DirecTV;

- Newspapers such as *Australian Daily Telegraph, Sun, The Times, New York Post* and *Wall Street Journal*;

- Book publishers HarperCollins.

As stated in his letter to shareholders in the company's 2007 annual report, Murdoch has a clear strategy:

> [To provide] a compelling combination of information and entertainment for the largest audience around the globe … in providing this content, we maintain what we believe is the ideal mixture of established, developing, and new businesses with significant potential. Our established properties – assets like our newspapers, film studios and broadcast television properties – maintain valuable brands and loyal audiences, while remaining the foundation upon which we develop and expand all our activities, as well as generating reliable cash flows to fund our new businesses. The businesses that I call our developing operations are already delivering profits but still have room for stronger growth as they continue to further penetrate new markets. Our third-generation assets – our newest businesses – are just starting their growth cycles and are poised to become the company's future growth drivers.

As far back as 1996 Murdoch was extolling the virtues of this approach when he said of News Corporation:

> We have positioned ourselves to take advantage of new frontiers, while remaining confident that our strengths and experiences of the past will allow us to prevail.

For News Corporation, awareness of the need to ensure both current and future financial soundness and business strategies that perpetuate both has endeared them to voters in the world's most admired company surveys.

5

Quality of goods and services

On five occasions a company that has led in quality of goods and services in the British survey has also won the overall most admired award. Tesco has done it twice and Reuters and Cadbury Schweppes once. In 2007, in recognition of its revival under Stuart Rose, Marks & Spencer achieved this double success too. But the incidence of coming top overall and for quality of goods and services is less than with quality of management, financial soundness or value as a long-term investment.

Between 1994 and 2007, there have been nine different winners of the quality of goods and services category in Britain's most admired company surveys: Cadbury Schweppes (four times), GlaxoSmithKline and Tesco (twice), and Whitbread, Reuters, the Daily Mail group, AstraZeneca, Diageo and Marks & Spencer (once).

Cadbury Schweppes was in every top 20 chart for quality of goods and services from 1994 to 2006. GlaxoSmithKline has also made the top 20 in every year bar two since 1994. Tesco has done well, as have Rolls-Royce (sixth in 1994, second in 2006), AstraZeneca and J Sainsbury. Other companies that have had success include Reuters, Whitbread, Manchester United, the Savoy Hotel, Capital Radio, Highland Distilleries and Thorntons. Overall, 107 companies have featured in the top 20 for quality of goods and services of Britain's most admired surveys between 1994 and 2006, the majority once or twice.

In America's most admired company surveys, between 1983 and 1995 there were only four firms that came top for quality of goods and services: Boeing, Dow Jones, Merck and Rubbermaid. But in the following 12 years there were ten winners: Coca-Cola, Mirage Resorts, Toyota, Omnicom, *New York Times*, Philip Morris, Anheuser-Busch, Kinder Morgan, FedEx and Nordstrom.

One possible explanation of this increase in the numbers of winners was put forward by A.G. Lafley, CEO of Procter & Gamble, who noted in 2003:[1]

> Over the last half of the 1990s, we were all a bit too shareholder focused, too growth-at-any-cost focused. I tried to get people to flip that around. If we create brands that make a difference to our customers and focus on the fundamentals, ultimately shareholder growth will take care of itself.

One of those fundamentals is the quality of goods and services. This may be related to specific attributes or a more general approach to the way a company goes about its business. Nordstrom was recognized for service features that included 'a positive attitude, thoughtful suggestions, consistent service and a lasting impression',[2] whereas in Procter & Gamble's case it was for a broad sweep of quality initiatives.

The results of the world's most admired company survey reflect what has occurred in the British and American surveys in recent years. No one company has dominated this survey and between 2002 and 2007 there were seven separate winners of the quality of goods and services category. Many have implemented Six Sigma, a set of practices designed to improve manufacturing processes and reduce defects to near zero.[3] For companies such as GE, 'Six Sigma is part of the genetic code of our future leadership'.[4] For others, such as Polaroid, Six Sigma was 'the fastest and most effective path to improving product quality, widening the company's customer base, and improving profitability'.[5]

New approaches to quality have seen a move from conformance to standards (the essence of total quality management) to one that is much broader, in which 'quality is a state in which value entitlement is realized for the customer and provider in every aspect of the business relationship'.[6] It has extended its reach from the factory floor to front-line customer-facing activities.

But improving the quality of goods and services has been an obsession in businesses for decades, ever since quality guru W. Edwards Deming's statistical process control and his 14 points programme for achieving quality (starting with 'creating a constancy of purpose' and concluding with 'taking actions to accomplish the transformation') transformed large parts of American and Japanese business processes.[7] All of these were designed to deal with 'the most challenging question confronting business leaders and management ... not "how do we succeed?" It's how do we stay successful?'[8] Continuous improvement, including that of the quality of goods and services (i.e. both internal processes and external products and services), was seen as one of the ways to achieve this.

Quality of goods and services by business sector

So how have the business sectors in the British surveys compared for quality? British engineering companies have led the way. Rolls-Royce has figured in the top 20 most admired companies for the quality of its goods and services for 13 of the 14 years to 2007, when it came fifth. Other companies that have featured regularly in the list are Balfour Beatty, Rotork and Pilkington. Many would agree with Sir Anthony Bamford, JCB's chairman, who commented in 2007 that the UK's innovative engineering capability remained world class as can be seen in motor sport, and in the defence, aerospace and marine sectors.

Food producers and processors championed by Cadbury Schweppes (even though it took a hammering in 2007, finishing at 164th, down from 11th in 2006) and Unilever have been among the best performers since 1994, and household and healthcare products producers GlaxoSmithKline, AstraZeneca, Reckitt Bensicker and Croda International all feature.

British retailers Tesco, Marks & Spencer, J Sainsbury, Boots, Burberry, Next and Selfridges have all rated well for quality, and some have plans to expand markets. Tesco, which has operations in 13 countries, announced plans to enter the American market and has been opening stores of about 10,000 sq ft branded Fresh & Easy. As Jenny Davey noted in an article in Britain's *Sunday Times* in June 2007:

> Most importantly the format will be fresh – an acceptance that it
> is impossible simply to transfer the Tesco format from Britain to
> America. It is an American store designed for American consumers.

Marks & Spencer, having only a few years ago slimmed down its overseas operations dramatically, has announced plans to open stores in the Asia-Pacific region, including Shanghai and Hong Kong. It has highlighted India and China as areas for future expansion.

The media have fallen in the quality of goods and services category since the 1990s as they have in others, with only BSkyB making a showing. Banks are not regarded highly for the quality of their products either. Indeed, between 1994 and 2007 only Schroders has appeared in the top 20, though a few insurance companies have made the odd appearance.

The performance of America's business sectors differs markedly from that of Britain's. Vehicles and hotels have done better (Toyota and Mirage) as have oil and gas and the energy sector in general. Moving stuff around (FedEx) is still a strong sector in America's most admired companies list. Pharmaceuticals and health and household were stronger in America in the past than they are now, whereas in Britain they have maintained a fairly high presence. Merck's earlier successes in the 1990s were not sustained, though Genentech featured in the 2006 and 2007 top 20 and Procter & Gamble has been highly rated for quality of goods and services for many years.

As in Britain, the spread of companies winning in the quality of goods and services category has increased in the past decade. In America's most admired survey, between 1983 and 1989 there were three winners, during the 1990s there were five, and between 2000 and 2007 a different company has won each year. This almost certainly reflects the more competitive environment that Lafley referred to, and the popularity of Six Sigma – largely through the pioneering work of GE – has reinforced this trend. There has been much more focus on quality in the 2000s than before as companies have increasingly recognized its importance as a source of competitive advantage. Indeed, the average score for this category, which had been steady at around 9, has risen since 2000. FedEx's score of 9.94 in 2007 was the highest score for an American company in the history of the surveys.

One customer at a time

Nordstrom has been described as 'the ultimate in customer service among mainstream retailers'.[9] Incorporated in Washington State in 1946 as the successor to a retail shoe business that started in 1901, Nordstrom is one of the leading retailers in America with 155 stores in 27 states. Like other retailers worldwide, Nordstrom is feeling the pinch caused by the 2008 economic downturn, but what factors have made it a most admired company?

Business highlights for 2006 included increased sales (up 10.8% to a record $8.6 billion, the fifth consecutive year of gains), a return on investment (ROI) of over 20% and sales of $388 per square foot on a 52-week basis. Gross profit was 37.5% on sales, which topped 2005's record of 36.7%, and earnings before taxes (EBT) 'exceeded $1 billion for the first time ever'.[10]

There is a famous story about Nordstrom. A man walked into a Nordstrom store with two recently purchased automobile tyres and said he wanted a cash refund. He doesn't have his receipt – the tyres were a gift, he says – but they're in perfectly good shape. The Nordstrom employee says he can handle this easily, takes the tyres, hands over $250 cash, and wishes the man a nice day. The fly in the ointment, of course, is that Nordstrom doesn't sell tyres. But it does pride itself on fabulous customer service and huge volumes of loyal return business.'[11] With such tales doing the rounds, it is not surprising that Nordstrom is so well regarded for the quality of its service. As the company's president, Blake Nordstrom, says:

> A focus on continuous improvement by our entire team is helping us enhance the customer experience – through service and merchandize – one customer at a time.

Nordstrom first gained high marks for quality of goods and services in the 1994 *Fortune* survey, which put it ahead of most other general merchandisers such as JCPenney, Dillards, Sears Roebuck and Kmart (but slightly behind Wal-Mart). It maintained this position throughout the 1990s, albeit in Wal-Mart's slipstream, and built a solid reputation for quality. Two years of 'dismal results' during the decade because of 'a regional buying structure that puts basic decisions about fashion mix and merchandising in the hands of local managers' didn't really harm the reputation of the company for quality. Indeed 'as the Seattle-based company has grown into a national chain, analysts say that its decentralized management is unique in an industry in which corporate headquarters increasingly make every purchase and fashion choice', and though this 'has caused intense growing pains', quality at Nordstrom remains paramount.[12] By 2006 it was top of the charts for quality, beating UPS and Walt Disney and demonstrating that its commitment to continuous improvement was not just a statement in the annual report.

What Nordstrom has been able to do is embed its capabilities for quality into the 'organizational socio-cultural fabric' resulting in 'barriers to imitation'.[13] This has allowed it to build competitive advantage on the back of the quality of its goods and services. Investing in new technology has improved decision-making for quality hot spots and continuous work on operating disciplines has allowed the quality process to be embedded. The effect has been that 'the nature and level of customer service at Nordstrom that generates its competitive advantage can be repeatedly revealed yet remain inimitable by Nordstrom's competitors'.[14]

There is no secret to Nordstrom's success. The company has instilled quality into its way of life. It has allowed localized decision-making for some of its processes, particularly those that are close to the customer, but takes a centralized approach to others, such as information gathering for decision processes.

Focus on plan A

Few companies have been subject to the vagaries of business fluctuation more than Marks & Spencer. Some of its challenges have been self-inflicted; others have been a result of market forces. But what has the company done to rectify the problems that saw it plummet in ratings for its quality of goods and services and then rise up phoenix-like from the ashes?

Marks & Spencer was rated highly for quality in the early most admired surveys. Indeed, in 1991 it was Britain's most admired company, with *The Economist* noting:[15]

Marks & Spencer started being nice to its employees, customers, suppliers and neighbours decades before it was fashionable to do so ... Marks & Spencer are a company people are fond of.

But as Judi Bevan also noted in her book about the company:[16]

Marks & Spencer, 114 years old and the second most profitable retailer in the world, the subject of three Harvard Business School case studies, five times winner of the Queen's award for export achievement and with cupboards groaning with trophies for managerial excellence, steamed on full throttle towards the iceberg.

In 1999 Marks & Spencer's ranking for quality in the most admired surveys plummeted and fell even further in 2001 – see figure 5.1 overleaf, which traces the quality ranking and scores for four leading companies.

Figure 5.1 Britain's most admired companies: quality of goods and services, 1994–2007

Four companies compared

Year	Cadbury Schweppes		Rolls-Royce		GlaxoSmithKline		Marks & Spencer	
	Position	Score	Position	Score	Position	Score	Position	Score
1994	9	8.2	6	8.3	1	8.7	5	8.3
1995	2	8.4	11	7.9	4	8.2	8	7.9
1996	2	8.3	20	7.6	12	7.9	5	8.2
1997	4	8.2	12	7.9	5	8.2	2	8.3
1998	1	8.7	15	7.7	4	8.6	6	8.4
1999	7	8.0	2	8.8	3	8.6	155	5.8
2000	1	9.1	3	8.4	6	8.1	106	6.5
2001	9	8.0	19	7.6	2	8.4	235	4.4
2002	1	8.8	18	7.7	28	7.4	50	7.1
2003	6	8.0	16	7.6	3	8.2	4	8.2
2004	1	8.4	5	7.9	7	7.8	64	6.8
2005	3	8.0	51	6.9	47	7.0	59	6.9
2006	11	7.9	2	8.3	1	8.3	6	8.0
2007	164	5.8	5	8.1	31	7.3	1	8.5
Average	15.8	8.1	13.2	7.9	11.0	8.1	50.4	7.4

As figure 5.2 illustrates, it is hard to sustain a reputation for quality – as Marks & Spencer and now Cadbury Schweppes have found.

Writing in *Harvard Business Review*,[17] Stuart Rose outlined the issues that would be critical in Marks & Spencer's recovery from the spring of 2004 when he took over as chief executive. As he noted, there were three things that Marks & Spencer had to deal with: 'product, store environment, and service. We had to fix all of them, and fast.' He adopted six principles: 'first battles first, don't even consider a plan B, clean house, invest in staff, lead with your strongest asset, keep it in perspective'. By having this focused approach, Marks & Spencer returned in 2007 to the top of the rankings for quality of goods and services.

As Rose showed, quality can only be maintained by vigilance and awareness of actions that might have an impact on quality or perceptions

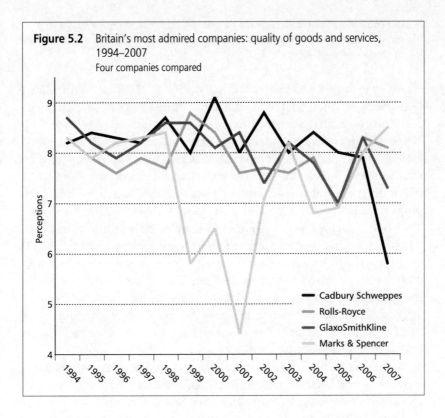

Figure 5.2 Britain's most admired companies: quality of goods and services, 1994–2007

Four companies compared

Cadbury Schweppes
Rolls-Royce
GlaxoSmithKline
Marks & Spencer

of it, leadership that inspires a quality approach and, most importantly, processes that foster the creation and maintenance of quality in goods and services from supplier management to stock control to the actions of the sales people on the front line.

Be innovative

When a leading biotechnology company, Genentech (founded by a biochemist, Herbert W. Boyer, and a venture capitalist, Robert A. Swanson, in 1976 and whose products include breast cancer drug Herceptin, Avastin, Rituxan and Raptiva), speaks of its success it is not only about profit but of bringing innovative new molecules to market. As it says in its 2006 annual report:[18]

Most of these molecules target novel mechanisms based on promising biology and could represent significant treatment advances. Over the next few years, we look forward to generating clinical data with new molecules and building our late-stage pipeline through advancement of these molecules.

As chairman and chief executive Arthur D. Levison, who joined Genentech in 1980, noted in the 2006 annual report that financial performance in that year was strong. Revenues of $9.6 billion were up 40% compared with 2005, pre-tax operating margins were 39% compared with 32% and cash flow from operations less gross capital expenditure was nearly $1 billion. By 2007 revenues had increased by 26% to $11.7 billion and the company was well on its way to achieving its Horizon 2010 project to discover, develop and manufacture life-enhancing medicines. Named as top employer by *Science Magazine* in 2007, 13th in the *Wired* 40 list and among the best companies for working mothers, Genentech is an employment force to be reckoned with. Its performance in America's most admired surveys reinforces the point. The company was second in the pharmaceuticals sector in 2006 and first in 2007, when it was top in innovation, people management, use of corporate assets, quality of management and quality of products and services. But what had it done to deserve the accolade for quality?

As well as its objectives for sustainable shareholder growth, it is the company's commitment to scientific excellence that has endeared it to those executives voting in most admired company surveys. Not fine words but 'translating basic scientific discoveries into novel therapeutics for significant unmet medical needs'.[19] Delivering high-quality pharmaceutical products is notoriously difficult with drugs being delayed because of clinical trials and a range of other social or political reasons. Genentech has a track record of delivery.

Forbes magazine summarized this success:[20]

At one point, Genentech had conducted 15 gigantic studies of its medicines without a single one coming up negative. Contrast that with the stench of failure in the drug industry, where experimental medicines are more likely to fail than succeed, and [some] pharmaceutical developers ... have seen their biggest bets bite the dust. Levinson says that based on the average success rates of drug companies, the chances of his winning streak were one in 300 million. Thanks at least in part to luck, Genentech has beat the drug industry's dismal odds – and thrived. In recent years, the world's first biotech – now a giant with $9 billion in annual sales – has launched cancer fighters Avastin and Tarceva, and Lucentis for age-related blindness.

Flawless execution, an 'incredible amount of expertise in delivering drugs to market and a process of designing clinical trials to understand patient risks as early as possible' are three of the factors that have led to the company being highly rated for quality.

Of course, the company's move into new market areas is risky and there is no guarantee that success will be as spectacular as it has been in the past (see Merck's performance in most admired surveys), and this is something of which the company is aware. The CEO's lack of hubris is marked: 'Says Levinson: There's nobody that asks "can we continue the hot streak" more than myself.'[21]

The virtues of continuous improvement

Takenaka was top in its sector for quality of goods and services in the world's most admired company survey in 2007, beating Skanska, Bouyges and Vinci. The firm's building and design work ranges from 'a modern tea room floating on a water garden', as part of the Sagawa Art Museum, to the Tokyo Tower and Midland Square, a 47-floor building in Nagoya. Takenaka provides total co-ordination of design, engineering, scheduling, estimation, purchasing and construction. This turnkey approach allows it to maintain quality control throughout the delivery of the 'product'.

Takenaka is one of Japan's leading construction and engineering companies with headquarters in Osaka and employing over 7,000 people worldwide. In the fiscal year ending December 2005, the company recorded revenues of ¥1,023.8 billion (approximately $8.7 billion), an increase of 4.6% over 2004. Operating profit was ¥19.5 billion (approximately $0.2 billion), an increase of 24.2% over 2004, and net profit was ¥17 billion, an increase of 73.5% over 2004.[22]

Established in the early 17th century, Takenaka is Japan's oldest architecture, engineering and construction firm. It has developed a philosophy:[23]

> To contribute to society by bestowing the best works to future generations. Architecture that responds both to the needs of the age and to the expectations of our clients is an asset to all of society, and endures as a symbol of the culture.

The company won the Deming quality prize in 1979 (named after W. Edwards Deming, an American management guru who advised Japanese companies on quality after the second world war) and was visited by Deming in the same year. Takenaka was one of the first construction companies in the world to introduce total quality management (TQM) processes into its business.[24] The effect was higher customer satisfaction, better project quality and higher market share.[25]

Takenaka tries to anticipate generational needs and maintain 'functionality, economic viability, artistry and freshness in society'. The company's president, Toichi Takenaka, also believes that:[26]

> As we face such issues as environmental protection, globalization and advanced accumulation and sharing of information, buildings standards have become increasingly sophisticated and diversified. With this in mind, we believe that the most important perspective is the concept of creating safe and comfortable people-friendly works of architecture.

To support these fine words the company has in place a series of processes:

> Firstly, gaining a clear picture of customers' needs. Bringing those needs together as a 'Quality of Design' and reflecting them in drawings and specifications. Faithfully building-in this quality of design in the workplace, and assessing it as a 'Quality of Conformance'. After completion, implementing quality assurance activities through after-sales service.

In an interview with *Forbes*, Takenaka gave his views on the strengths and direction of the company.[27] Training of employees in the culture of the company was identified as another way of ensuring that there was continuity of approach to quality:

> We emphasize the training and education of employees in our overseas offices. Some key personnel are sent to Japan to study for up to a year, and we regularly invite 10 employees a year to Japan for two weeks' training. We also arrange visits to ongoing projects and to our offices, as well as sightseeing trips to historic places like Kyoto.

Furthermore, the president emphasized the continuous improvement that was inherent in the company:

> Another important environmental area is intelligent buildings. We use energy-efficient systems in those buildings, such as the vapor

crystal system, which produces ice slush during off-peak hours when electricity rates are lowest. The slush releases cool temperatures during the day and provides efficient air-conditioning at a lower running cost.

What Takenaka has shown is that to deliver quality takes years of continuous improvement. However, two further things are important: the leader of the company showing a passion for quality and the ability to 'join up' company processes over time.

Is everybody happy? If not, fix it

When Mirage Resorts, a Las Vegas hotel and casino operator, was voted America's most admired company for quality of goods and services in 1996 it was the first time that any company from the leisure sector had won any category in the survey. The company was also eighth in the overall rankings that year, one place behind Microsoft but ahead of Hewlett-Packard and Motorola. Mirage Resorts built on this success in 1997 and finished second ahead of Procter & Gamble, Berkshire Hathaway and Johnson & Johnson. In 1999 it came top for quality yet again. The fact that the company was a leading provider of hotels, resorts and casinos in Las Vegas showed that the quality emblem was not just confined to technology or pharmaceuticals.

Steve Wynn, the owner of the company, is a leader with a difference. In 2006 *Time* magazine described him as:[28]

> The anti-Trump, hiding the bling, de-gilding the chandeliers, putting the Ferrari dealership in the back. The greatest creator of spectacle has redefined spectacle as an inner experience – or at least as much of an inner experience as you can have while playing blackjack.

In May 2006, *Time* recognized him as one of the world's 100 most influential people. He became a billionaire in 2004, and was appointed to the board of the John F Kennedy Center for the Performing Arts by President George W. Bush in 2006.

Before winning its first award, Mirage Resorts had given its shareholders a 22% return on investment between 1985 and 1995, putting it ahead of Procter & Gamble, on a par with Johnson & Johnson and a few points behind Coca-Cola.

In 1996 Wynn explained his approach to quality to *Fortune*:

Let's be honest, a slot machine is a slot machine. It's a commodity. The only difference between ours and one in Atlantic City and one in London is that you keep coming back to our slots because you have buddies, you have a little warm spot there.' Wynn's strategy is simple. Is everybody happy. If not fix it. 'We tell our people, if you see a hotel guest with the tiniest frown on her face don't ask a supervisor, take care of it. Erase the charge, send the dinner back, don't charge for the room.

Again, though, the key to quality is converting such ideas into action, making them part of the company's DNA and not just single events or campaigns. Mirage Resorts achieved this in three ways:

- Investing in employee education and training. At the time, this included in-house 'equivalency degrees' (equivalent to a bachelor's degree) on site. But another strategy, which attracted higher costs as noted in the company's 1998 SEC filing, was 'to ensure a smooth transition, the company hires replacement employees prior to the departure of transferring employees'.[29]

- Providing employee recognition. In 1996 the company persuaded George Bush senior and his wife Barbara to hand out the employee of the year award at Mirage Resorts.

- Empowering employees to deal with quality problems on the spot.

The effect on employee turnover of such activities was dramatic: Mirage's staff turnover in 1996 was 12% compared with 43% for competitors.

As with other examples, leadership emphasis on quality has been important. Speaking at a Milken Institute economic think-tank in 2007, Wynn reflected that his investment in employee training and benefits was a key factor in creating what became the number two company on *Fortune*'s most admired companies list. With outstanding customer service as his hallmark, Wynn has since successfully set up Wynn Resorts and is expanding internationally.

Performance of such high standards was bound to attract investors. And it did in 2000 when MGM acquired Mirage Resorts for $6.6 billion in a hostile takeover. It is a fair enough assumption that without Mirage Resorts's high reputation for the quality of its products and services this would never have happened.

6

People management

In 2008 Indra Nooyi, chairman of PepsiCo, stated the simple fact that 'if you appoint the right people, many of the worries are reduced'[1] – an observation that is borne out by the results of most admired company surveys worldwide. During the past ten years or so, the British company that has finished top in the ability to attract talent category in most admired surveys has finished top in the overall survey on five occasions (Tesco three times, GlaxoSmithKline and BP once). In America's most admired surveys, winners of this category (later called people management) invariably finished in the overall top 10 (such as Microsoft, GE, FedEx and Procter & Gamble). Good people management can increase the value of intangible assets such as employee know-how and company culture, which are considered important by chief executives. Since intangibles can represent up to 75% of the value of a company, paying sufficient attention to talent can make the difference in achieving high returns.

This is why Virgin Mobile (winner in Britain's most admired survey in 2006) has put so much effort into talent activity and why Cadbury Schweppes has consistently focused on this area since 1994 (finishing in the top five for talent management on no fewer than eight occasions). These companies see managing talent as a hard rather than a soft issue, and the ability to attract and retain talent is high on the board's agenda. In PepsiCo's 2006 annual report, Nooyi said that talent sustainability is:

> [A key focus] reflecting our belief that people hold the key to
> PepsiCo's success. Our company is known to many as an academy
> company, a place where people grow and business leaders develop.
> We are also committed to building a work environment where all of
> our associates can achieve a better quality of life and know that, as a
> business, we cherish them.

There is an added benefit. Companies find it easier to recruit and retain talent once they have a reputation for being a good employer. In 2000 *Fortune* reported that some of the leaders in talent management in America saw their investment paying off. GE had 200,000 applicants for 10,000 vacancies; Microsoft had 180,056 applicants for 10,233 vacancies; and Wal-Mart had an incredible 3.1 million applicants for 85,000 vacancies.

A study by the UK's Chartered Institute of Personnel and Development (CIPD)[2] noted that 'persistent skills shortages, the changing demographics of the UK workforce, its increasing diversity and the work–life balance agenda' had all contributed to the war for talent. These forces had led to labour shortages and increased competition for skills. This was not just a European phenomenon. Following a study carried out by Bersin and Associates, the American Society for Human Resource Management noted in 2007 that the gap in the leadership pipeline 'is a leading challenge for organizations'. It concluded that 'clearly, the issue that emerges from the study is that organizations are realizing the urgency of treating talent as a corporate asset and managers are beginning to act on it'.[3] The same is true in Australia, New Zealand and Japan, according to Manpower's 2007 Talent Shortage Survey. There is as much focus now on talent than when McKinsey conducted its famous War for Talent survey in 1998.[4]

There have been some imaginative responses to the challenge:[5]

> William J. Amelio, CEO of Lenovo, the world's third largest computer-
> maker, calls his global workforce strategy, 'worldsourcing' ... To retain
> workers in China, PepsiCo's snacks unit funnelled nearly 300 extra
> people into its talent assessment programme ... and promoted three
> times as many managers.

This appears to be true across business sectors. As one commentator noted:[6]

> The job market for skilled people is so hot. I also have heard similar
> messages at ... companies I've visited recently, including eBay,
> Microsoft, Google and Yahoo!, as well as from managers at companies
> including Procter & Gamble and Fidelity Investments.

The best at people management

The best companies in Britain for their ability to attract, develop and retain talent have been Marks & Spencer, Virgin Mobile, Cadbury Schweppes, Johnson Matthey, Tesco, Unilever, GlaxoSmithKline, Vodafone, Balfour Beatty and HSBC. A few companies have managed a sustained run. Cadbury Schweppes's record was mentioned at the beginning of this chapter, but others that were in the top 20 in this category in the first *Management Today* survey in 1994 and are still highly placed are Glaxo-SmithKline (Glaxo in 1994) and Vodafone. Some, such as Tesco, have been consistently placed. Others such as Rentokil, Schroders and Reuters were early successes but no longer feature in the upper tiers. However, Unilever stands out in this category: since 1994 it has been in the top six no fewer than 11 times.

The leaders in America's early most admired company surveys for talent/people management were companies such as IBM and Hewlett-Packard. Indeed, IBM sustained a good record during the 1980s but fell away subsequently. By the 1990s Merck and then Microsoft had appeared on the scene, the latter topping the chart in 1994 and still in the top 20 by the 2006 survey. Coca-Cola, Wal-Mart, Motorola and Home Depot figured highly during the 1990s, and Intel was in the top 20 in 1996 and 2006. But it is the performance of Procter & Gamble that stands out. It came second in the 1996 survey and has remained in the top 20 for talent/people management ever since, coming top in 2004 and 2006 and second in 2007.

In the world survey Procter & Gamble has been dominant and with General Electric has monopolized the top rankings for talent/people management since 2003, although Walgreen and Intel have also featured several times. Microsoft won in 1999 and has been highly rated in other years.

The inclusion of Enron in the lists is perhaps ironic. It came second for people management in 2000 in the American and world surveys. It was, of course, top in innovation in America from 1996 to 2001.

The best sectors at people management

There have been shifts in the performance of particular sectors in talent management since 1994.

There was a period when banking was considered a safe sector to work in. Then came big bang, mega mergers (such as that of Lloyds Bank and TSB, the largest banking merger in the UK) and a vast range of new

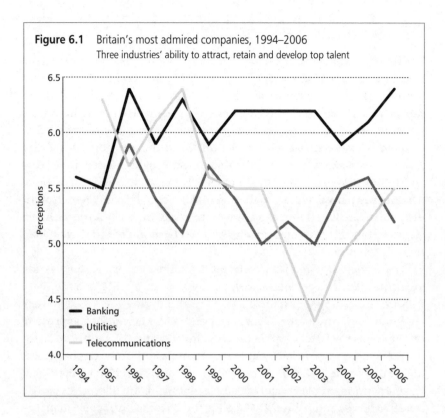

Figure 6.1 Britain's most admired companies, 1994–2006
Three industries' ability to attract, retain and develop top talent

financial instruments and ways of marketing, such as bancassurance, and suddenly banking began to take on an exciting dimension. This is reflected in perceptions of the ability of financial services companies to attract and retain talent. In the period 1994–96 the financial services sector attracted 8% of votes in the talent category, growing to 10% between 1997 and 1999 and 16% by 2002. Between 2003 and 2006 the sector was getting 17% of the votes for its ability to attract and retain talent. However, the recent credit crunch and sub-prime mortgage crisis have damaged perceptions of banks' talent management skills.

The media sector was the most highly rated sector for talent until 1996, getting around 13% of votes, but by 2003–06 it was attracting only 6%. If the resurgence of WPP, Pearson and Reuters in higher positions in the most admired charts in 2007 continues, it is likely that the media's share of votes for talent management will increase.

As is true with other categories, the performance of individual sectors can fluctuate considerably as figure 6.1 shows.

Several sectors have kept their share of the vote in this category fairly consistent. Pharmaceutical companies such as GlaxoSmithKline have long been regarded as being good at attracting talent. In the early years of the survey they were able to attract around 10% of the votes, a level that was more or less maintained until 2006, with a peak in the late 1990s and a slight downward trend thereafter. In 2007, GlaxoSmithKline was still third in the ratings. Oil companies have also had a fairly consistent share of the votes at 6–8%, though again there has been a slight fall in recent years.

From 1994 to 1997 retailers attracted some 11% of the votes for their ability to attract and retain talent, increasing their share slightly thereafter before falling back to 11% by 2006.

One sector that has experienced a big decline in the talent category is engineering, which has seen its share of the vote fall between 1994 and 2006. In an article in *The Times* in January 2008, Sir James Dyson lamented students' desertion of engineering subjects. He wanted Britain to go back to its roots as a hub of creative engineering. Perhaps only then will the sector's reputation as a source of talent improve. The utilities sector has done even worse: in 260 entries over a 13-year period, it did not get a single entry in the top 10 for its ability to attract and retain talent.

In America there has been a far greater emphasis on talent in the technology sector and this goes back to the very early days of the surveys. During the early 1980s over half of those firms that made it into the top three of the talent category were technology based. Hewlett-Packard and IBM dominated the top positions. There was also strong representation in the pharmaceuticals sector, with Merck as the dominant force during that period.

Over one-third of the top positions in the talent category during the period 1995–97 were filled by computer and data services companies (mainly Microsoft) and 20% by electronics companies, with strong performances by Motorola and Intel. The high regard for technology-based companies in this category has continued ever since with the electronics and computer and data services sectors doing well. In contrast with Britain, which had few highly rated electronics or computer companies in the talent category but did have some telecommunications companies, telecommunications companies did not feature in the upper echelons of the American surveys.

American financial services companies have on occasions done well in the talent category. JP Morgan made the top three in the 1980s and Citigroup and American Express in the 2000s. About 20% of top three entries for 2003–07 were finance based, about the same as in Britain. This figure is roughly the same as that for soaps and cosmetics, with Procter & Gamble – the talent factory – performing best.

Promote internal talent but also bring in fresh blood

Unilever has a long track record of success: second in the talent category in 1991, fourth in 1997, second in 2002, top in 2005 and fifth in 2006.

In 2006 Unilever had income of nearly €40 billion and profit of over €5 billion. Unilever's products included such famous brand names as Flora, Bertolli, Blue Band, CiF, Comfort, Domestos, Dove, Hellmann's, Knorr, Lifebuoy, Lipton, Lux, Ponds, Omo, Radiant, Signal, Sunsilk and Vaseline.[7] Its stated mission is:

> To add vitality to life. We meet everyday needs for nutrition, hygiene and personal care with brands that help people feel good, look good and get more out of life.

Figure 6.2 Britain's most admired companies: ability to attract and retain talent, 1994–2007
Four companies compared

Year	Unilever		Rentokil Initial		Tesco		ICI	
	Position	*Score*	*Position*	*Score*	*Position*	*Score*	*Position*	*Score*
1994	2	8.5	5	8.1	47	6.6	55	6.5
1995	2	8.0	8	7.7	11	7.5	31	7.0
1996	24	7.2	18	7.3	2	8.3	53	6.8
1997	4	8.1	19	7.5	1	8.2	41	6.9
1998	10	7.6	21	7.4	1	8.6	16	7.5
1999	5	8.0	21	7.3	1	8.8	173	5.1
2000	5	8.0	63	6.4	4	8.1	69	6.3
2001	7	8.1	64	6.4	3	8.4	36	6.7
2002	2	8.4	54	6.6	4	8.1	97	6.1
2003	6	7.8	42	6.7	1	8.5	110	5.8
2004	4	8.2	151	5.3	3	8.2	94	6.0
2005	1	8.6	203	4.4	3	8.3	127	5.7
2006	5	8.1	233	4.1	4	8.2	30	7.2
2007	14	7.5	191	4.8	2	8.3	121	6.0
Average	6.5	8.0	78.1	6.4	6.2	8.2	75.2	6.4

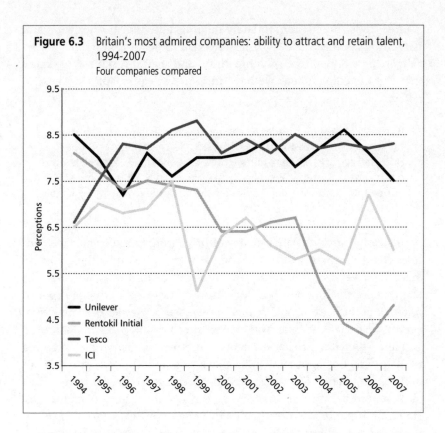

Figure 6.3 Britain's most admired companies: ability to attract and retain talent, 1994-2007

Four companies compared

But does the vitality Unilever seeks to add externally extend internally to its management of talented people? The company has undergone many changes, and as recently as 2006 it redesigned its organizational and governance structure and introduced new operating procedures. The One Unilever programme had led to cuts in senior management (including about half of those one level below the board in 2007). It also launched a major outsourcing deal for many of its support processes with Accenture. All of this was bound to have had an impact on how the company managed its people.

Figures 6.2 and 6.3 show Unilever's performance in the talent category compared with Tesco, which has won the category four times in the past decade, and also against two companies which did well in earlier years. ICI came top in 1990.

Unilever summarized part of its approach to talent management through the twin objectives of growing and harvesting. Patrick Cescau, chief executive, speaking at the World Food Business Summit in Paris in June 2006, noted, appropriately or ironically, that this growing and harvesting approach had to be flexible, had to adapt to the times – 'in a globalizing world of intense competition and specialist skills ... we know that the incredible talent we have in Unilever can adapt'. But he also noted:

> It is hard for a senior leader to change the very behaviour that made him or her so successful in the first place. So we are doing all the things necessary to help facilitate the new behaviours. We've changed our incentive systems. Regrettably, we have had to change some of our people ... and the new senior leaders in Unilever are acting as role models for the new behaviours.

Instead of sticking with a policy of promoting to senior management roles those nurtured within the company and who know the company mores and values, Unilever opted for a mix of nurturing home-grown talent and attracting new people with fresh ideas. This principle applied to the appointment of Paul Polman, previously at Nestlé, as its new chief executive in 2008. Polman was chosen ahead of internal candidates. He had also worked at Procter & Gamble, another company much admired for its people management. Unilever was not afraid to face up to difficult decisions when new talent was needed. Indeed, when the company issued its 2005 profits warning (the first in the 75-year history of the Anglo-Dutch multinational), it ditched its two chairman structure, reorganized the company and went to market to persuade its clients, shareholders and employees to have faith in the company.

At the same time, Cescau outlined part of the company's approach to the economic challenge:[8]

> I will never say, for example, that about 30 per cent of our people are not good enough, that would be terribly demotivating. Besides, we have been working with the new organizational model very successfully for several years in Latin America. Now I put people from that continent in vital places. That is how I give the implementation a face.

A focus on internal talent seems to come through here, to complement the healthy dose of new blood. It is also interesting to note that talent is on the CEO's business dashboard.

There are lessons to be learnt from Unilever's experience:

- Top management are actively involved in 'talent'. The CEO knows it is important to talk about talent as well as about the bottom line.

- The company is not wedded to a single system and is prepared to change things if one approach was not working. Every effort is made to 'take the people along', but occasionally there is a need to introduce new ingredients into the mix. It is a fine balancing act to keep internal talent motivated while bringing in new players.

- Unilever did all it could to make sure that its employees knew what was going on. The motivation of talented individuals is a critical management activity; if they feel excluded or in the dark, they may become disaffected and may well leave.

In Unilever's case the message is clear. Nurture your own talented people where possible and give them opportunities to progress within the business. But also bring in fresh blood when fresh thinking is required or there is no suitable internal candidate.

Build on the shoulders of those who came before

Walgreen, an American food and drug retailer, has featured in the top three of its sector in America's most admired company surveys for the past ten years or so. In 2004 it came second in the talent category in the world's most admired company survey and in 2006 it came third, just behind long-term stars Procter & Gamble and General Electric. Walgreen is one of the fastest growing retailers in America and continues to lead the chain drugstore industry in sales and profits. Furthermore, Walgreen was cited as one of Jim Collins's good to great companies. As Collins noted:[9]

> From December 31 1975 to January 1 2000, $1 invested in Walgreen beat $1 invested in technology superstar Intel by nearly two times, General Electric by nearly five times, Coca-Cola by nearly eight times, and the general stock market (including the NASDAQ stock run up at the end of 1999) by over fifteen times.

Such a performance could not have been achieved without a group of highly talented people.

There are over 5,461 Walgreen stores in 47 states (by comparison Boots has around 1,500 stores and the merged Alliance Unichem some 3,000) and the company has around 15% of the American retail market for prescriptions, serving over 4 million customers every day. With nearly 200,000 employees Walgreen has a lot of people to manage. The company was 45th in the *Fortune* 500 list of the largest US-based companies. In 2006 it had sales of $47 billion and earnings of £1.75 billion.

Walgreen entered America's most admired company charts at number three in the food and drugs sector in 1994 and has remained in prominent positions ever since. In 2006 it was top of its sector and in 2007 it was second behind a rapidly rising star, Whole Foods Market.

David W. Bernauer, Walgreen's CEO, reported in the company's 2006 annual report:

> We all build on the shoulders of those who came before us, and work to improve this company for those who follow. The challenge is to take advantage of people's minds across Walgreen. No way do all ideas flow from the corporate office. We're taking the time to listen – really listen– to folks from the stores to headquarters about what's working and what's not ... our greatest challenge is also our greatest opportunity – to attract and develop the people who will lead Walgreen 10, 20 and 40 years from now. With our growth, there's no time for 'slow cooking'. We're in a 'microwave' mode, where new folks reach management levels quickly. Investments in recruitment, training and development are consequently a top priority.

And he was indeed building on the shoulders of those who came before. The founder of the company, Cork Walgreen, had a particular knack in finding talented people to work for him:[10]

> The contrast between Jack Eckerd [head of a rival chain] and Cork Walgreen is striking. Whereas Jack Eckerd had a genius for picking the right stores to buy, Cork Walgreen had a genius for picking the right people to hire.

There are lessons to be learnt from Walgreen's experience:

- Hiring the right people is fundamental to the success of the company and has been since its foundation.

- The company puts a strong emphasis on 'home-grown' and cultivating internal talent (although the CEO had been brought in from outside the company).

- The company has a policy of committing to internal promotion where possible. This is attractive to career-minded individuals and helps attract and retain top talent.

- There is investment in talent that is not only financial but also in time and the creation of opportunity, tapping into the knowledge that exists within the talented employee and giving space to ideas.

Given this background, it is not surprising that Walgreen has a range of programmes for ensuring that diverse talent is encouraged. Walgreen's success in this area has put it ahead of retailers such as Carrefour, Groupe Auchan and Ito Yokado in the world's most admired company rankings.

Take talent very seriously

One of the principal attributes of companies that do well in the talent category is that they have excellent programmes in place for both recruitment and retention. There has been evidence of this since the early days of most admired company surveys. For example, in *Fortune* in January 1984, John Young, CEO of Hewlett-Packard, talked of 'creating the kind of environment where people see their futures here ... you have to compete for people – get their attention and loyalty'. Two years later, Clifton Garvin Jr, CEO of Exxon, talked of his people as being the number one strength of the company. Nowhere is this more evident than in Google.

Google's rise has been astonishing. As David Vise noted in his book *The Google Story*:[11]

> Not since Gutenberg invented the modern printing press more than 500 years ago, making books and scientific tomes affordable and widely available to the masses, has any new invention empowered individuals, and transformed access to information, as profoundly as Google.

In 1998, Google's founders Larry Page and Sergey Brin set in train the seeds for what was to become one of the fastest growing companies in history. By June 2006 Google was valued at $117 billion (Microsoft at $230 billion, Disney at $65 billion and McDonald's at $41 billion). In the eight years of its existence the company had risen to be one of the top three in the United States. By 2007, Google was one of the five most popular sites on the internet and the world's largest search engine. It is often said that it takes 20 years to build a reputation, but the Google timeline is on warp speed. Google didn't even feature in the upper echelons of the most admired company lists until 2006, when it popped up as second for innovation, behind Apple, and third for people management, behind Procter & Gamble and General Electric. Google was eighth overall in the 2007 *Fortune* most admired company rankings – ahead of such established giants as Microsoft, PepsiCo and Wal-Mart – finishing with even higher scores than the year before in innovation and people management.

But Google had not found it easy to get enough talented people on board. In 2005, Sergey Brin told the *Wall Street Journal*:

> Can we hire the quality and quantity of people we want to? No. We're underinvesting in our business because of the limitations of hiring.

Google recognizes the importance of getting a good fit between its employees and the organization. A huge amount of effort goes into the recruitment process to make sure employees have the right level of talent and cultural attributes for the company before they become a Googler (the name given to employees). The hurdle for joining Google is set high. The company's philosophy for attracting the best is based on three principles: 'It's tough to get into Google; all hires are talent; we cherish our culture.'[12]

In Europe, there are two aspects to the company's quest to get the right people. In operations, it has individual hiring plans for the top cadre and has developed multinational (and 'meaningful') sourcing capabilities in France, Germany and Poland to attract the right people to its business, and there is an inclusive approach whereby all Googlers can have a say in the hiring process. In programmes, it has plans for recruitment from colleges and universities, but it also places a good deal of emphasis on referrals from employees, seeing this as the cornerstone of the process. In all of this the company strives to balance new hires with internal promotions.[13]

Once someone has joined Google, a sophisticated 'on-boarding' process takes place in which the employee is assigned a buddy for a year. A mix of formal and informal development activities and the ability to spend time in pursuit of self-development (Googlers are allowed to spend 10% of their time on their own specified projects) promotes a culture of innovation and loyalty. Many employees also get the chance to 'design their own working environment', and as one HR specialist noted: 'They can pick their own job titles, they can pick their coffee machines, they can just do anything they want.'[14]

Google also puts great emphasis on personal development as part of its retention process. The high costs of recruitment mean that every effort needs to be put into retention if the return on this investment is to be maximized. So Google's leadership talent development process is seen as 'an ongoing integrated cycle', involving regular profiling of talent and a talent review, development planning at both the individual and regional level to ensure that development needs are both understood and met, and a series of development activities including allocation to programmes, coaching, and so on.[15]

Talent attraction and retention in Google are high. The company believes the reasons for this are threefold: 'Create a fantastic brand and working environment; hire the very best people; develop them through a blended approach.'[16]

The talent factory – no coincidence

In 2006 *Fortune* hailed Procter & Gamble as a veritable CEO factory, as human resources head Dick Antoine noted:

> When people do leave, we stay in touch with them, and they tell us they miss being surrounded by talented, high-energy colleagues. But we're very proud of our alumni, who tend to do pretty well elsewhere.

Three alumni sit on Procter & Gamble's board: James McNerney, CEO of Boeing; Scott Cook, founder and chairman of Intuit; and Meg Whitman, CEO of eBay.[17]

In an article in *Harvard Business Review* in June 2007,[18] Douglas Ready and Jay Conger noted some of the things that made Procter & Gamble great in talent management. The first was functionality: 'The processes themselves, the tools and systems that allow a company to put the right people with the right skills in the right place at the right time.' They highlighted the need to link talent management processes directly to the CEO's agenda. The second was vitality: 'The attitudes and mind-sets of the people responsible for those processes – not just in human resources but throughout the line, all the way to the top of the organization.' This idea of energizing a wide variety of players in the talent process was also found in the CIPD's study of the need to get both the board and line management involved.[19]

The third area is the creation of opportunity for talented people within the organization. Like Tesco, Procter & Gamble has a CEO who is a long-serving company man. A.G Lafley started working for the company in 1977 as a marketing assistant for Joy dishwashing liquid. Procter & Gamble invests time and energy in the careers of its employees, a fundamental requirement if a company is to do well in the ability to attract and retain talent category. It has been doing this for a long time, building up knowledge and systems in the process. In their classic 1992 *Harvard Business Review* article 'What Is a Global Manager?', Christopher Bartlett and Sumantra Ghoshal noted:

> A transnational's greater access to the scarcest of all corporate resources, human capability, is a definite advantage when compared with strictly local companies, or old-line multinationals, for that matter. Scores of companies like IBM, Merck, and Procter & Gamble have recognized the value of harvesting advanced (and often less expensive) scientific expertise by upgrading local development labs into global centers of technical excellence.

In the 15 years since the article appeared Procter & Gamble has sustained its competence in managing talent to maximize advantage both for the company and for its employees.

Building for the long run

In his book *The World is Flat*, Thomas Friedmann reminds us that competitive advantage comes to those who understand the new forces that are at play in global competition.[20] Attracting and retaining talented people clearly is a powerful agent in the source of competitive advantage.

Not surprisingly, given the interest shown in the subject, a number of surveys of talent management have been conducted. *Fast Company*, for example, concluded that seven principles should be applied in the management of talent:[21]

- Instil a talent mindset at all levels of the organization.

- Create 'extreme' employee value propositions (EVPs) that deliver your people's dreams – the EVP is the compelling reason why a talented person would want to work for your company. Crafted in the extreme, an EVP will enable a company to capture more than its fair share of talent. You will know that you've got the four elements of the EVP right when:

- great company =
- great leaders =
- great job =
- attractive compensation.

- Build a high-performance culture that combines a strong performance ethic with an open and trusting environment.

- Recruit great talent continuously.

- Develop people to their full potential.

- Make room for talent to grow.

- Focus on retaining high performers.

A 2007 report from the CIPD, 'Talent: Strategy, Management, Measurement', suggested that such things as 'a proactive, strategic approach to talent management' and support for talent management flowing from the top of the organization were important to success, as were performance tracking and the joining up of talent policy with other aspects of the employment relationship (such as pay).

7

Value as a long-term investment

Value as a long-term investment (VLTI) is one of three 'financial' categories that are covered in most admired company surveys – the other two being financial soundness and use of corporate assets – and therefore one of the areas traditionally used to assess company performance. Between 1994 and 2007 there were 11 different winners in the VLTI category in Britain's most admired surveys and nine in America's.

On seven occasions the company that came top in the VLTI category in the British survey also came top overall: Rentokil in 1994, Reuters in 1997, GlaxoSmithKline in 2000, Shell in 2001, Tesco in 2003 and 2006 and Marks & Spencer in 2007. On another three occasions the winner of VLTI came second overall.

The winners of the VLTI category in the American survey since 1994 were Coca-Cola, Cisco, GE, Microsoft, Citigroup, Medtronic, ExxonMobil, Berkshire Hathaway and CHS, again across a wide range of sectors. But the American survey is characterized by three distinct periods of perception: a stable period from 1983 when there was less of a flip-flop of perception than later (IBM won for four consecutive years and Merck won three times); the 1990s, when Coca-Cola won for five consecutive years; and from 2000, when six different companies won the award over an eight-year period. IBM won in the VLTI category and overall in 1984, 1985 and 1986 in the early surveys. However, by 2000 the relationship was less strong. GE, overall winner in 2000, did not make the top three for VLTI; likewise in 2001, the winner for VLTI, Citigroup, did not finish in the top 10 overall. By 2007, the winner of America's VLTI award, CHS, did not feature at all in the top 20 overall most admired companies; though it is not surprising that Berkshire Hathaway, a stalwart of VLTI and second in 2007, finished fourth overall.

Several familiar names have dominated the world's most admired company surveys since the turn of the century: Citigroup, Procter & Gamble, Berkshire Hathaway, Home Depot and ExxonMobil. The diversity and number of winners in such a short period of time show, once again, just how changeable are the perceptions of long-term value.

The business sectors most admired for VLTI

The winners of the VLTI category have come from a wide range of sectors – services to food manufacturing, information technology to retailing. But perceptions of a company's value as a long-term investment can vary substantially from one year to another.

Two things may explain this. The first is the volatility of the stock market. For example, Dow Theory Forecasts noted that 'long-term buys are our top choices for 24- to 48-month gains. In general, long-term buys are investment-grade stocks with solid finances'.[1] With 24 months regarded as long term it should not be surprising that VLTI lists change frequently. There also has to be a relationship between the perception of long-term value and what is actually happening on the stock market. The relative 'stability' of the early part of the 1990s, the technology bubble of the late 1990s and the dynamism of the bull market in the 2000s may have been factors in voter perceptions of value. There were five winners of the VLTI category for the seven years till 2006, compared with three winners for the last seven years of the 1990s. Second, there is the question of fashion in stocks. Even the staples of oil and gas, retailing, and health and household have shown volatility when it comes to peer perception.

There have been significant changes since the surveys started, such as the increasing success of financial and 'fun' companies in the VLTI category. Most notable is the rise of the financial services sector. Before Big Bang, the 1986 deregulation of the London stock market, which became one of the Thatcher government's sweeping reforms of the British economy, the financial services sector was a safe haven for a limited number of financial institutions. Closely regulated and mildly competitive, the banks in particular were seen as a good, safe repository for investment funds. But from October 1986, a new regime brought about radical changes, making the sector much more exciting, and hundreds of finance companies located to London (there were more than 500 banks in the City and Docklands in 2007). The changes appear to have had an effect on perceptions of the financial services sector as a source of long-term investment value. In the early years of the survey, financial services companies constituted some 8% of all votes, but by 2006 the figure had nearly doubled. Mergers of companies such as Lloyds and TSB, the growth of RBS and the global aspirations of HSBC have persuaded voters in the survey that the sector is a source of long-term value – although the sub-prime crisis and the credit crunch will have an effect on individual banks' VLTI, the view of the sector's VLTI as a whole may not be affected.

The broad-based 'leisure' sector is also seen as a contender for long-term investment. From 2003, positive perceptions of this sector as a source of long-term value had tripled as a percentage of the overall vote, with such companies as SAB Miller and Diageo included in the top 20 together with Carnival. This $11 billion revenue, 75,000 employee corporation, according to its 2006 annual report, is one of the largest vacation companies in the world, with a portfolio that includes Carnival Cruise Lines, Holland America Line, Princess Cruises and Seabourn Cruise Line in North America; P&O Cruises, Cunard Line and Ocean Village in the United Kingdom; AIDA in Germany; Costa Cruises in southern Europe; and P&O Cruises in Australia. 'Fun' is increasingly seen as a source of value.

Other sectors are closely related to the performance of the economy. Engineering, for example, did well during the mid-1990s before falling back at the end of the decade. However, the sector has enjoyed a resurgence as a result of the performance of Rolls-Royce, Weir Group, IMI and Halma, and by 2006 engineering companies accounted for about 10% of companies perceived as having the greatest long-term investment value. Oil and gas also got around 10% of votes over the whole period.

But the sector that has been getting the biggest share of the votes in recent years is that given the broad title of 'support'. By 2006 some 11% of votes were cast in favour of support services companies such as Serco, Compass and Capita.

Serco's mission statement is 'we improve services by managing people, processes, technology and assets more effectively'.[2] In 1964, the company won one of the British government's first outsourced contracts, which was the operation and maintenance of the UK Ballistic Missile Early Warning System at RAF Fylingdales. Today its activities range from providing IT services to the financing, leasing and building of new facilities, including hospitals and transport systems, as well as their day-to-day operations.

Between 2002 and 2006 Serco's revenue nearly doubled from £1.3 billion to £2.5 billion. Profits went up from £57 million to £112 million and by 2006 there were 40,000 employees. It would be possible to paint a similar picture for Capita, whose diversification from its traditional payroll base to huge government contracts has led to significant growth. The advent of services companies as creators of long-term value from the outsourced 'non-core' processes of other organizations is a phenomenon. Thomas Friedmann, author of *The World Is Flat*, believes that 'the best companies outsource to win, not to shrink',[3] a view that has increased perceptions that support services companies offer value as a long-term investment. Of course, such a fundamental reshaping of the traditional business model is not without its critics. Lou Dobbs has referred to offshoring – one possibility within the outsourcing model – as 'Exporting America' and has raised the political stakes on this aspect of outsourcing.[4]

American companies seen as having long-term investment value fall into a broad spread of sectors. During the 1980s technology and pharmaceuticals stood out in this category; by the 1990s it was the turn of the beverages sector, with Coca-Cola coming top for five consecutive years between 1993 and 1997. In the new millennium oil and finance became dominant. Since 2002, the winners of the world's most admired company survey for value as a long-term investment have been drawn from the finance, health and household and oil sectors.

Shareholder value

Shareholder value is what GE, America's most admired company for value as a long-term investment in 1999, saw as critical in determining its own executive performance. It said in its 2001 annual report:

> We support compensation policies for senior executives that provide challenging performance objectives and motivate executives to achieve long-term shareholder value.

Warren Buffett's philosophy is to look for investments with 'favourable long-term prospects' (Berkshire Hathaway was winner of the value as a long-term investment category in 2005).

Alfred Rappaport, a professor at Kellogg School of Management, Northwestern University, is believed to have coined the phrase shareholder value in 1986, when he noted the limitations of some of the more traditional ways of valuing a company and came up with an alternative: shareholder value = corporate value – debt.[5] In this definition, corporate value had two components: present value of cash flow from operations during the forecast period and residual value (value beyond the forecast period). By evaluating company performance in this way and looking at how the 'direct linkage between competitive strategy and shareholder value' allowed those evaluating a company's performance to translate business strategies into 'the dollars of value that they create', Rappaport added a new dimension to the assessment of company performance. Perhaps value as a long-term investment, certainly since the mid-1980s, is a proxy for perceptions of shareholder value creation.

There is other evidence to support this perception. Companies such as Wal-Mart, Coca-Cola, Berkshire Hathaway, Walt Disney and General Electric, top performers in America's most admired company surveys, have, in past years, also been top-tier performers in annual shareholder returns, giving percentages of over 20% and as high as 35%. This supports the view that for most large companies, maximizing shareholder value, though often requiring 'fundamental strategic and organizational change, is a worthwhile business activity since the potential for value creation is so enormous'.[6]

Shareholder value is clearly a contributor to the perception of executives when they cast their votes in the value as a long-term investment category. But there is also a good chance that the unmeasurable 'gut feel' also played a part.

How do individual companies ensure that they deliver long-term value?

Building success for the long term

Perhaps it is surprising that a company in an unglamorous business should be regarded highly for value as a long-term investment. But Wolseley, a supplier of heating and plumbing products, building materials and services, has done well in Britain's most admired company surveys since 1995, when it finished 14th in the VLTI category, coming top in 2005 ahead of Tesco. In 2006 the company reported sales of over £14 billion and around 78,000 employees serving customers through over 5,000 branches in 28 countries. In the same year, when revenue was up nearly 26% on the previous year and trading profit up 25%, it made 53 acquisitions (31 in North America and 22 in Europe) for which it paid over £900 million.

With the American housing market showing no sign of recovery, at least in the short term, perceptions of Wolseley's value as a long-term investment may change.

Figures 7.1 and 7.2 illustrate Wolseley's performance in the long-term investment value category between 1994 and 2007 and compare this with three other companies.

Calm seas with lots of activity under the water

Since its formation in 1997 after the merger of Grand Met and Guinness, Diageo has become one of the world's leading premium drinks businesses. Its brands include Smirnoff, Johnny Walker and Baileys. The company trades in over 180 countries and is quoted in both New York and London. The word Diageo is derived from the Latin for day (*dia*) and the Greek for world (*geo*). As the company notes: 'We take this to mean every day, everywhere, people celebrate with our brands.'

In 2007, Diageo reported sales of £9.9 billion compared with £9.7 billion in 2006; operating profit was £2.16 million compared with £2.04 million in the previous year, although overall profit was down from £1.9 billion in 2006 to £1.5 billion in 2007.

In 2002, Diageo came eighth in the overall most admired company ranking and sixth for value as a long-term investment. Under its CEO, Paul Walsh, the company had adopted a strategy that involved disposing of peripheral companies and concentrating wholly on drinks. This involved the sale of Diageo's food arm Pilsbury for $10.5 billion and 'helped to put some sparkle back into the world's biggest booze business', according to *Management Today*. Figure 7.3 compares Diageo's performance in 1996 and 2006 and shows how it has increased its scores in seven categories including value as a long-term investment.

In 2005, Walsh commented:[9]

> One of the things I find quite interesting is how analysts and journalists use statements like 'stable cash flow' about Diageo. They don't realize it's like a graceful swan going down the river, they don't realize the activity going on under the water.

Once again, double-digit growth appears to be a feature of those companies valued as long-term investments, and in his 2007 annual review Walsh noted that this had occurred internationally, with North

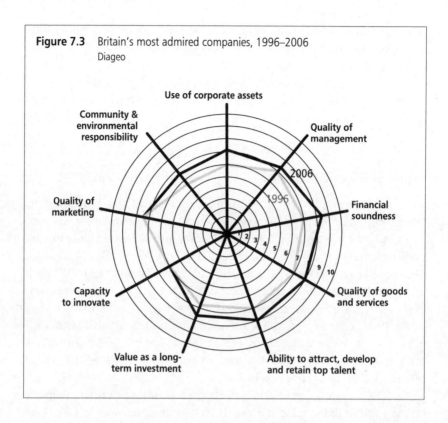

Figure 7.3 Britain's most admired companies, 1996–2006
Diageo

America in particular delivering strong top- and bottom-line growth. It was also reported that 91% of Diageo employees are proud to work for the company. So growth and growth potential would appear to be two characteristics that strengthened the perception of long-term value, backed up by a workforce willing and able to deliver strategy. Reinvesting in the business, in particular £100 million in the Scotch whisky business in Scotland, also augured well for Diageo's long-term value.

A further characteristic of Diageo's reputation for long-term investment value, spread of risk, mirrors that of Wolseley. So when Bloomberg reported the 2007 figures it was quick to point out:[10]

> Increased sales of higher-priced spirits in the US, Brazil and Asia offset slowing European demand for Guinness stout and premixed vodka beverages. Sales in North America, the distiller's most profitable market, haven't been affected by a recession in the housing market that has cut disposable income.

The fact that a company can weather economic storms in one geographic area or product line by counterbalancing financial hits with revenues from another sector seems to count a lot when executives decide whether a company's reputation as a long-term investment is sound.

By spreading risk across international markets and focusing on its core drinks business:[11]

> Diageo provides a clear example of a company that understands and leverages its core competence. Rather than pursue multiple strategic thrusts at the time of the merger, the company put its faith in its ability to build global drinks brands and it created an organization that allowed it to extract value from that ability. In a difficult market, Diageo still managed nine per cent organic growth.

As mentioned earlier, Diageo also invested in existing businesses, such as whisky in Scotland, and new ones as the market consolidated, pursuing a strategy of 'taking a stake in small and nimble companies ... that can deliver new ideas'.[12]

Without investing in the future a company will not be thought to have great value as a long-term investment.

Consistency in shareholder focus

In 2006 ExxonMobil hit record levels of income at $39 billion and a return on capital employed of 32%. Such a performance was instrumental in the company achieving the top spot in the financial soundness category in America's most admired company survey in both 2006 and 2007, and the highest ranking in 2004 and 2006 and third position in 2007 for value as a long-term investment. In its 2006 annual report, the company stated that shareholder value had grown in the year with a total return of 39%. Over the previous five years $92 billion had been paid out in dividends.

ExxonMobil's reporting shows that it has a clear understanding of its core competencies. There is no ambiguity in what it does and where it is going, even though the company operates in a volatile market affected by politics. In 2006 'consistency – in our shareholder focus, in our long-term approach' was one of the company's five principal business values, the others being integrity, discipline, reliability and ingenuity. If a company such as Exxon promotes such a long-term perspective, it is a step towards achieving a reputation in this area. Other companies do not always articulate this as clearly as part of their 'mission'.

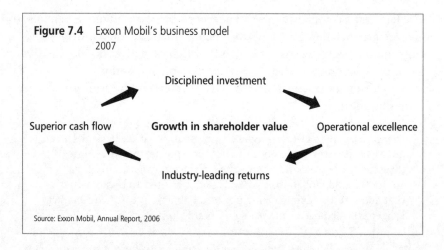

Figure 7.4 Exxon Mobil's business model 2007

Disciplined investment

Superior cash flow   **Growth in shareholder value**   Operational excellence

Industry-leading returns

Source: Exxon Mobil, Annual Report, 2006

With ExxonMobil there is once again an element of spreading risk within the core business. In 2006 it reported over 60 projects in development, including upstream projects in West Africa, Malaysia, Azerbaijan, Norway and Canada, as well as a $700 million investment in technology research and development. Furthermore, in common with others in the sector, ExxonMobil really does take a long view. As Rex W. Tillerman, the company's chairman and CEO, noted:[13]

> By 2030 we expect the world's energy needs will be 60% greater than in 2000, with the majority of that demand being met by fossil fuels.

As figure 7.4 shows, the company has a 'disciplined and straightforward approach: taking a long-term perspective and focusing on generating growth in shareholder value while managing risk'.

According to its annual report, in 2006 ExxonMobil's invested $20 billion in new projects and developments, an increase of $2 billion on the previous year. The company subjects its projects to a rigorous approval process to 'ensure that each project is technically, operationally and financially robust', and the scale of the projects – the company expects to invest £10 billion in the East Area Project off the coast of Nigeria – demonstrates why this should be the case.

Oil companies have other problems to contend with which might have an impact on perception of their value. For example, the Exxon Valdez affair rumbles on 20 years after the oil spillage in Alaska, showing that the long view must take environmental considerations into account.

The company is well aware of this and among other actions it has given $100 million to Stanford University's Global Climate and Energy project, the mission of which is 'to conduct fundamental research on technologies that will permit the development of global energy systems with significantly lower greenhouse gas emissions'.[14]

Venturing to succeed

Nokia has done well in the world's most admired company surveys and the Finnish telecommunications giant has a solid financial reputation. In 2006 the company's sales were over €41 billion, a 20% increase on 2005, and net profits were €4.3 billion, a 19% increase on the previous year. Mobile phone sales were the biggest segment of revenue at nearly €25 billion, but there was also significant growth in multimedia sales at nearly €8 billion, up 32% on the previous year, and sales of networks at nearly €7.5 billion.

This is not a bad set of results for a company that started as a wood pulp mill in 1865 in a small town in the south-west corner of Finland. What were the characteristics of the company's performance that led to its being so admired?

The first thing that stands out once again is the geographic spread of business activity. In 2006, 38% of Nokia's sales were in Europe, down from 42% in the previous year as sales grew in Asia-Pacific from 18% to 20% and in China from 11% to 13%.

Second, there is a mix of acquisition and organic growth in achieving financial targets. Nokia continues to grow organically but has also been bolting on additional services as part of its portfolio. Acquisitions in 2006 and 2007 included Twango (media sharing), Loudeye (Digital Music Platforms), Intellisync (synchronization software) and LCC International (wireless networks), as well as joint venture activity with Siemens, to widen the revenue base and mitigate risk. In so doing Nokia is building a 'competitive product portfolio with products that are preferred by our current and potential customers to those of our competitors'. Clearly the company sees its long-term value being both preserved and enhanced in part by developing its product portfolio. In the late 1990s Nokia established Nokia Ventures Organization to build on its knowledge and ensure the success in investments in this area. According to Nokia's website:

Nokia Ventures Organization approaches the identification of new business opportunities from two directions: Identifying broad opportunity spaces based on industry analysis and developing new ventures based on Nokia employees' ideas as well as on innovations from external sources.

An article in *Business Strategy Review* said:[15]

[It was a] way to create and develop new businesses outside the natural development path or current focus of core businesses. It was realized that different corporate venturing situations required different solutions.

Interestingly, Nokia Venture Partners, part of the ventures organization but operating at arm's length from the parent company as a venture capital fund, invests in new ventures where:

Nokia can add value through technical expertise in the due diligence phase and gets an insight into new technologies, markets and business models being developed in the outside world.

The third area of note with regard to long-term investment value is Nokia's investment in research. It has 1,100 people working in the Nokia Research Centre and it also undertakes joint research projects such as those with the University of Cambridge in the UK. As mobile communications converge with other media, Nokia, whose success is based on constant innovation, will also be in a strong position to shape the industry and this will be crucial to longer-term success.

Verbund and competitive advantage

With revenues of over €52 billion in 2006 (up from €42.7 billion in 2005) and net income at over €3 billion in 2006, chemicals company BASF is one of the leading companies in Europe. The world's most admired company survey put it at number one in Germany in 2006. BASF has more than 160 subsidiaries, 150 production sites worldwide and over 95,000 employees.

One thing that has differentiated the company from its competitors is its 'integrated approach to manufacturing, research and its overall management philosophy'. This philosophy, together with the 'maximum integration of infrastructure, processes, energy and waste management, is known as *Verbund*, a German word meaning linked or integrated to the maximum degree'. But in BASF terms *Verbund* is more than simple integration:[16]

[It represents] entire interlocking value chains, from chemical building blocks produced primarily for BASF use to cyclically resilient specialty and fine chemicals that offer higher returns. BASF's investments and acquisitions highlight more than market opportunities; they also demonstrate the expansion of value chains, a key concept for understanding Verbund. Value chains, capital investments and management's approach to market opportunities together enhance BASF's overall returns, serve customers and consistently make high-quality products.

The point is that *Verbund* – linking together value chains – allows resources to be used efficiently:[17]

Our *Verbund* is one of BASF's greatest assets when it comes to using resources efficiently and BASF use the concept in all of its regions and globally. Worldwide, BASF operates six *Verbund* sites and more than 150 production sites in proximity to our customers. In our *Verbund*, we link production plants intelligently to save resources and energy. The largest *Verbund* site in BASF Group is located in Ludwigshafen, Germany. This was where the *Verbund* concept was developed and optimized before it was applied to other sites around the world.

BASF has *Verbund* sites in Antwerp, Belgium; Geismar, Louisiana; Freeport, Texas; Kuantan, Malaysia; and Nanjing, China. This is a most effective business model, offering economies of both scale and scope to BASF divisions (of which there are 14 marketing to business partners in over 200 countries).

In pursuing its aim to earn a premium on the cost of its capital, BASF uses value-based management that 'encourages all employees to act in an entrepreneurial manner'. This is done by linking value targets to performance-related pay. Improving the cost structure, a disciplined approach to capital expenditure and maximizing growth opportunities are three elements of BASF's strategy which contribute to its performance as a long-term value adding company.

Spreading risk and investing in the future

Between 1994 and 2006 in the value as a long-term investment category, there were 11 separate winners in Britain's most admired company survey and nine in America's, making it one of the most diverse categories. Perceptions of value in a company are influenced by culture, geography, the performance of national economies and the volatility or otherwise of the stock market. Overall, though, value as a long-term investment seems to be a proxy for shareholder value.

There is plenty of evidence to support this view. One study took the top ten companies from the overall American results over the period 1983–2004 and found that the portfolio of most admired companies had annual returns of 17.7% compared with 13% achieved by the least admired companies. Considered over five years, the annual return was 16.51% compared to only 10.27%.[18]

Another study found that a portfolio of most admired companies consistently outperformed the stock market while one of least admired companies underperformed. Over a period of five years, the study concluded that the cumulative five-year returns for most admired companies were 125%, whereas for least admired companies they were just 80%. Even when a portfolio of all shares listed on the New York Stock Exchange, the American Stock Exchange and NASDAQ were taken into account, the results still showed that most admired companies outperformed the index by on average 3.7% per year.[19]

8

Capacity to innovate

Not only do much admired companies use innovation to launch new products or improve processes, they also achieve competitive advantage by being innovative in the way they deal with customers and manage people.

Between 2006 and 2008 Apple Computer was rated the most innovative company in America and in 2008 it was also the most admired company overall. It had a brilliant track record in coming up with innovative products such as the Mac, iPod and iPhone that transformed the market. Apple's philosophy of saying no to a thousand things and working on a few key products has paid off.

America's most admired companies for innovation have in recent times come from a broad range of sectors. As well as Apple and Google, top companies since 2003 have included FedEx, United Healthcare, Nike and 3M. Citicorp featured regularly in the early years of the survey during the 1980s, but like other American finance companies it has dropped off the lists for innovation. And between 1996 and 2001 the innovation award went to Enron, only a year before it went bust for innovative accounting.

Britain's most admired companies for innovation have included companies such as Burford from the property sector, Tesco from retail, BSkyB from the media and ARM holdings from technology. That innovation is not confined to technology alone is highlighted by the fact that Tesco has won the category three times, although it must be said that Tesco's innovative skills in loyalty cards and supply chain management have a lot to do with technology.

Figures 8.1 and 8.2 compare the performance of four British companies in the innovation category.

Figure 8.1 Britain's most admired companies: capacity to innovate, 1994–2007
Four companies compared

Year	BSkyB		Pilkington		Cable & Wireless		Vodafone	
	Position	Score	Position	Score	Position	Score	Position	Score
1994	–	–	12	7.5	82	5.9	23	7.0
1995	–	–	24	6.9	206	4.5	20	7.0
1996	–	–	9	7.6	177	5.2	61	6.4
1997	10	7.7	28	7.0	109	5.8	30	7.0
1998	3	8.2	25	7.0	82	6.2	19	7.2
1999	1	8.9	42	6.5	171	5.1	23	7.0
2000	1	8.5	64	6.5	160	5.2	27	7.1
2001	1	8.4	6	7.9	199	4.6	90	6.0
2002	3	7.8	5	7.6	203	4.8	88	6.1
2003	1	8.1	6	7.7	202	4.1	56	6.3
2004	6	7.4	4	7.4	199	4.3	14	7.1
2005	4	7.8	3	8.0	220	3.9	20	7.1
2006	37	6.8	9	7.5	204	4.8	47	6.7
2007	1	8.4	–	–	199	4.6	95	6.1
Average	6.2	8.0	18.2	7.3	172.4	4.9	43.8	6.7

However much people may bang on about the importance of innovation, in the history of the British most admired company surveys only one company that finished top in innovation also came top overall (Tesco in 1998 and 2005). The 1995 innovation winner, British Land, came in 20th in the overall chart and Burford, 1997's most innovative company, came in 36th overall – a similar overall ranking to that of ARM Holdings, the 2006 innovation winner. Furthermore, the capacity to innovate has the lowest correlation with financial soundness at 47% and with only a 63% correlation with value as a long-term investment.

The results of the American surveys paint a similar picture. In 2007, for example, Apple, Google and FedEx were the top three in the innovation category but did not make the top five overall. In 2006 only Apple and

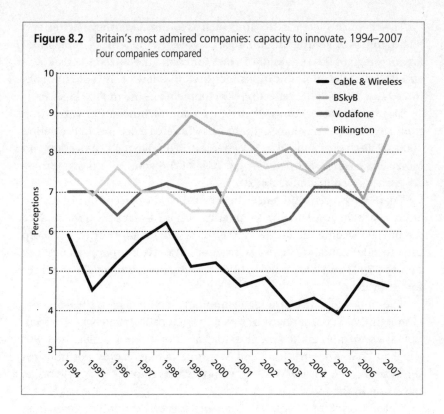

Figure 8.2 Britain's most admired companies: capacity to innovate, 1994–2007
Four companies compared

in 2005 only FedEx from the top three most innovative companies made the top 20 overall.

The business sectors that are most innovative

Between 1994 and 2006, 21 British sectors out of 24 were represented in the innovation category. Companies in sectors such as heavy construction and house building are generally not regarded as innovators, although some property developers, notably British Land and Quintain, have done well over the years.

The finance sector's increased share of the vote over the period 1996–2006, from 1% to 13% by 2006, was the largest of any sector, reflecting the innovations of companies such as Man and ICAP as well as more traditional finance businesses, no doubt driven by new legislation, greater competition and a more discerning consumer base. By 2006 finance was considered the most innovative sector in Britain.

The chemicals sector, with firms such as Johnson Matthey, Victrex and Pilkington, was getting around 10% of votes by the end of the period. Engineering got 9% as a result of votes for companies such as Rolls-Royce and Rotork. Telecommunications increased its share of the vote from 5% in 1994 to 8% in 2006, reflecting developments in the mobile business.

The media sector, however, saw its share of innovation votes drop from 13% to 4%. The retail sector has also suffered a decline. In the period 2000–02 Tesco, Iceland, Dixons, Next, Selfridges, French Connection and Morrisons ensured that retailers got 23% of the votes for innovation. By 2006 only Tesco made the top 20.

There have been differences between sectoral perceptions of innovation in Britain and America. In America over a 20-year period the finance sector has become much less highly regarded for innovation. Citicorp used to ride high and Charles Schwab has also made an appearance, but between 2003 and 2007 not one finance company has made the top three for innovation.

The opposite is the case for technology. In the period 1984–86, and although IBM was dominant in other characteristics, there were no technology companies in the American top three for innovation. By the 1990s this had changed, with Intel and Motorola taking leading positions for innovation. And in 2003–06 companies such as Apple and Google began to feature in the top three.

In the world's most admired company surveys technology companies such as Nokia, Apple and Intel have featured in the top three for innovation along with Walt Disney, Procter & Gamble and FedEx.

Innovation is essential for any business's long-term prosperity and survival, but as *Fast Company* noted in 2004:[1] 'Truth is, some of the most innovative companies in the history of American business have been colossal failures.'

Innovation: beyond the petri dish?

There are differing views about what constitutes innovation. A study by an American consulting firm, Blessing White, put a definition of innovation in context:[2]

> **Invention** – creation of something completely new, whether it is a product, service, or process. This is something that makes other products or processes redundant.

Innovation – which is the creation of a substantially new approach on an existing product, service, or process. This is something that enters the market or process and competes with others.

Stepped improvement – small changes, e.g., speeding up a process.

Innovation can be big and dramatic, an invention (a big 'I'), or a small change (a small 'I'). In other words, one person's invention is another's innovation. In organizations such as Procter & Gamble, there are likely to be myriad innovative ideas across all the business processes. As the company's CEO, A.G. Lafley, told *Fortune* in 2006:[3]

Narrowing the focus makes a difference, so we focus on eight to ten core technologies where we want to be world-class. I don't know how it happens, but in every case I've been associated with over almost 30 years, the focus gets diffuse. More projects get started than anybody can manage. At the corporate innovation-fund level we had way too many; we went through every one in detail and chucked two-thirds.

The key is to identify those innovations that will make the biggest difference and pile corporate effort into them. Or as Steve Jobs of Apple told *Business Week*, the 'seed of Apple's innovation' was 'saying no to 1,000 things'.[4]

The type of company that has won the category has broadened in recent years. 3M, which came second in the innovation category in 1990, was described by *Fortune* in January 1990 as functioning 'like a kind of corporate petri dish that fosters the spirit of innovation in its scientists and engineers'. Each year the company held a private trade show to display its 'bountiful innovation produced from over 115 research labs'. In 2001 it was financial companies such as Charles Schwab and Citigroup in the top three for innovation, and in 2006 UnitedHealthcare.

Perceptions of what is innovative have gone beyond the petri dish to embrace an organization's processes, services, human resources marketing and indeed every aspect of the business. It is often the result of a convergence of the big idea with smaller ones, balancing, as Blessing White put it, 'innovation and the day job'.

In order to innovate more effectively, Procter & Gamble has moved from a research and development (R&D) approach to one of connect and develop (C&D). In their *Harvard Business Review* analysis, Neil Huston and Nabil Sakkab concluded:[5]

Most companies are still clinging to what we call the invention model, centered on a bricks-and-mortar R&D infrastructure and the idea that their innovation must principally reside within their own four walls.

But in spite of the introduction of improvement processes, they concluded that 'these are incremental changes, bandages on a broken model'. This was the situation faced by Procter & Gamble in 2000 when the 'invent it yourself model' clearly wasn't working. So the company moved to greater collaboration with smaller entrepreneurial companies which were eager to sell their intellectual property or form industry partnerships. Given the perception that Procter & Gamble's approach to innovation was not capable of sustaining the required levels of growth, the company adopted the C&D model, which, as the CEO said, enabled the company to:

identify promising ideas throughout the world and apply our own R&D, manufacturing, marketing, and purchasing capabilities to them to create better and cheaper products, faster.

Procter & Gamble start idea searches with the top ten customer needs:[6]

Once a year, we ask our businesses what consumer needs, when addressed, will drive the growth of their brands ... This inquiry produces a top ten needs list for each business and one for the company overall. The company list, for example, includes needs such as 'reduce wrinkles, improve skin texture and tone ... which do we want to license, sell or co-develop further?' The answers provide an array of broad targets for our innovation searches and, as important, tell us where we shouldn't be looking.

In other words, start with a real problem or issue and focus your innovative resources, across the board, on to solutions.

Innovation, innovation, innovation (and profit)

One company that appears to have captured the essence of these multiple forms of innovation is BSkyB, which has a great track record for innovation in the British most admired company surveys. In 1997 it was tenth behind such firms as Orange, Glaxo, Reuters and Tesco. The following year it came third and in 1999 it came top, which it was again in 2000, 2001 and 2003 and again in 2007.

In 2006 BSkyB's revenues were £4.1 billion, up 8% on the previous year working on a gross margin of 61%. Profits were £877 million, up 7% on the previous year, and the dividend pay-out was up by 34%. The company had over 8 million subscribers for its DTH (direct-to-home) service and 1.5 million subscribers for its Sky+ service. Part of its success was based on its ability to offer innovative products and services to its customers, starting with digital TV and moving on to integrated digital decoders and personal video recorders and then to high definition TV. But as BSkyB pointed out in its 2006 annual report:

> This isn't innovation for its own sake. It's first, last and always about our customers. It's about what new technology can do for them, and how we can use it to make Sky better.

This ability to match its innovation to the wants of its customers, often creating demand – a skill of the most successful innovative companies – had allowed the company to take a lead over its competitors.

Three things stand out in BSkyB's approach:

- The idea of collaborative partnerships, rather than inventing everything in house. This is a concept the company has in common with Procter & Gamble in its C&D model. BSkyB is working with companies such as Vodafone and Intel to leverage each other's innovations and technologies to develop new customer services.

- Embracing the big 'I' of innovation in a client-facing way with the launch of high definition TV in 2006. For BSkyB this means:[7]

> Offering such a comprehensive HD service has been a huge technical challenge for us as a business, and has involved everyone from the transmission teams, to customer support, to marketing. We've also been working with Sony on co-marketing the huge advantages of HD, and there have been some great offers for people buying both a Sky HD box and Sony HD-Ready TV.

This is collaborative big 'I' innovation in action and demonstrates the importance BSkyB puts on innovation.

- The focus on continuous improvement as part of the innovation process. Grouping channels in the packages offered to make the buying process easier for customers is one such innovation that combines technology applications with a customer focus;

developing Sky+ to help people record or delay programmes for their convenience is another.

Indeed, BSkyB was recently likened to another innovation winner as 'TV's Tesco' by one commentator, though not without criticism. The report noted:[8]

> BSkyB clearly knows how to do business, as illustrated by new subscription figures (8.6 million with a target of 10 million by 2010). Given the siege mentality in the media trade, this is remarkable. Sky's gamble of expanding beyond its core TV business, to offer telephony and broadband internet access appears to be paying off ... what Sky has become is the Tesco of pay TV.

BSkyB offers some good lessons in innovation:

- Get the balance right between the big 'I' of invention and the continuous improvement of innovation.

- Make innovation customer focused and offer innovative services that people want rather than those that look good in the tool room.

- Make sure innovation is profitable or the investment will drag you down.

Two fundamentals: execution and investment

One thing that has been noted by a number of companies, including Apple and Procter & Gamble, is the need to convert innovation into meaningful, value-added applications. Without such a convergence of business need and innovative activity the process is pretty much a waste of time. ARM Holdings is a good example of where this has taken place. The company makes microchips for MP3 players, mobile phones and a wide range of other products. In 2006 it was voted Britain's most innovative company, never having featured before in the most admired company rankings.

In 2006 ARM's revenues were £263 million (up from £232 million in 2005), made up of a broad mix of licences, royalties, sales of development systems and services. By 2007 the company was growing at twice the rate of the semiconductor industry as a whole. Its CEO, Warren East, said in the 2006 annual report that he was pleased with the 'strong licensing momentum' which 'confirmed the market share gains of the company'.

Underpinning this growth was the reallocation of resources to the development of leading-edge technology in the intellectual property division and management focus for growth. Company performance showed healthy growth in an incredibly price sensitive market with competitors in lower-cost economies than the UK. East described the company as 'being the architecture for the digital world', a pretty big claim. But its success in getting its technologies into everyday items from washing machines to televisions to cars means that there is some justification for it. ARM's products 'enable companies to design and market their electronic devices more quickly and more economically' to give end-users intelligence, reliability and security.

ARM knows full well that the digital revolution is ongoing and strives to stay ahead of the game through a process of continuous improvement as well as invention. The 2006 annual report states:

> Technology will continue to evolve. ARM's digital architects are a vital part of that evolution – they create products that are, and will continue to be, fundamental to the implementation of the digital world.

This is perhaps the little 'I' of innovation. However, ARM also seeks innovation with a big 'I'. For example, 90% of the innovation in the motor industry is a result of electronics and ARM's products have been instrumental in this, improving such things as brakes, intelligent wheel systems and fuel consumption (by up to 40%). This requires the company to work proactively with end-users, a point also raised by GE in its approach. ARM also has a keen commercial perspective; it is not interested in having innovation for innovation's sake. As the annual report states:

> Our technology makes it easier and more cost effective for companies to design and make advanced digital products. Our role is not only to innovate, but also to take structural cost out of the process: we enable the retail cost of electronic devices to be reduced.

Three lessons can be learnt from the example of ARM Holdings:

- Innovation is continuous improvement.

- Innovation should be relevant to users.

- Innovation should add value to the bottom line by helping to reduce the costs of processes.

Saying no to a thousand things

Without focus the effort and energy put into innovation are likely to be diffused and may not lead to anything meaningful. Apple Computer recognizes this. In 2006, with net sales of over $19 billion and income of nearly $2 billion, it was voted the most innovative company in the world, and it held on to the top spot in 2007.

Apple's story is one of a company recognizing strategic mistakes and taking action to regain pre-eminence in its field. It is also one of how leadership matters: while Steve Jobs was out of the picture between 1985 and 1997 Apple struggled in its business performance as a result of poor marketing and confusion in product lines (too many models). After Jobs's return, a focus on innovation was one of the keys to its revival, but according to *Fast Company* innovation is also the company's problem. As it noted, the failure to license its operating system in the 1970s, not maximizing on the educational PC market and the poor design of its Newton pen based computing system (way ahead of its time) are examples of failure to capitalize on innovation:[9]

> That Apple has been frozen out time and again suggests that its problems go far beyond individual strategic missteps. Jobs may have unwittingly put his finger on what's wrong during a keynote speech in Paris. 'Innovate,' he bellowed from the stage. 'That's what we do.' He's right – and that's the trouble. For most of its existence, Apple has devoted itself single-mindedly, religiously, to innovation.

As Jobs put it, it's 'saying no to 1,000 things' so as to concentrate on the 'really important' creations. This is view shared by GE's CEO Jeffrey Immelt with his emphasis on focus on a few critical innovations. But Apple has also invested in its innovation effort at a time when many companies are slashing their R&D funds. The results are staggering. The iPod and the iPhone are the most influential new technology product for years and Apple's desktop computers are not only design icons but also have a huge fan club of users. Much of the credit for the turnaround in fortunes must go to Jobs, the man who founded Apple in 1976, was ousted in a power struggle with CEO John Sculley in 1985 but returned in 1997 to shift the company onto a new plane.

Figure 8.3 compares Apple's overall performance in America's most admired company survey with that of Microsoft. Whereas Microsoft's performance has been reasonably consistent if gradually declining, Apple's performance has been volatile but has been on an upward slope

Figure 8.3 America's most admired companies: overall performance, 1993–2007
Two companies compared

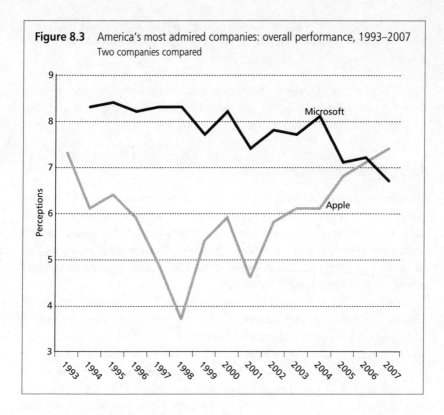

in recent years, culminating in its success in taking the top spot overall in the 2008 survey (including first place for innovation ahead of Nike, Procter & Gamble and Starbucks, among others).

Jobs was asked about why Apple seemed to have its innovation act together when other companies failed to do so:[10]

> You need a very product-oriented culture, even in a technology company. Lots of companies have tons of great engineers and smart people. But ultimately, there needs to be some gravitational force that pulls it all together. Otherwise, you can get great pieces of technology all floating around the universe. But it doesn't add up to much. That's what was missing at Apple for a while. There were bits and pieces of interesting things floating around, but not that gravitational pull.

In his view the gravitational pull was getting people on the front line – sales, business development and marketing – to inform innovation in product design and specification. But even this isn't enough:

We have a second goal, which is to always make a profit – both to make some money but also so we can keep making those great products.

As well as focus, Apple's success is because of its innovative people. Having the right people, people who care about innovation and can deliver it, is crucial if innovation is to be effective.

Game changing innovation

Innovation can range from a small series of incremental changes to a big killer application. But if a company can achieve breakthrough innovation and make it work, the rewards can be dramatic. A.G. Lafley, CEO of Procter & Gamble, has cited 'game changing' innovation as a route to revenue and profit growth.[11] PepsiCo has also sought to do this with its quest for game changing innovation.

Although PepsiCo made the final 19 of Jim Collins's 'Good to Great' list, it, together with its arch rival Coca-Cola, just failed to get through to the 'Great 11'.[12] The battle between PepsiCo and Coca-Cola for domination of the American beverages market is one of the most fascinating in corporate history, full of challenges and responses, strategic errors (such as Coke's disastrous reformulation of its basic recipe in 1986, which forced a relaunch of the original version of the drink as Coca-Cola Classic) and fight-backs. It has been a roller-coaster ride in which innovation has played a big part.

This battleground was made more challenging by consolidation in the food and beverage industry between 1997 and 2002, with the result that PepsiCo faced fewer but stronger competitors. It had to do something that would strengthen its competitive position. In a paper published in 2002, Sankaran Venkataraman noted that:[13]

Four attributes have served to fuel PepsiCo's growth and endurance. They may be characterized as:

I.   Muscular Global Brands and Consumer Goodwill

II. Robust Technology/Manufacturing Platforms

III. Powerful and Flexible Go-To-Market Systems

IV. Global Footprint

PepsiCo also recognised that innovation could fuel growth.

Nowhere is this competitive battle better exemplified than in America's most admired surveys where three companies have fought to lead the beverages industry sector since 1984. In that year Anheuser-Busch came top, Coca-Cola second and PepsiCo third. Coca-Cola then had a couple of years' domination before conceding to PepsiCo, which came top from 1989 to 1991. Coca-Cola then came top from 1992 until the beginning of the millennium. In 2003 PepsiCo was back on top and was also winner of the innovation category in the world's most admired company survey.

In 2006, PepsiCo had net revenues of $35 billion (up from $32 billion in 2005) and an operating profit of over $7 billion (up from $6.7 the year before). The company saw innovation as the key to growth, both strategically and operationally. Indra Nooyi, the CEO, noted in the company's 2006 annual report:

> Innovation demands that we constantly look around the next corner to ensure we're providing products that our consumers and retail customers want. We have a relentless focus on innovation, as new products consistently deliver 15% to 20% of our total growth. In 2006 alone, our North American businesses introduced new products that totalled greater than $1 billion in retail sales. More strategically said, we're focused on game-changing innovation. Clearly, we need to keep our existing big brands fresh while developing products and venturing into new categories.

This enlightening statement shows how PepsiCo has adopted the 'game changing' approach of Apple, GE and Procter & Gamble, while also paying attention to smaller, incremental changes.

As Nooyi stated, PepsiCo is disciplined about innovation:

> We've developed a very strong pipeline for 2007 and beyond, including new products like Flat Earth vegetable and fruit crisps from Frito-Lay, and new beverage entries such as Izze, a sparkling beverage made with 70% fruit juice, and Naked Juice, a line of all natural juices and juice smoothies, acquired in January 2007. And we'll expand on our successes, such as introducing Baked Walkers crisps in the United Kingdom.

For PepsiCo, innovation is the lifeblood of the company.

The Pilkington paradox

Pilkington Glass, based in St Helens, is one of the few survivors of this industrial heartland and its survival may in large part be because of its ability to innovate.

Established in 1826, Pilkington developed the idea of forming a ribbon of glass by floating the melted raw materials over a bath of molten tin. This replaced the traditional grinding and polishing process and was to become the universal method for the manufacture of high-quality flat glass. The company's continued ability to innovate has resulted in the development of K glass with coatings, automotive, laminated, fire-resistant, bullet-proof and energy-saving glass, solar-controlled and thermatic insulation glass, and, most recently, self-cleaning glass.

Between 1990 and 2006 Pilkington came top in its sector for innovation in Britain's most admired company survey, with the exception of 2000 when it came second. It also finished in the top ten for innovation in Britain's most admired company surveys for six consecutive years from 2001, with a highest position of third in 2005 ahead of BSkyB and Carphone Warehouse, both notable for their innovative qualities. Being held in such high esteem does, however, highlight potentially positive and negative relationships between other characteristics, specifically the quality of its products, financial soundness and its value as a long-term investment. This is called the Pilkington paradox and is illustrated in figure 8.4.

Figure 8.4 shows an apparent trade-off between innovation and value as a long-term investment. Voters are aware that development and innovation in products and processes could be a significant drain on the company's financial resources, which can put it in a precarious position.

Despite continued efforts to reduce costs, in June 2006 Pilkington was acquired by Nippon Sheet Glass. Inevitably, global competition has taken its toll on Pilkington's performance, but also building a strategy based on a capability such as innovation puts pressure on other key performance indicators. The skill is to encourage and manage the right amount of innovation.

Innovation: a platform for business success

Innovation can be a tremendous platform for success, but business history is full of companies that were first to market with much admired innovative products but which did not achieve their potential competitive advantage

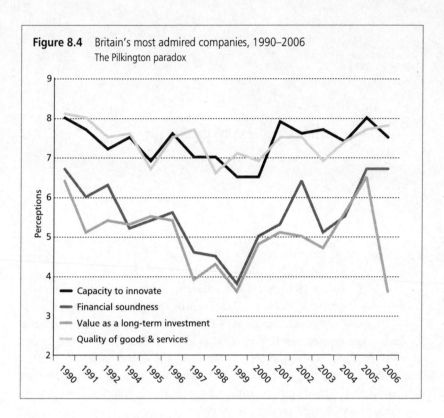

Figure 8.4   Britain's most admired companies, 1990–2006
The Pilkington paradox

- Capacity to innovate
- Financial soundness
- Value as a long-term investment
- Quality of goods & services

because of a failure of application. Pilkington was highly focused on innovation but did not give enough attention to other business fundamentals. Innovation on its own will not make a business successful, but Apple and PepsiCo have shown that innovation and business acumen will pay off.

Some companies such as Tesco (three times a winner in the innovation category) appear to be able to strike the right balance: just enough innovation to stay fresh and for it to be a continuous process, since one off innovation is rarely good enough. Others such as GE, with its research centres, strive for big 'I', too, as Immelt has said:[14]

> If you're going to run a central research center, you've got to pick areas you're going to own no matter what. Nobody can do ceramic aircraft engine parts better than GE. We will own that space for 50 years. Rolls-Royce, Pratt & Whitney won't ever touch us. That's the research center – that's what they do because we said, That's what you have to go do.

9

Quality of marketing

Since 1994, the seven companies that have performed best in the quality of marketing category in Britain's most admired company surveys have been British Airways, Cadbury Schweppes, Tesco, Orange, GlaxoSmithKline, BSkyB and Marks & Spencer. There is no equivalent category in the American most admired company survey, but later in this chapter we look at the marketing approach of FedEx, PepsiCo and Coca-Cola, all companies highly rated for the quality of their products or services.

Four companies that did well in the quality of marketing category in Britain's 1994 survey also did well in more recent surveys (BA, GlaxoSmithKline, Cadbury Schweppes and Berkeley Group). However, 53 companies have made the top 20 just once and a further 19 only twice. So how do companies that have a good track record in being admired for their marketing prowess, such as Tesco, Unilever, BP, Next and AstraZeneca, do it when other companies that spend huge amounts on marketing do not?

The importance attached to marketing within a company is clearly important. When Jeffrey Immelt took over from Jack Welch at GE, he stressed 'marketing and customers while pulling back on some internal processes such as the six sigma quality programme'.[1] Todd Stitzer, CEO of Cadbury Schweppes, had been vice-president of marketing, and perhaps it is no coincidence that Charles Dunstone, founder of Carphone Warehouse (second in the quality of marketing category in 2006), has his roots in sales and marketing.

Sir Alan Sugar's company, Amstrad, which pioneered low-cost computers, won Britain's most admired company award for quality of marketing in 1991 – the only time it appeared in the overall most admired charts. (Sir Alan sold Amstrad to BSkyB in 2007 for £125m; by then his property fortune far outweighed his electronics business.) As with GE and Cadbury Schweppes, a strong marketing awareness on the part of the CEO was a factor in the success of the company.

For others, marketing includes a diverse set of activities stemming from a 'social and managerial process by which individuals and groups obtain what they need and want through creating and exchanging products and value with others'.[2] This definition reduces marketing to its basic core, but in companies such as Diageo or Rolls-Royce (fifth and seventh in the quality of marketing category in 2006) it takes on a more complex form.

Most companies use their brand or brands, the most visible aspect of a company's marketing, as a 'corporate ambassador and consumable possession'.[3] Many will try to persuade their clients that the brand is not simply a logo or advertising campaign.[4] Wal-Mart, for example, took eight pages in the September 2005 issue of *Vogue* to promote its brand to new market segments. As Tim Ambler, a marketing professor at London Business School, says: 'Brand equity is one of the most valuable assets.'[5] If there is congruence between an organization's values, employees' values and brand values, the resulting synergy should encourage a strong brand which is genuinely 'lived' by employees.

All these aspects of the marketing mix – the brand, the advertising campaign, how the culture is translated through marketing activity – will influence perceptions of a company's quality of marketing.

Quality of marketing winners

More than 100 companies have made it into the top 20 in the quality of marketing category since 1994. Retailers have featured strongly, as have travel companies. But the list has also included Manchester United, a world famous soccer club, British Oxygen, Canary Wharf, a property group, and Spirax Sarco, a global steam systems and heat exchange company.

Marketing success is no guarantee of overall success, although Cadbury Schweppes, GlaxoSmithKline and Tesco won both the quality of marketing award and the overall award in 1995, 2000 and 2003 respectively. But British Airways finished 52nd in the overall chart when it came top for marketing in 1994; Orange was 18th overall in 1998 having won the marketing award; and BSkyB finished 19th and 22nd overall in 2001 and 2004 when it won the marketing category. There is around a 65%

correlation between marketing and both financial soundness and value as a long-term investment. This suggests that marketing should perhaps be better aligned with financial measures for it to be most effective.

Among retailers, Tesco has been in the top 20 for quality of marketing in every survey since 1995, the only company to manage such a sustained run; Next did well from 1995 to 2003 but has tailed off in recent years; Sainsbury's made the top 20 in 1994, 2002 and 2006; and Marks & Spencer made it only twice: 17th in 1994 and, following a shift in its marketing strategy, top in 2007. In this category 16 retailers have featured in the top 20, but only six have made it on more than one occasion. If part of the role of marketing is to be consistently admired for it, retailers have some work to do.

The financial services sector has a poor track record in the marketing category. Only one bank, HBOS, has featured in the top 20 since 1994 and only Aviva and Legal and General in the insurance sector, although a few speciality finance companies have made the lower reaches. Banks spend huge amounts of money on marketing, but this is clearly not reflected in perceptions of quality as judged by voters in Britain's most admired company surveys.

Companies involved in food and beverages have done consistently well over the four periods of the survey. Cadbury Schweppes was in the marketing top 20 in every survey from 1994, when it came third, since when it has been first on three occasions and in the top three in eight of the 13 years to 2007. Unilever has also done well, making the top 20 nine times, though it has never been ranked higher than fourth.

In the pharmaceuticals sector, GlaxoSmithKline came top in the marketing category in 2000 and 2002 and second in 2001 and 2003. AstraZeneca has also made the charts in seven out of eight years to 2006, finishing in eighth place, ahead of GlaxoSmithKline, in 2006.

Among the oil companies, Shell featured in the marketing top 20 in the early years of the survey, but it was not until 1998 that BP joined it, since when BP has been ahead of Shell in every year to 2007.

World travellers

The track record of British Airways in the marketing category is among the best: top in 1994, in the top 20 for ten of the next 12 years, third in 2006 and second in 2007. The company has managed to stay ahead in a market that is often turbulent, is often a target for politicians and environmentalists, and, with the advent of low-cost airlines, is extremely competitive.

British Airways is the UK's largest airline, flying to over 500 destinations. In 2006/07 it carried some 33 million passengers, revenue was up 3.4% on the previous year to over £8 billion and profit was £600 million. In the company's 2006/07 annual report, chief executive Willie Walsh spoke optimistically about the future, reaffirming the 'BA Way', with 'values based on heritage and the best traditions', and an emphasis on 'delivering service'.

The company adopted the 'world's favourite airline' mantra some 20 years ago and used it extensively in its marketing campaigns. The object was to project a global image for a multinational customer base and advertising was targeted at key markets such as New York and London. For a long time the mantra and reality were in synch and the claim to be the world's favourite airline was justified. The supporting advertising campaign was one of the most notable in airline history. Replacing the 'we'll take good care of you' theme, which had been the core of its previous campaigns, the new campaign, launched over 15 years ago, featured commercials which showed, among other images, 'the Manhattan skyline rotating slowly through the sky'.[6] It was undoubtedly one of the talked about advertisements in the company's history.

BA's logo and branding have also undergone change as part of various marketing campaigns. In 1997, under former chief executive Bob Ayling, the company changed its tailfin design from the Union flag to 'world images', sparking controversy and criticism, not least from the prime minister at the time, Margaret Thatcher. Although the new images did reflect BA's global nature, they somehow missed another of the company's fundamentals, its Britishness, which had become associated with quality travel. In 2001 a new CEO, Rod Eddington, dropped the world images and reinstated the Union flag. The company still flies the flag. To refresh the marketing approach BA appointed a new advertising agency (BBH) in 2005 and a new emphasis was added to its campaigns, in particular a response to competition from easyJet and Ryanair with lower prices and advertising to back this up.

Marketing was not just about the brand on BA's tailfins or its slogans. It complemented all of these with some highly focused marketing campaigns to specific segments. Segmentation, targeting and positioning, one aspect of the classic marketer's toolkit, were implemented most professionally by the company. For example, business travellers, one of the most lucrative segments, have regularly been targets of BA's marketing. Its flat bed seats, from 2003, prompted a multimedia campaign including online advertising. The launch of the 'Fresh First' service in 2007 was also targeted at business people. BA was the winner of the 2007 Condé Nast Readers

Travel Awards (though it was fourth in the business travel category, behind Singapore Airlines). And BA has its 'world traveller' class to invoke a feeling of belonging to the company in non-business travellers. Lower prices, emphasizing additional features and head-on marketing have also been responses to low-cost competition.

The BA brand took a knock in 2007. The company:[7]

> [Faces] a battle once again to restore its reputation among passengers ... the business that once advertised itself as the world's favourite airline has to overcome the bigger threat of being labelled an enemy of consumers.

Its reputation took a further battering after the chaos that accompanied the opening of Terminal 5 at London's Heathrow. To overcome that setback will be a marketing challenge as great as any that the company has faced.

Figure 9.1 Britain's most admired companies: quality of marketing, 1994–2007

Four companies compared

Year	British Airways		Cadbury Schweppes		Rolls-Royce		BSkyB	
	Position	Score	Position	Score	Position	Score	Position	Score
1994	1	8.8	3	8.5	43	6.6	–	–
1995	5	7.9	1	8.6	26	6.9	–	–
1996	6	8.2	1	8.6	19	7.4	–	–
1997	2	8.5	13	7.8	51	6.9	3	8.4
1998	6	7.8	5	7.8	15	7.5	4	8.1
1999	25	7.1	11	7.6	7	7.9	3	8.4
2000	14	7.5	2	8.1	32	6.9	7	7.8
2001	14	7.4	6	7.8	44	6.6	1	8.6
2002	7	7.7	4	7.8	44	6.6	16	7.3
2003	55	6.3	3	8.1	13	7.4	5	8.0
2004	12	7.5	2	8.1	13	7.4	1	8.4
2005	9	7.7	3	8.3	11	7.6	1	8.4
2006	3	8.1	1	8.4	7	7.9	51	6.7
2007	2	8.3	28	7.0	36	6.8	4	8.1
Average	11.5	7.8	5.9	8.0	25.8	7.2	8.7	8.0

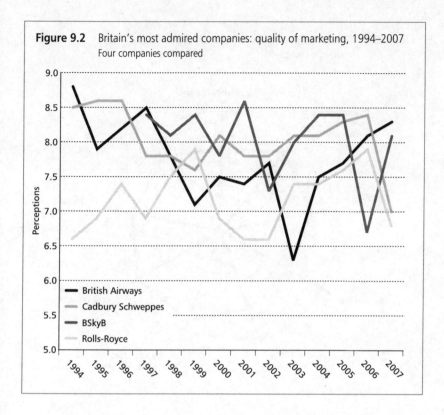

Figure 9.2 Britain's most admired companies: quality of marketing, 1994–2007
Four companies compared

Figures 9.1 and 9.2 compare the performance of British Airways in the marketing category since 1994 with that of three other companies.

Brands that people love

Although it fell out in 2007, Cadbury Schweppes had been in the marketing top 20 every year between 1994 and 2006 and came top three times (1995, 1996, 2006). CEO Todd Stitzer believes that one the factors that have made the company successful is that it creates 'brands that people love'.[8]

In its 2006 annual report, Cadbury Schweppes reported a marketing spend of £693 million, a 2% increase on 2005, and a marketing figure which equated to 9% of revenues.

For Cadbury Schweppes:[9]

Consumers are at the heart of the business. We are committed to listening to them and acting responsibly in their interests and

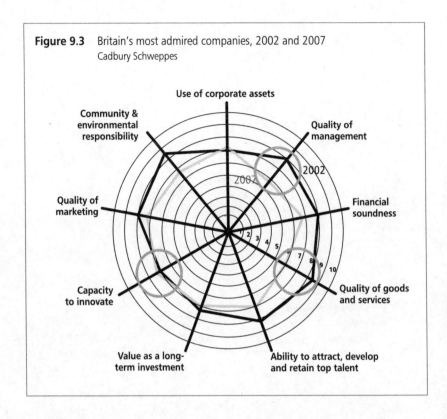

Figure 9.3 Britain's most admired companies, 2002 and 2007
Cadbury Schweppes

have done this successfully for generations. This Marketing Code of Practice ensures we continue to meet our responsibilities to our consumers.

- Accurate and truthful.
- Attentive to local sensitivities.
- Supporting sensible consumption and balanced lifestyle.
- Protecting children.

It is this type of sophisticated approach to marketing that has underpinned its reputation for quality of marketing, even when some of its other business indicators have been under pressure (see figure 9.3).

By issuing a global marketing code of practice, Cadbury Schweppes set the agenda for all its marketing activities and clear ground rules for those within the company responsible for marketing activity. By emphasizing 'sensible consumption and balanced lifestyle', it has taken on board increasing concerns about health and obesity. The company made a commitment that:[10]

Copy, sound and visual presentation will accurately represent all
material dimensions of products advertised, including taste, size,
content and nutrition and health benefits.

Claims about health benefits should have a sound nutritional basis as
well as reflecting 'moderation in consumption and portion sizes appropriate to the social and cultural setting portrayed'. The company has
undertaken to ensure that:

Prior to release, all advertisements and promotions to children will be
reviewed at an early stage for the appropriateness of the activity and
then checked against this code before being signed off by business
unit general managers. In addition, there will be a periodic review of
business unit activity by regional and global management to ensure
that interpretation of the code is aligned locally, regionally and
globally.

It also takes pains to be sensitive to local, cultural and political needs and
religious sensitivities.

Ensuring global compliance is one of the toughest tasks facing a
company in any discipline, but especially marketing. Cadbury Schweppes
appears to have succeeded better than many other companies.

Big ticket, big brand

Rolls-Royce employs 38,000 people in 50 countries. The company's 2006
annual report states:

The Group has a balanced business portfolio with leading positions in
the civil and defence aerospace, marine and energy markets. There are
approximately 54,000 Rolls-Royce gas turbines in service. The Group
provides high-value, product-related services to customers throughout
the operational lives of our gas turbines.

In 2006 the order book was worth £26.1 billion, up from £24 billion the
previous year, split almost equally between Europe, the Americas and the
Middle East/Asia. Underlying profits before financing costs in 2006 were
£748 million, an increase of 10% on 2005.

According to the 2006 annual report, four of Rolls-Royce's five core
strategic drivers are market related: address four global markets; develop
a competitive portfolio of products and services; grow market share and

installed product base; add value for customers through the provision of product-related services. The fifth, invest in technology, capability and infrastructure, is designed to support these initiatives. Since becoming chief executive in 1996 after 20 years with the company, Sir John Rose has put strong emphasis on the global nature of the business and the need to develop new markets.

Rolls-Royce has a rich heritage and strong values. In the words of Sir John Rose:

> For 100 years Rolls-Royce has powered the world's most advanced machines on land, at sea and in the air. Our engines powered the Spitfire during World War II, and Concorde, the world's first supersonic airliner. Our Trent family of engines now makes travel possible for millions of passengers by powering half the world's latest generation of wide-body aircraft.

The company's operating values are:[11]

- Reliability – our customers place their trust in us
- Integrity – at the heart of the way we operate and behave and also in the quality of the products and services we deliver
- Innovation – we strive to be open minded and flexible in our work

And its vision is:

- Trusted to deliver excellence
- Trust – we never assume trust, we must earn it, each and every day
- Delivery – we are only as good as our last success
- Excellence – this must be our standard. A way of life, the way that we operate

Rolls-Royce has extended the brand to include aftercare services. An example is TotalCare, which is a long-term product support package for airlines that has grown from covering just 2% of the company's installations at the turn of the millennium to just over 50% in 2006.[12] This can only have been achieved through skilful marketing. In the civil sector Rolls-Royce has also been successful, signing a 15-year TotalCare engine services agreement with UPS in 2006 covering 40 RB211–535s powering 757 freighters.

Better service, greater sales, and higher profits

FedEx has a straightforward marketing proposition: 'We promise to do whatever it takes to meet your needs.'

In 2007, the company had revenues of over $35 billion, up from $32 billion in 2006, and it made a profit of over $2 billion, 12% more than the previous year. The chairman and founder, Frederick W. Smith, noted in the 2007 annual report that:

> Though customers may begin talking to us about one or more of our services, they sometimes end up telling us what they really want to accomplish is better service, greater sales, and higher profits.

This explains why the company has sought to broaden its range of products and services, making acquisitions that deepen its capability and broaden its range of services.

In a case study of FedEx in 2007, brand consultants Landor reported that:

> Between 1997 and 2000, FedEx acquired a number of transportation companies, including Viking Freight and American Freightways, highly-regarded LTL carriers, and World Tariff, the leading customs information company for carriers around the world. Numerous challenges were presented by these acquisitions. By linking these businesses to the FedEx brand, would FedEx be credibly perceived as a diversified transportation services provider with global reach?

Their solution was:

> To create a brand architecture and naming strategy that would extend the FedEx brand without compromising the brand's integrity. The resulting system uses a different color and descriptor to distinguish each operating company, from FedEx Ground green to FedEx Custom Critical blue. The system thereby communicates the broad diversity of the product offering while building the core brand.

FedEx organizes its approach to its brand proposition around the theme of 'Access':[13]

> Access to networks that provide connectivity and choice in more than 220 countries ... our customers have the flexibility to operate and innovate, to respond to changes quickly and to lead change.

This commitment to satisfying customer need for access with a full range of services is the essence of FedEx's marketing approach. At an investors' meeting in 2007, Raj Subramaniam, senior vice-president of marketing, described the brand values that are enshrined in FedEx's approach:

> Peace of mind for our customers … the manifestation of this brand will be different for different markets … but the cornerstone is the same … a strong value proposition.

Cola wars

In the worldwide marketing war between PepsiCo and Coca-Cola for market share marketing has a crucial role.[14] The effort that has gone into marketing by both companies has been a dynamic sequence of challenge and response.

According to the two companies' 2006 annual reports, PepsiCo's 2006 revenue was $35 billion, up 8% on 2005, and net income was $5 billion, up 12% on 2005. Coca-Cola also had net income of around $5 billion in 2006 but it achieved this on much lower net revenue of $24 billion. PepsiCo has 168,000 employees and Coca-Cola has 70,000, of whom 49,000 were outside the United States. Coca-Cola has 400 brands in 200 countries.

In this tit-for-tat battle there is little to choose between the two protagonists. Figure 9.4 shows how PepsiCo, Coca-Cola and a third rival, Anheuser-Busch (underestimated in its reputational achievements), slugged it out over the years in America's most admired company surveys for the overall position, and this is very much reflected in their marketing competition.

The Pepsi–Coke battle has been going on for more than 100 years. Pepsi Cola's 1903 slogan 'Exhilarating invigorating aids digestion' was met by Coca-Cola's 1905 campaign called 'Revives and sustains' and in 1906 'the great national temperance'. Pepsi Cola's 1939 'twice as much for a nickel' was met by Coca-Cola's 1945 campaign 'you hear the voice of America'. And so it went on from 'it's the real thing' to 'the choice of a new generation' to 'can't beat the feeling' to 'be young have fun drink Pepsi'.

Both companies have an obsession with markets and customers. Muhtar Kent, Coca-Cola's chief operating officer (now chief executive), said in the company's 2006 annual report:

Figure 9.4 America's most admired companies: overall performance, 1983–2007
Three companies compared

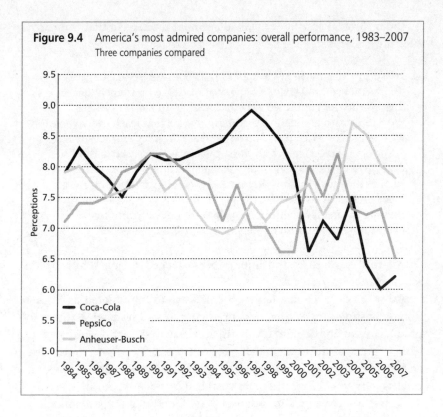

The year 2006 saw our Company's Manifesto for Growth translated into action in our global marketplace. In fact, it was the year in which we restored our ability to execute in a firm and disciplined manner. The Coca-Cola Company has grown across our product portfolio and our global geography. We have grown our core sparkling beverage business, expanding new products like Coca-Cola Zero to new markets … We, however, are not content. The Coca-Cola system remains constructively dissatisfied because there is much work to be done. Despite competitive pressures, opportunities abound for the sustainable long-term growth of our system. In 2006, the growth of the nonalcoholic ready-to-drink beverage industry outpaced the world's gross domestic product growth. We firmly believe that growth will continue as worldwide markets gain increasing economic and purchasing power. In the next decade, nearly 1 billion new consumers will enter the global marketplace. Sparkling beverages are a significant growth opportunity in the markets we serve.

Indra Nooyi, PepsiCo's CEO, had a similar message in that company's 2006 annual report:

> We sit squarely in the sweet spot of the Food and Beverage space – convenience ... We have a big global reach – with tremendous opportunity for continued growth ... Our go-to-market systems provide us with a mosaic of distribution arms that reach everywhere we operate cost effectively and with great efficiency and speed – ensuring our products are always available ... We have demonstrated that we have the strategic acuity to spot shifting consumer interests, such as the move to non-carbonated beverages and the increasing focus on health and wellness ... We know how to build a brand's personality and leverage our mega-brands, not only into line extensions but also into entirely new platforms.

All this emphasizes the importance attached to marketing by the senior management team.

Coca-Cola's three key targets for 2007 were highlighted as inspirational consumer marketing; enhanced commercial leadership (the right products through the right channels, and 'renewed franchise leadership'. Nooyi spoke of an ideal match between 'PepsiCo people, capabilities and great brands with opportunity. Specifically, this includes our structural advantages'. Then the company had 'a track record of success in acquiring attractive tuck-in businesses and then integrating them quickly and efficiently'.

The lessons of the two companies' marketing efforts are clear. They have one overriding characteristic: they are obsessed with the brand and its values and try to ensure that nothing is done to dilute either. But they also take care to understand the markets they operate in, assessing market size, market share and local consumer tastes and how they are changing. On the operational side they make sure that the local infrastructure matches their marketing objectives. Last but not least, the leaders of both companies instil in their companies a marketing mindset.

The Marks & Spencer new style of marketing

A new approach to marketing has been a major contributor to the change in fortunes of Marks & Spencer since 2006. Figure 9.5 shows how Marks & Spencer's ratings in Britain's most admired company surveys declined between 1994 and 2001.

But then Sir Stuart Rose and key members of his team started to work

Figure 9.5 Britain's most admired companies, 1994–2001
The decline and fall of Marks & Spencer

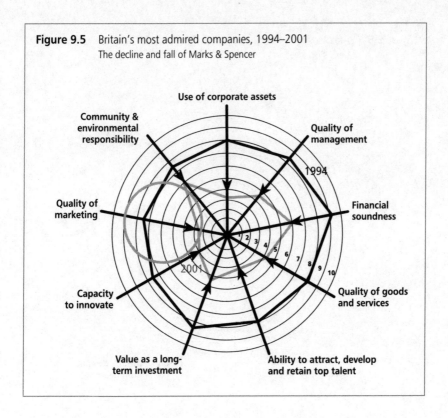

their magic. Between 2001 and 2007 a focus on increasing brand awareness enabled the company to drag itself from the edge of the precipice, as shown in figure 9.6 overleaf.

For a company that not long before had never felt the need to indulge in television advertising or offer customers the ability to pay by credit card this was a new style of marketing, with an emphasis on brand values backed up by highly sophisticated advertising. There was a total change in marketing strategy. The company went from minimal advertising to successful campaigns covering all media, using Twiggy, a model who had become famous in the 1960s and who 40 years later was an inspired choice to be the face of M&S. But advertising would not have worked if other key business attributes had not been in place too, specifically attractive distribution outlets and the right product set backed by a workforce that understood the messages put out by the marketing campaigns. By 2007, Marks & Spencer had exceeded 1994 levels for marketing recognition.

Figure 9.6 Britain's most admired companies, 2001 and 2007
Marks & Spencer

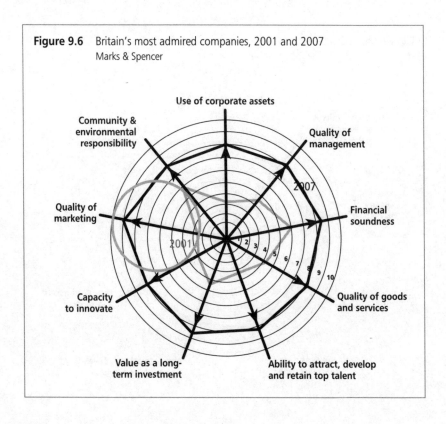

10

Community, social and environmental responsibility

Community, social and environmental responsibility (as it is known in the British most admired company surveys) or social responsibility (in the American surveys) is still not considered as important by those who take part in the surveys as most other categories and it has low correlations with quality of management (47%), capacity to innovate (44%), financial soundness and value as a long-term investment (51%). This may change because of growing public interest in the environment and social responsibility.

In 1996, according to *Management Today*, 267 companies in the world published corporate social responsibility (CSR) reports; in 2006 there were 2,235. In the US as many as 90% of the *Fortune* 500 companies have specific CSR statements.[1] In the past decade corporations have taken the initiative on CSR, often in response to outside pressure and/or as part of marketing strategies rather than simply complying with the regulations.

Socially responsible companies

Winners of the community, social and environmental responsibility (CSER) category in early most admired company surveys included representatives from the business services, telecommunications, retailing and energy sectors. Companies such as Rentokil and Iceland were recognized for the quality of their community work. By 2007 the leaders also came from the extractive industries (BHP Billiton), pharmaceuticals (GlaxoSmithKline and AstraZeneca) and engineering (Rotork). And in 2007, there was even a bank, the Co-operative Bank, in one of the top spots. Interest in CSER has grown considerably over the past 20 years as companies recognize its importance to their reputations.

The efforts made by oil and gas companies have been recognized in that their share of the vote in the category has increased from about 3% in the early 1990s to around 15% by 2007.

Few banks or insurance companies featured in the top 20 British most admired companies for community and environmental responsibility until the Co-operative Bank's impressive fourth place in 2007. The average score for banks in the CSER category in 1994 was over 2 points below the average score for the top 20 companies overall, but the gap had closed to just over 1.5 points by 2007. Insurance companies' average performance was worse than that of the banks in 2007.

Retailers' average score in 2007 for CSER was even worse and the sector's average score has declined since 1994. From being in a decent position for most of the 1990s they are now one of the worst-performing sectors in this category.

The utilities sector has also done poorly in recent years. In 1999 there were six utility companies in the CSER top 20; in 2006 not a single utility company made the top 20.

In America the story is somewhat different.

Johnson & Johnson came top in the category three times in the 1980s, scored well in the 1990s and was second in 2003. UPS has done well in recent years, coming first in 2005 and 2006 and second in 2007. But all in all there has been great diversity in the types of companies that have made the CSER top 20, from furniture manufacturer Herman Miller in the late 1990s to McDonald's in the early 2000s and fast-growing Whole Foods Market in 2007.

In the CSER category in the world's most admired company surveys there has been similar diversity, with UPS making a strong showing, coming top in 2003, 2005 and 2007. In 2006 Tesco was the winner, which must have been a relief. International Paper and Anheuser-Busch were also top performers in 2006 (and Anheuser-Busch was third in 2005).

A change in emphasis in CSER?

In the 1990s CSER was very much about corporate citizenship. Johnson & Johnson's 'Credo' emphasized honesty, integrity and putting people before profits. As *Fortune* noted in 1990:

Every few years, in a kind of conference of bishops, the company gathers senior managers to debate the Credo's contents, a process meant to keep its ideals fresh.

In 1982 Johnson & Johnson had recalled 31 million bottles of Tylenol capsules after seven people died from taking some that had been laced with cyanide. The loss accounted for nearly one-fifth of the company's revenue. But Tylenol was soon back on the shelves in tamper-proof bottles and within a year the company recovered most of the market share it had lost as a result of the crisis. Johnson & Johnson's actions were based on its belief in honesty, and were a model for crisis strategy. CSER at this time meant an understanding of the effect the company's actions had on the community.

It was this understanding that propelled Body Shop to the top of the category in the British most admired surveys in the 1990s for three consecutive years. Opened in Brighton, England, in 1976 (next door to an undertaker), Body Shop's natural products and social awareness struck a chord among buyers of cosmetics. A charismatic, environmentally committed chief executive, Anita Roddick, added to this perception of Body Shop as a leader in this area. Roddick's views on the lack of environmental and social sensitivity of the cosmetics industry made her something of a campaigner and in the late 1980s and early 1990s Body Shop formed alliances with Greenpeace and Friends of the Earth. In 2007 the company was still campaigning and noted in its *Values Report*:

> Our 'Stop Violence in the Home' campaign is now running in 47 markets and has raised over £2 million to help victims of domestic violence.

A further important focus of CSER in the earlier periods of the surveys was equality of opportunity, later diversity. Microsoft has put countless initiatives in place for minority groups, including women. This has worked so well that over 30% of the company's UK board is drawn from them.[2] Similarly, according to its website, Unilever, which came top in the CSER category in 2004, has built its approach:

> [By understanding] the importance of diversity and that's why it is a critical component of our business strategy and an integral part of everything we value and do. At Unilever, we have a diverse consumer base with a diverse array of needs.

The company had mirrored this broader diversity within its own organization, allowing it to:

> Develop powerful consumer insight and incorporate it throughout our business. We seek and welcome unique talents and perspectives at Unilever, because they strengthen us as a company and help us on our journey to add vitality to life in a variety of ways.

Cadbury Schweppes, winner of the CSER category in 2002, has adopted a similar approach in its diversity policies. It says on its website:

> We value diversity and value employees from varied backgrounds as they enrich our culture and support our commercial success. Our diversity practice helps us to attract the best people to Cadbury Schweppes and allows us to reflect the diversity of the world around us better – our consumer base and the communities in which we operate. We aim to reflect diversity in both our workforce and in our leadership teams. Through a culture of inclusiveness, we also aim to inspire the best in our people, earn their trust, increase their engagement and promote pride in our company.

In both Unilever and Cadbury Schweppes, attention was drawn to the need to match the diversity of the client base with the diversity of the company.

Community, social and environmental responsibility has evolved from being about compliance with ethical business practices, to something that is more proactive. Companies now make a virtue of taking a lead on CSER. Furthermore, a wider range of companies see it as important. During the 1990s around 40% of the leaders in the CSER category in the British most admired company surveys were retailers, about 10% were from the oil and gas industry and 10% were water companies.

By 2000 this had changed. Between 2001 and 2007 no retailers made the top three. Instead, 20% of the top three were pharmaceutical companies (compared with none in the 1990s), 10% were from the oil and gas industry (the same level as in the 1990s) and 10% from the telecommunications sector.

A permanently rising expectation curve

Sustainability is now firmly on the corporate agenda. That Shell and BP have been in the CSER top 20 for the past ten years reflects in part the perception of what they have been doing about sustainability. BT has also done well over the years, coming top in 2005 and 2006 and making the top 10 in the category for 12 of the last 13 years. Only Cadbury Schweppes comes anywhere close to this achievement.

In 2006 BT had revenues of £20,223 million, up 4% on the previous year; profit before tax was £2,495 million, up 15%. Sir Christopher Bland noted in the company's 2007 annual report:

> As the corporate social responsibility agenda evolves, so does our strategy. We are, for example, increasingly emphasizing three new priorities:
>
> - tackling climate change. We are committed to cutting our CO_2 emissions by 80% from 1996 levels by 2016 and to helping customers and suppliers cut theirs through the more effective use of communications technology. The fact that our chief executive, Ben Verwaayen, is chairing the CBI's climate change task force indicates how seriously we take this issue.
>
> - enabling sustainable economic growth. We are increasingly integrating sustainability in all our business processes.
>
> - helping to build a more inclusive society. We are looking at the ways in which communications technology can help to build a fairer, more inclusive society.

Bland drew attention to the Dow Jones Sustainability Index, a measure of how companies do in this area across the world and in which BT had been number one in its sector for six consecutive years and had negotiated the world's biggest green energy contract in 2004, a pioneering move at the time which meant that much of BT's electricity needs were met from environmentally friendly energy sources from suppliers such as nPower. He noted that there had been a 'permanently rising curve in expectation' that had come from employees as well as customers. This was more influenced by a groundswell of opinion and evidence than by government or legislative factors. That BT had recognized this and taken action at an early stage gave it a first-mover advantage.

BT's charter included a series of objectives which included:[3]

- Reducing the amount of CO_2. BT had reduced its UK CO_2 emissions by some 60% over a ten-year period to 2006 against a targeted 80% reduction by 2016. Improving efficiencies in energy consumption was the driver behind this target, which includes 'buying all of BT's

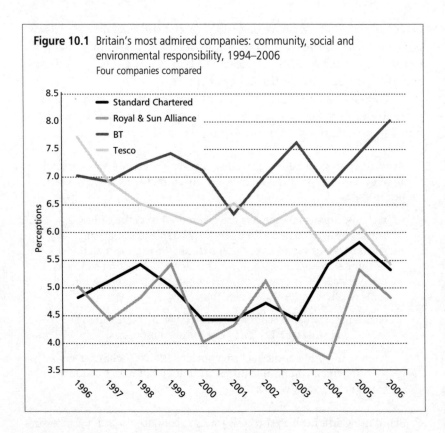

Figure 10.1 Britain's most admired companies: community, social and environmental responsibility, 1994–2006
Four companies compared

UK electricity from low carbon sources including renewables and combined heat and power'.

- Influencing customers by creating products and services that use less energy.

- Influencing suppliers by tightening procurement procedures.

- Engaging employees to be energy efficient.

BT also decided to:

- Appoint a board level 'inclusive society champion' to take responsibility for delivering all the social inclusion targets, which focus on increasing access to technology and making BT an inclusive company.

- Establish a social responsibility unit to work closely with charities such as ChildLine, the UK's free, confidential, 24-hour helpline for children in distress. (BT has been a partner of ChildLine since 1986 and has sponsored its awards since 1991.)

- Develop a strategy, 'Connectivity', which gives more people access to communications technology.

- Develop content that benefits a wide range of users from small businesses to the community as a whole.

- Develop capability to use the technology. This includes programmes to support older people and people with disabilities.

- Create 'an inclusive culture' in the workforce.

A most compelling aspect of BT's performance has been its willingness to regard CSER as a long-term strategy. This has led to a board-level appointment and getting employees, suppliers and customers involved in the process to ensure effective implementation of the company's strategies.

Thinking outside the can

Anheuser-Busch likes to think 'outside the can'. In a 2005 report entitled *Environmental, Health and Safety* it stated:

> As one of the world's largest recyclers of aluminum cans, the Anheuser-Busch Recycling Corporation recycled a whopping 804 million pounds of cans in 2004 – more than 125 percent of the number of cans that the company's breweries use to package their products.

Anheuser-Busch has a strong track record in community, social and environmental responsibility, coming third in 2005 and 2006 in the world's most admired company survey in this category. According to its 2006 annual report, the company had gross sales of nearly $18 billion in 2006, up from $17 billion in 2005, and profits of $5.5 billion.

Among the CSER achievements that the company listed in its 2006 annual reports are the following:

- In 1993 it recycled one can for every can used in beer production.

- In 1994 it issued a company-wide commitment to environmental excellence policy and its first environmental quality manual.

- In 1995 its theme park SeaWorld California became the first zoological park in the US to breed whitetip reef sharks; in the same year Hubbs-SeaWorld Research Institute opened a hatchery, which breeds and releases more than 350,000 juvenile white sea bass annually.

- In 1996 the installation of bio-energy recovery systems was completed at six breweries. Anheuser-Busch International began conducting environmental audits in overseas breweries.

- In 2000 an environmental management system was implemented at all facilities. That year also marked an 11% reduction per dollar of sales in the amount of waste sent to landfills.

- In 2004, the company reduced the thickness of 30-pack can packages, saving 2.8 million pounds of paperboard. It also increased use of web-based electronic forms and included upgrades that enhanced electronic routing, signing and workflow processes. With approximately 15,000 employees using 350 e-forms, there were major reductions in time, money and paper consumption.

Anheuser-Busch invested in CSER not only because it was the right thing to do but also because it paid off financially.

Common commercial sense for all

When Whole Foods Market's co-founder, John Mackey, posted anonymous notices on the internet against a potential acquisition target, he undermined his and the company's reputation for being a leader in corporate social responsibility. Described as the 'gold standard' for organic and natural foods grocers,[4] Whole Foods Market won the Green Power Partner of the Year award from the US Environmental Protection Agency (EPA) for a second consecutive year in 2007.

Mackey, who had established a reputation as a maverick, apologized for his 'error in judgment'. But there is no denying that this business has grown so fast on the back of its perceived community, social and environmental responsibility, so much so that it was third in the CSER category in America's most admired company survey in 2007.

Whole Foods Market appears to have demonstrated that it is possible to be 'cool' and make money. Indeed, in its 2007 letter to stakeholders the company says that its business is about:

Selling the highest quality natural and organic products available, satisfying and delighting our customers; supporting team member happiness through profits and growth; caring about our communities and our environment.

Whole Foods Market opened its first store in 1980 in Austin, Texas, at a time when there were hardly any natural food supermarkets in America. In 1984 the company began to expand, first organically but then through acquisitions of the Whole Foods Company in 1988 and other natural foods chains throughout the 1990s, including Wellspring Grocery (North Carolina), Bread & Circus (Massachusetts and Rhode Island), Mrs Gooch's Natural Foods Markets (Los Angeles), Bread of Life (Northern California and Florida), Fresh Fields Markets (East Coast and Midwest), Merchant of Vino (Detroit) and Nature's Heartland (Boston). As the company notes in a 2007 press release:

Whole Foods Market started our third decade with additional acquisitions of Food for Thought in Northern California and Harry's Farmers Market stores in Atlanta. In 2001, Whole Foods moved into Manhattan, generating a good deal of interest from the media and financial industries. 2002 saw an expansion into Canada and in 2004, Whole Foods Market entered the United Kingdom with the acquisition of seven Fresh & Wild stores.

According to its annual stakeholders' report, in 2006 Whole Foods Market had sales of $5.6 billion, a 19% increase on the previous year. Return on capital was 40%. Economic value added increased by $39 million to $64 million and the company's cash flow was over $450 million. This had been achieved with a full commitment to CSER. As the company notes:[5]

We walk our talk when it comes to our core values. The stores featured over 30,000 natural and organic items, and the emphasis on the highest quality perishable foods, which are about 67% of our sales, broadens our appeal beyond our core natural and organic food customers.

The company's CSER philosophy is described as follows:

Sustainable Agriculture – We support organic farmers, growers and the environment through our commitment to sustainable agriculture and by expanding the market for organic products.

Wise Environmental Practices – We respect our environment and recycle, reuse, and reduce our waste wherever and whenever we can.

Community Citizenship – We recognize our responsibility to be active participants in our local communities. We give a minimum of 5% of our profits every year to a wide variety of community and non-profit organizations. In addition, we pay our Team Members to give of their time to community and service organizations.

Integrity in All Business Dealings – Our trade partners are our allies in serving our stakeholders. We treat them with respect, fairness and integrity at all times and expect the same in return.

Since its foundation Whole Foods Market has initiated a wide variety of environmental projects. In 2006 it purchased renewable energy credits:[6]

[to offset 100% of] the electricity used in all of its stores, facilities, bake houses, distribution centers, regional offices, and national headquarters in the United States and Canada. The renewable-energy commitment – the largest in the US and Canada to date – makes Whole Foods the only Fortune 500 company to offset 100 percent of its electricity use through wind energy credits.

Whole Foods Market is a good example of a company that has whole-heartedly embraced CSER:

- It was founded on a premise of environmentally sound product acquisition and marketing, in a similar way to Body Shop, for a long time one of Britain's most admired companies for CSER.

- It has clear targets and accountability for the CSER aspect of its business, published in a way that leaves no ambiguity about what the company stands for.

- It has an inclusive approach to gaining the commitment of its employees to the principles of sustainability on which the company was founded.

Reflecting the attributes of the community

Diversity has been one of the long-standing definitions of CSER and it is in this area that a lot of progress has been made.

UPS has an excellent track record in the social responsibility category in the American survey, coming top in 2004, 2005 and 2006 and second in 2007. Its stance and actions on diversity have contributed to this success. The company's head-to-head battle with its arch rival FedEx, the intensity of which has seen the two interchanging positions over the past few years, is shown in figure 10.2.

In 2006 UPS's chairman and chief executive, Michael Eskew, was able to announce that revenue had increased by 11.7% on the previous year to $47.5 billion and operating profit by 8% to $6.6 billion. An astonishing 3.9 billion packages and documents were delivered and 7.9 million customers were serviced every day. The company has more than 427,000 employees and its workforce, according to its 2006 annual report, is 'multicultural, multidimensional, and reflective of the broad attributes of

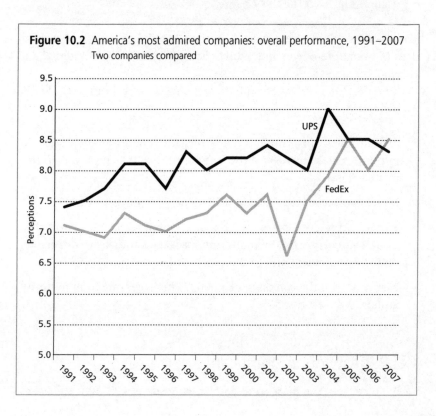

Figure 10.2 America's most admired companies: overall performance, 1991–2007
Two companies compared

our global communities'. In every year since 1999, UPS has been ranked by *Fortune* as one of the 50 best companies for minorities. In 2005 it was recognized in *Hispanic Business* magazine's Corporate 100 list as one of the leading companies providing career opportunities for Hispanics, and it has also been named a top corporation for women business enterprises by the Women's Business Enterprise National Council.[7]

UPS policies that engender diversity include employee ownership (employees own a significant amount of shares and are encouraged to increase their ownership stake through employee stock purchase plans and matched share ownership schemes such as the UPS Savings Advantage), equal opportunity and promotion from within, which have contributed to the preferred employer status. It has also established the UPS Diversity Steering Council whose vision, according to the company's 2006 annual report, is to:

> Ensure that workforce, customer, and supplier diversity remain a
> visible core value that is integral to our business, our community
> relationships, and The UPS Charter.

The steering council is co-chaired by the CEO and the senior vice-president of human resources and public affairs. It includes both internal and external members.

Measures of how successful these policies have been include the following:[8]

- African-Americans, Hispanics, Asian-Pacific Americans and other minorities make up 35% of the company's 348,400 employees in the United States.

- Minorities accounted for half of UPS's new employees in 2005.

- Women represent 28% of the US management team and 20% of the overall workforce, holding jobs from package handlers, to drivers, to senior management and to the UPS board of directors.

- Nearly 30% of the company's 63,000 US managers are from minority groups.

CSER: growing in significance

In the history of the most admired company surveys, CSER is the lowest rated category of all the categories covered. In over 20 years of American surveys, for example, the mean score of all of the winners is 8.39 compared with a mean score for quality of management of 9.24. The highest ever score for CSER, achieved by UPS, is just 9.00. In the British survey the mean score for winners of the CSER category at just 7.94, compared with 9.17 for financial soundness. The highest score for CSER in the British survey, achieved by Cadbury Schweppes in 2002, is 8.5. However, the surveys do show an increase in the perceived importance of CSER over recent years, reflecting the view that:[9]

> To be socially responsible in their approach to customers, staff, the environment and the supply chain has become essential for corporates.

Companies that communicate their CSER initiatives effectively can reap the benefits of higher customer satisfaction. Starbucks has done this with its CSER initiatives with the charity agency CARE. And there are financial benefits:[10]

> For a typical company with an average market value of approximately $48 billion, one unit increase of CSR rating would result in approximately $17 million more profits on average in subsequent years, a substantial (not to be ignored) increase in financial returns.

It is evident that a commitment to community, social and environmental responsibility is becoming an essential feature of a most admired company:[11]

> Corporates know that if they don't have diversity and equality among their staff and step up energy-saving and recycling programmes their business will suffer.

Research from most admired company surveys suggests that if this is not the case now, it soon will be.

11

Use of corporate assets

A corporate asset is defined as an economic resource that is controlled by the company and is expected to provide returns today and in the future.[1]

When Hanson, a diversified batteries to locks, fertilizers to bricks conglomerate led by James Hanson and Gordon White, finished top in the use of corporate assets category of Britain's most admired survey in 1992, the company was recognized for the unique skills of buying and turning underperforming businesses into profitable ones. It had a formidable reputation for sweating assets to the maximum and in some of its businesses was making operating profit margins of over 50%. Conglomerates were in vogue in the early 1990s and in addition to Hanson, other ones that did well in the 1992 survey were BTR (rubber, plastics, medical and consumer goods) and Tomkins (manufacturing acquisitions).

But the vogue passed. Focus replaced diversification and for most companies 'sticking to one's knitting' became the key to success. By 2007 the companies in the top 20 for the use of corporate assets focused on a core business, with the top five being made up of Marks & Spencer, Aggreko, Tesco, easyJet and Intercontinental hotels. These companies are as focused as it is possible to be.

The nine winners of the use of corporate assets category in Britain's most admired company surveys between 1994 and 2007 have been from industries ranging from services to oil, retailing and property. Only three companies, Tesco, BP and Rentokil, have won on more than one occasion, and BP and Tesco have each won three times between 1998 and 2007.

Between 1994 and 2006 only British Land and Wolseley have stayed in the top 20 of Britain's most admired company survey for the use of corporate assets. Tesco entered the top 20 in 1995 and has stayed in it every year since with the exception of 1996; in 2007 it came third. BP too has had a good run from 1996, finishing in the top 20 in every year and in number one position in 1999, 2000 and 2001.

In America, there have been 13 winners of the use of corporate assets category since 1984 from a range of business sectors, including technology, pharmaceuticals and oil and gas, and in contrast to the British survey where the only financial firm to win the category was Lloyds TSB in 1997, there has been a strong representation from the financial sector. Berkshire Hathaway has been top in the category in the American survey six times since 1990, and it has also won the category in the world's most admired company survey, most recently in 2002, 2003 and 2005. Citigroup was also in the top spot in 2001.

Since 1999 the use of corporate assets category in the world's most admired company survey has been a little different from those of Britain and America as a few companies have dominated. Berkshire Hathaway and ExxonMobil have each won several times, with only Home Depot and Procter & Gamble getting a look in.

Business sectors and use of corporate assets

Until the mid 1990s, firms involved in engineering such as Siebe, Smiths Industries, Tomkins, BTR, GKN and Hanson all featured in the use of corporate assets category in Britain's most admired company surveys. In 1995 Smiths Industries, BTR, Hanson and GKN took four of the top five spots. In later years it was more specialized engineering companies such as Rotork, Halma and Kidde which made the top 20.

As the conglomerates involved in engineering became less admired, companies in the financial services sector became more highly rated. In 1997 Lloyds TSB came top for the use of corporate assets and in later years it and other financial sector businesses such as Provident, Royal Bank of Scotland, AMVESCAP and Man have made the top 20. Following the sub-prime crisis, banks' ratings in this and other categories are bound to fall, and it will be interesting to see which, if any, remain admired.

Companies in other sectors including retail, food production, oil and gas and leisure have all been rated at least reasonably highly for their use of corporate assets, but in recent years it is the 'support' services sector

– companies such as Serco, Capita, Compass and Bunzl – which has made a strong showing.

There has been a good spread across business sectors in America's most admired company surveys in the use of corporate assets category. Technology, which is not a favoured sector among British voters, has had some winners (IBM and Cisco), as have pharmaceuticals, retail, 'moving stuff around' (which invariably means UPS or FedEx) and beverages. But in the past few years it is energy companies that have been most admired in the category, taking over from financial services companies.

'Goodwill is the gift that keeps giving'

In the American most admired company surveys, Berkshire Hathaway's performance for use of corporate assets – as well as financial soundness and value as a long-term investment – has been notable.

In 1990 *Fortune* analysed Warren Buffett's performance to gain insights into how he had made the company into a world beater. 'I'm in the capital allocation business,' said Buffett. 'My job is to figure out which business to invest in.' And how did he do that? 'I'm not like a steel executive who can only think about how to invest best in steel … I've got a bigger canvas.' Buffett's tactics for investment included reading 'hundreds and hundreds of annual reports'. A fan of Benjamin Graham, Buffett chose to ignore the financial markets' fluctuations but 'only to buy shares in companies whose intrinsic value is higher than their stock price'. This approach had been so successful and the company had used its assets so well that by 2007 Buffett was able to pledge 85% of his Berkshire Hathaway stock to five charitable foundations, with the lion's share going to the Bill & Melinda Gates Foundation.

A crucial point about Buffett's philosophy is that:[2]

> Businesses logically are worth far more than net tangible assets when they can be expected to produce earnings on such assets considerably in excess of market rates of return.

It would seem incumbent therefore on companies hoping to gain a reputation for the use of corporate assets to make clear just what economic goodwill they have – though this is a challenge since it is only now that intangible assets are gaining in prominence. The lesson is clear: make sure that intangible as well as tangible assets are identified and their use maximized. This includes people as well as brand value. In future, the use of corporate assets category is likely to give a good deal of weight to the use of corporate intangible assets. As Buffett says, 'Goodwill is the gift that keeps giving.'

This is reinforced by another of Buffett's beliefs – 'asset heavy businesses generally earn low rates of return'[3] – which might also indicate whether a company will be regarded highly for the use of its corporate assets. Once again, the Berkshire Hathaway approach recognizes the importance of intangibles such as brand value.

Buffett's letter to shareholders in 2006 perhaps says it all:

> Our gain in net worth during 2006 was $16.9 billion, which increased the per-share book value of both our Class A and Class B stock by 18.4%. Over the last 42 years (that is, since present management took over) book value has grown from $19 to $70,281, a rate of 21.4% compounded annually.

That over 30,000 shareholders attended the 2008 annual general meeting is testament to the success of Berkshire Hathaway and its use of corporate assets.

High-powered asset use

Kinder Morgan has done very well in recent years. Between 1997 and 2007 it has provided a 1,393% return on investment.[4] It publishes an asset map as part of its corporate communications and it is proud to note:[5]

> Management got no money for cars, jets, financial planning, or any other privileges in 2006. We are currently below competitive levels for comparable companies in this area of our compensation package.

Kinder Morgan Energy Partners was set up in 1997 by Richard Kinder, William Morgan and a group of investors. Kinder, who receives a salary of $1 a year with no bonuses, stock options or restricted stock grants, was named CEO of the year for 2005 by Morningstar. Kinder Morgan has achieved its success through organic growth and acquisition (such as the $1.4 billion acquisition of Santa Fe Pacific Pipeline Partners in 1998).

In the American most admired company surveys Kinder Morgan's performance stands out, particularly in 2005 when the company achieved the highest ever score for the quality of its management. That year and in

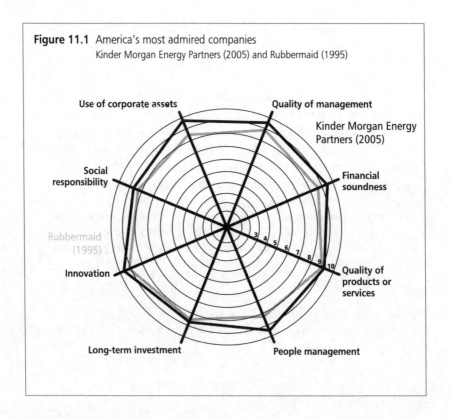

Figure 11.1 America's most admired companies
Kinder Morgan Energy Partners (2005) and Rubbermaid (1995)

2007 the company also came top in the use of corporate assets category. Figure 11.1 compares Kinder Morgan with Rubbermaid, another company that did well in the surveys in the 1990s.

Kinder Morgan Energy Partners is one of the largest pipeline companies in America, worth around $20 billion. But what is its philosophy for getting the most out of its corporate assets?

The first thing of note is the detail that goes into Kinder Morgan's presentation of its asset utilization performance and future (always adding a rider cautioning against the placing of undue reliance on any 'forward-looking statement'). For example, in November 2007 the company made a detailed presentation to Wachovia in response to a question about infrastructure opportunities in North America. The system map showed tangible assets (products, pipelines, terminals, natural gas pipelines, natural gas storage and processing facilities) as well as intangible assets (project management capabilities and timescales, supplier management capabilities and precedent agreements). The presentation ended with an analysis of future prospects, including expansion and extension capabilities. Kinder Morgan was demonstrating not only the company's existing 'hard wired' capability (pipelines and so on) but also its capabilities and competences (things that do not show in the balance sheet but are crucial intangible assets).

Another example of the effective use of corporate assets is a presentation to UBS in September 2007. The trademark system map, showing the company's physical assets, was complemented by details of how the solid asset base (products pipelines, natural gas pipelines, terminals and CO_2 transportation and sales) had been able to generate stable fee income, a consistent track record (on total distribution, net debt to total capital and net debt to EBITDA) and significant historical returns. The Kinder Morgan strategy was clearly articulated:

- focus on stable, fee-based assets which are core to the energy infrastructure of growing markets;

- increase utilization of assets while controlling costs;

- leverage economies of scale from incremental acquisitions and expansions;

- maximize benefit of a unique financial structure which fits with strategy.

Kinder Morgan focuses its efforts on maximizing returns on its core assets. Of the $1 billion of capital invested since 1998, the bulk had been in expansion into the core segments of which products and natural gas pipelines were the largest recipients. It has also been divesting itself of non-core assets. In February 2007 the company exited the retail utility business with the sale of Terasen Gas to Fortis for C$3.7 billion.

The Kinder Morgan message is clear:

- Be transparent in how you are using the company's assets.

- Do not veer from the core business.

- Let everyone know that you are in for the long haul.

Sustaining an admirable reputation

Lloyds TSB is one of Britain's five biggest banks. It is a result of a merger in

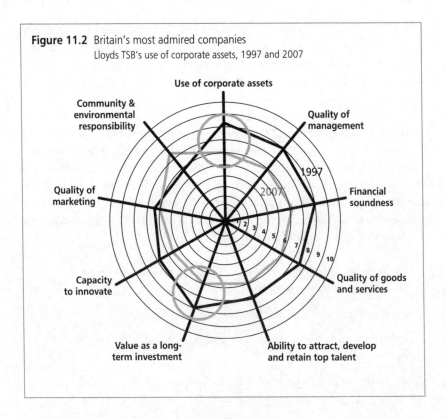

Figure 11.2 Britain's most admired companies
Lloyds TSB's use of corporate assets, 1997 and 2007

1995 of two banks that have long histories: Lloyds had been founded in the 17th century and Trustee Savings Bank (TSB) in the 19th century. The merger proved successful and the bank's performance in the most admired company surveys improved steadily in the latter half of the 1990s. In 1997 it came top in the use of corporate assets category.

At the time the bank set out its governing objective, which was to maximize shareholder value. To achieve this it aimed to be a leader in its chosen markets, to be the first choice for its 16 million customers and to reduce day-to-day costs through increased effectiveness.

These are clear, focused and targeted objectives. This clarity no doubt influenced those voting in the survey, together with the bank's achievements against performance measures: profit, share price and cost reductions through the merger, which all came in on target or exceeded expectations. But the bank was unable to sustain this position. By 1999 it was down to 16th place in the use of corporate assets rankings and by 2000 it was out of the top 20.

Figure 11.2 illustrates perceptions of Lloyds TSB's performance in all categories in 1997 and compares it to 2007. In the overall rankings the highest position it achieved was ninth in 1998. In 2007 it came 133rd.

Figures 11.3 and 11.4 compare Lloyds TSB's performance for use of corporate assets with that of three other companies and show just how much perceptions of a company's ability can change over the years.

Figure 11.3 Britain's most admired companies: use of corporate assets, 1994–2007

Four companies compared

Year	Lloyds TSB		Tesco		British Land		Rentokil Initial	
	Position	Score	Position	Score	Position	Score	Position	Score
1994	20	7.1	91	6.2	3	7.9	1	8.3
1995	19	7.1	11	7.4	14	7.3	13	7.3
1996	8	7.6	39	6.9	2	8.1	73	6.4
1997	1	8.1	12	7.4	7	7.6	2	7.8
1998	6	7.3	1	8.3	2	8.0	70	6.4
1999	16	7.2	3	7.7	10	7.4	90	6.0
2000	23	7.0	5	7.6	64	6.5	117	5.9
2001	30	6.8	3	7.7	111	5.8	112	5.8
2002	70	6.4	9	7.5	77	6.3	1	8.0
2003	106	5.9	1	8.2	35	6.6	16	7.2
2004	140	5.5	4	7.6	32	6.8	102	6.0
2005	107	5.9	1	7.7	41	6.7	215	4.2
2006	156	5.6	3	7.6	14	7.3	235	4.2
2007	146	5.9	3	7.8	21	7.0	212	4.3
Average	60.6	6.7	13.3	7.5	30.9	7.1	89.9	6.3

Indeed, in the case of Lloyds TSB, the bank has been returning to favour. Eric Daniels has held the ship steady since he took over as CEO in 2003. What is more it seemed in 2008 that Lloyds TSB had managed to 'steer clear of toxic waste' by its conservative avoidance of the securitizations that had precipitated the sub-prime mortgage crisis and had caused bankers across America and Europe to, in the words of Patrick Hosking at *The Times*, take 'collective leave of their senses'.[6] Despite pressure from

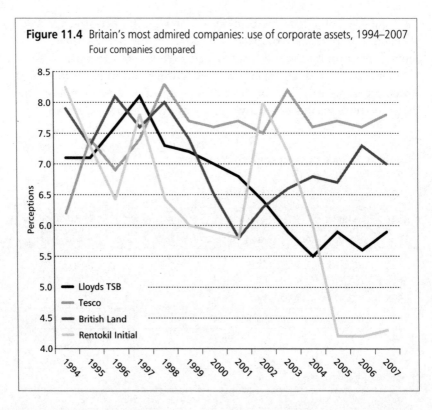

Figure 11.4 Britain's most admired companies: use of corporate assets, 1994–2007
Four companies compared

those at investor road-shows and 'one to one meetings with big share-holders', Daniels and his board had held firm. By 2008 it was beginning to look as if Lloyds TSB had avoiding squandering its corporate assets as a result of its risk aversion and conservative decision-making. However, by the time this book went to press in late October 2008, Lloyds TSB, having been apparently nudged by the prime minister towards a takeover of struggling British bank HBOS, was itself found, like so many of its counterparts worldwide, to be short of capital and had agreed to a government bail-out on terms that many of its shareholders disapproved of.

Asset return through acquisition

BHP Billiton made the *Fortune* Global 500 companies in 2007 with revenues of $32 billion, profits of $10 billion and assets worth over $48 billion. It was second in its industry sector behind Anglo American, but ahead of Rio Tinto and Occidental Petroleum among others. As a national champion its track record in the world's most admired company survey was evident from 2003, when it entered the Asian charts in fourth place behind Singapore Airlines, Samsung Electronics and News Corporation. But it was its audacious plan to combine with Rio Tinto in November 2007 that really brought the company to the market's attention and highlighted the issue of the use of corporate assets.

BHP Billiton is one of the worlds largest 'resources' companies, involved in steelmaking raw materials, copper production, coal, uranium and aluminium production. It is also a significant player in oil and gas. It prides itself on having:[7]

- a world class diversified asset base

- stable and increasing cash flow

- cost savings and operational efficiencies to provide strong returns and margins

- a range of premium growth options

- a committed and engaged workforce

- an overriding commitment to sustainable development.

The company has over 38,000 employees in more than 100 operations in 25 countries. Market capitalization at 30 June 2007 was in excess of $165 billion. In 2007 the company generated revenue of $47.5 billion and profit attributable to shareholders of $13.4 billion. Chairman Don Argus was proud of his company's achievements and noted in the 2007 annual report that 'it is comforting to see the strategic direction of a company delivering on its objectives'. He outlined the company's strategy for its asset utilization:

> To ensure we have a suite of long-life, low-cost assets, diversified by geography and commodity, that can be expanded and that are largely export-oriented. The growth opportunities implicit in this strategy mean we can move quickly to increase capacity from an existing operation when we determine that global demand warrants such an expansion.

This strategy indicates a sustainable approach to the use of corporate assets. On the one hand the company plays to its strengths. It is a resources company and investments in its core competences are clear from its strategic activities, such that:[8]

Global demand for our products has enabled us to benefit from our high-quality asset base and from our decisions over the past seven years to reinvest in our business through organic projects and acquisitions.

On the other hand the spread of resources within the core business allowed sufficient flexibility to take advantage of market opportunities or deal with any threats to a single business area or geography. How a merger with Rio Tinto would affect the company and its use of corporate assets is impossible to know.

People before products

In late 2007 *The Times* reported:[9]

> The relentless march of Starbucks across the world's high streets stumbled yesterday after the coffee chain said it would open fewer stores as customers went to cheaper rivals. The fall in custom marks the group's first decline since the ubiquitous chain floated in 1992.

Starbucks' success has to a large degree been built on the back of intangible factors. As its website says:

> We always figured that putting people before products just made good common sense. So far, it's been working out for us. Our relationships with farmers yield the highest quality coffees. The connections we make in communities create a loyal following. And the support we provide our baristas pays off everyday.

Starbucks is proof of the point made by Warren Buffett that a company's intangible assets can carry more weight than its tangible assets. Its focus has been unremitting and this has paid off in terms of its performance in America's most admired company surveys. Starbucks came second overall in 2007 (up from fifth in 2006), and in its industry sector it finished top overall as well as in innovation, people management, quality of management, quality of products and use of corporate assets. As *Fortune* noted in March 2007:

> Starbucks is green, it's humane, it's politically correct, it sells a popular product and provides a comfy place to hang out and consume same – what's not to like.

In the 2006 fiscal annual report, Howard Schultz, chairman of Starbucks, was able to say of his Seattle-based company that it had a critical responsibility 'in serving our customers more than 40 million times a week and the commitments we've made to more than 145,000 partners (employees)'. By 2006 Starbucks had 12,440 stores in 37 countries, and had increased revenues to $7.8 billion (up 22% on the previous year) and earnings to $564 million. The company could report 15 consecutive years of over 5% store sales growth. As *Fortune* also noted:

> Investors have no complaints: If you had put $1,000 into Starbucks stock when the company went public in 1992, you'd have been $52,718.10 to the good at year-end 2006, vs. just $3,515.30 for the S&P 500.

What was Starbucks' philosophy for getting the most of its corporate assets?

There is evidence that this is more fluid than it was. Before 2006 the strategy was to open more stores in both America and internationally. But at some point this kind of core organic growth gets tricky. Not saturation, but enough. Starbucks' objective of 40,000 outlets is a considerable stretch. This is where the Starbucks brand – a corporate asset of immense value – comes into play. It is what Schultz has been most passionate about. He warned executives about watering down the Starbucks experience and commoditizing the brand.

One thing of note is the potential for diversification which, as we have seen, presents challenges to many companies and goes somewhat against the overall theme. In the case of Starbucks it is the type of diversification that involves stretching the brand beyond its core. So in 2006 it was noted in the company's annual report that it had succeeded in:

> Extending our unique brand experience well beyond our retail stores in new and imaginative ways that resonate with customers all over the world.

By this Starbucks meant its ready-to-drink beverages, new speciality coffees for grocery shoppers and entertainment, including the company's first movie and book offerings. The strategy for this was based on plausible assumptions. Behind the record growth and high margins were some indicators that the company had done just about as much as it could with its existing store sales. Comparable store sales in 2006 were 7% up on the previous year, but this was a lower figure than 2005 at 8%, 2004 (10%) and 2003 (8%). Likewise, operating income was slightly down (though earnings were up). This is a business with a strong franchise that provides the opportunity for further sales in each store and further roles for the brand in the 'coffee experience' area. In-store sales of music and its own iTunes area are two such brand extensions. But diversification strategies and brand extensions have to be cleverly planned and skilfully executed. Virgin's airline and some other brand extensions may have worked well but excursions into the cola, cosmetics and bridal businesses did not.

Summary

The most admired companies in the world

A reputation, hard won over decades of successful business, can fall in an instant. Keeping that reputation is a constant challenge to even the best companies. Companies that sustain an admirable reputation:

- have processes that enable a long-term, continuously improving approach;

- learn from their performance and make adjustments to improve it. They protect the things they do well and fix things that are not going well;

- not only listen but also hear. They are able to cope with and adapt to adversity, evolving their business strategies accordingly;

- invest in the businesses which they are admired and withdraw from those in which they are not;

- have some shared characteristics, such as strategic focus, a commitment to the long term, increasing utilization of assets while controlling costs and leveraging economies of scale;

- stay continuously aware of their customers' needs;

- instil the principles of partnership in the company and see shareholders as partners;

- have vision and courage, but equally if not more important in practice the ability to execute strategy;

- are able to deal with criticism and crises.

Quality of management

The quality of a company's management is one of the two most important factors in determining overall corporate reputation. The other is financial soundness. Companies that are most admired in this category have managers who:

- are confident, accessible, wily and shrewd, and show personal commitment to the company;
- convey authenticity and have the right touch with different groups of stakeholders;
- create an all-round balance of dynamism and conservatism, with high visibility when it is appropriate and a low profile when it is not – in other words, are able to 'read the runes' and present the right image at the right time;
- have good timing and pitch, and avoid coming across as arrogant;
- have a vision and communicate it clearly, along with communicating the company strategy to achieve the vision clearly;
- give a clear sense of direction in what they expect with regard to individual and corporate performance;
- make sure all the company's managers have the right mindset;
- are aware of the dangers of hubris.

Financial soundness

The importance of doing well in the financial soundness category is demonstrated in its relationship with success in others such as quality of management, value as a long-term investment and even the ability to attract and retain talent. That is why companies like HSBC, Shell and Tesco in Britain and ExxonMobil, Microsoft, IBM and Coca-Cola in America have generally done well in the overall most admired surveys. Their reputations for financial soundness have informed other factors.

However, further analysis reveals that there are some common strategies and practices that these companies adopt to ensure their continuing success. Companies that are most admired for financial soundness:

- need to be profitable but are also able to demonstrate strength in other financial indicators. Perceptions of financial soundness come from a combination of long-term and short-term financial measures;

- ensure that there is always a new generation of assets to supplement those currently providing revenues and replace mature assets producing declining revenues;

- keep their stakeholders informed about what is going on. They are open about adverse changes in the financials and say what the company will do to put them right;

- have sector intelligence and use this to best effect – in other words, when the financial reputation of their sector is good they should take advantage of it; when it is poor they act to counter any negative effects.

Quality of goods and services

There has been a greater emphasis on quality of products and services in Britain and America since 1996. Reputational leadership in quality of goods and services is earned from each and every interaction with stakeholders. Companies that are successful in doing this:

- are led by managers who ingrain quality into the fabric of the company;

- have processes to support this quality mindset – Six Sigma is an example – that lead to embedding the company's capabilities for quality into its DNA;

- focus on continuous improvement in their products and services;

- invest in employee training and benefits – a key factor in creating outstanding customer service;

- ensure that their supply chain management is excellent.

People management

Companies that are admired for their ability to attract and retain talent:

- make the attraction, retention and development of talented people a strategic priority, which is discussed and dealt with like any other strategic investment;

- manage talent as a hard not a soft issue. Getting it right adds value to the bottom line. The successful integration of talented people into an organization's systems and processes can add value to both tangible and, more importantly, intangible assets;

- have CEOs who are actively involved in talent management, who know what is going on and are involved in sorting out succession issues;

- know that retaining talent is as important as attracting it;

- achieve a healthy and stimulating mix in promoting or appointing internal and external candidates;

- invest in branding the company as a leading employer of top talent;

- cherish and nurture talented employees.

Value as a long-term investment

Companies that are valued as a long-term investment are likely to be valued highly overall. There is a strong relationship between this and other financial categories. Companies that are most admired for their value as a long-term investment:

- execute strategy over the long term and in a joined-up manner. *Verbund* or the integration of strategies maximizes economies of scale and scope;

- have a good spread of risk, minimizing the effect of financial downturns in one sector or market;

- reinvest in the business;

- focus on their core business support services.

Capacity to innovate

Companies that are most admired for innovation:

- have CEOs who play an active part in driving and supporting innovation. It is not enough to rely on the innovation 'champion' or 'champions' to do so. Big investments in innovation will need board approval, so the CEO has to be fully involved in understanding the implications and be ready to argue the case;

- get the balance right between the big 'I' of invention and the little 'I' of innovation, and view innovation as continuous improvement as well as dramatic invention;

- say no to a thousand things and ensure there is a focus on innovation and not a diffusion of effort, as Apple and GE have demonstrated – 'Narrowing the focus makes a difference';

- make innovation everyone's job for continuous improvement. Inclusivity in the innovation process is an important characteristic in some organizations;

- don't let innovation float around and make sure that it is customer focused and relevant to end-users;

- make sure innovation adds value to the bottom line

Quality of marketing

Companies that are most admired for quality of marketing:

- build up information about their customers' needs and make sure that their products and services continue to meet those needs;

- maintain their brand strength, their hunger for market information and 'market-oriented' research and development;

- have an obsession with the markets in which they choose to operate, with the brand and how they might stretch it into new products or services, and internationally;

- take care of their brands – they put huge effort into maintaining and enhancing brand image. Brand values are clearly articulated and permeate almost every aspect of the company's activity, from the way it trains its employees to the way it presents its company report and accounts. Nothing is left to chance;

- back up a powerful brand with well thought through marketing and business processes – for example, British Airways, whose marketing track record is excellent, found with its Terminal 5 experience that goodwill can be lost if the reality is different from the message;

- understand the importance of all the factors in the marketing mix.

Community, social and environmental responsibility

Companies that are most admired for community, social and environmental responsibility:

- are genuinely committed to CSER and do not just use it for marketing advantage;

- develop and communicate a clear strategy for CSER;

- see CSER as contributing to profitability today and absolutely necessary for future profitability;

- have strong board-level support for CSER initiatives. Some companies choose to do this by appointing a board-level 'champion' for CSER. Furthermore, if a company increases the quality of its community and environmental disclosure, its environmental reputation will increase;

- have strategies to engage a broad range of stakeholders including employees and customers;

- ensure the supply chain is integrated into the company's CSER initiatives;

- have measurable targets and objectives for CSER.

Use of corporate assets

Companies that are most admired for their use of corporate assets:

- are generally highly focused, choosing to 'stick to their knitting' and use assets in support of the core business. The days of the highly successful diversified conglomerate seem long gone. But some companies have to some extent been successfully diversified through brand stretching;

- give weight to the use of intangible assets. 'Goodwill is the gift that keeps giving';

- prioritise initiatives that ensure maximum added value to the company's assets, whether they be tangible or intangible;

- demonstrate the use of corporate assets over and above the performance of other companies in their business sector;

- publish details of tangible and intangible assets in a transparent way.

Appendix 1

Most admired company surveys: methodology

Three surveys have been used in this book. The British survey has been in place since 1990 run first by *The Economist* and since 1994 by *Management Today*. America's and the world's most admired companies surveys have been run by *Fortune* since 1983 and 1997 respectively.

In the British survey the people asked their views include chairmen, chief executives, finance and other senior directors from the leading companies that are polled each year as well as sector analysts from leading investment firms. These 'informed spectators' are asked to rate organisations in their particular industry sector on a scale of 0 (poor) to 10 (excellent) for the various categories from quality of management to community and environmental responsibility. The overall score is derived from the total score firms get across all categories.

The American and world surveys have a similar approach. In 2007 the British survey covered 22 industry sectors and the world survey 27 industry sectors. The American survey began in 1983 with 25 industry sectors, but by 2007 this had expanded to 63 (see table overleaf).

In Britain the industry sectors are arrived at by reference to a number of sources, including stock exchange listings, newspapers such as the *Financial Times*, analysts, business editors and the Institute of Actuaries. Once the sectors are decided the top ten companies in terms of market capitalisation at a specific time are identified. A company is included in the survey if it meets the following criteria:

Industry	No. of sectors
Transport ('things that move')	10
Stores and distributors	8
Finance	7
Computers	7
Natural resources	6
Consumer products	5
Power	5
Shelter	5
Contracted services	4
Media	3
Precision	3

- It is publicly owned.

- If it has dual nationality, it is predominantly British (for example Unilever and Shell).

- It is quoted on the London Stock Exchange.

Such criteria help to maintain a degree of continuity. As a result almost all the top 100 and approximately 90% of the top 200 public companies in the UK are included in the survey. Some sectors disappear over time, such as textiles; other sectors merge, such as electricity and water into utilities; and new sectors are introduced, such as construction, which itself has been split into home and heavy construction. However, throughout the period of the British survey many sectors have remained broadly similar.

In America the starting point is the largest 1,000 companies by revenue plus the top foreign companies operating in the country. The companies are sorted into 65 industry sectors and the top ten companies in each sector are included in the survey. As in the UK, 'informed spectators', senior executives and analysts are asked to rate companies within their sector on a ten-point scale in eight categories, one fewer than in the British and world surveys. The overall rating is then reached by summing the scores of the individual categories.

The world survey includes companies with turnover greater than $8 billion (347 in 2007). The rating process is similar to that of the American and British surveys. Senior executives and analysts are asked to rate companies in each industry in nine categories using a 10-point scale, with 10 seen as excellent and 0 as poor.

These three surveys provide a substantial amount of data. In Britain, for example, the annual rankings take into account some 156,000 ratings by those surveyed across 24 industry sectors. Over 15 years that makes 2.34 million individual ratings, which rises to more than 10 million when the American and world surveys are taken into account.

An additional analysis was undertaken on the industry sectors to provide comparisons of performance over time. The total number of times a company from a particular sector, for example finance or utilities, appeared in the top 3, 10 or 20 in a particular time period (usually three years) in a particular category was calculated as a percentage of the total. So, for example, if the finance sector had six entries out of a total of 60 for 1994–97, in this book that is described as a 10% share of the vote and is used to establish the relative performance within and between sectors.

Note that the industry sectors referred to in the appendix tables are what *Fortune* or *Management Today* would have used at the time the survey was carried out. They may not be the sectors the companies operate in at the present time. For example, Berkshire Hathaway appears in various sectors: publishing and printing in 1990–94; diversified financial in 1996–97; and insurance: property and casualty since 1998. The names of companies may also vary, appearing as they were reported at the time. For example, BP has been British Petroleum and BP Amoco.

Development of most admired company survey categories

Category	Britain's most admired companies	America's most admired companies	World's most admired companies
Management	Quality of management (1990)	Quality of management (1983)	Management (1999); Management quality (2007)
Finance	Financial soundness (1990)	Financial soundness (1983)	Financial soundness (1999)
Products	Quality of products or services (1990)	Quality of products or services (1983)	Product/services (1999); Quality of products & services (2002)); Product/service quality (2007)
People	Ability to attract, develop and retain top talent (1990)	Ability to attract, develop and keep talented people (1983); Employee talent (1998); People management (2005)	Getting/keeping talent (1999); Employee talent (2002); People management (2007)
Investment	Value as a long-term investment (1990)	Long-term investment value (1983); Value as a long-term investment (1988); Long-term investment value (1998); Long-term investment (2004)	Long-term investment value (1999); Long-term investment (2007)
Innovation	Capacity to innovate (1990)	Innovativeness (1983); Innovation (2002)	Innovativeness (1999); Innovation (2002)
Marketing	Quality of marketing (1990)		

Category	Britain's most admired companies	America's most admired companies		World's most admired companies			
Social responsibility	Community and environmental responsibility (1990)	Community and environmental responsibility (1983)	Social responsibility (1998)	Social/environmental responsibility (1999)	Social responsibility (2002)	Community/environment (2007)	
Use of assets	Use of corporate assets (1992)	Use of corporate assets (1983)		Wide use of assets (1999)	Use of assets (2000)	Use of corporate assets (2002)	Use of assets (2007)
Globalisation				International acumen (1999)	Global business acumen (2000)	Globalness (2002)	

Appendix 2

Most admired companies: overall rankings

1 Britain's most admired companies, 1990–2007

	1990		1991	
Rank	Company	Sector	Company	Sector
1	Shell	Oil & gas	Marks & Spencer	Drapery & stores
2	Glaxo Holdings	Health & household	Shell	Oil & gas
3	Marks & Spencer	Drapery & stores	Glaxo	Health & household
4	J Sainsbury	Food & groceries	Rolls-Royce	Engineering
5	Bass	Drinks & tobacco	Unilever	Health & household
6	ICI	Chemicals	Redland	Building, timber & roads
7	Greycoat	Property	Tesco	Food & groceries
8	British Petroleum	Oil & gas	J Sainsbury	Food & groceries
9	Unilever	Health & household	Bass	Drinks & tobacco
10	Grand Metropolitan	Hotel, catering & travel	Guinness	Drinks & tobacco

Source: *The Economist*, 1990; 26 January 1991

1992 / 1994

Rank	Company	Sector	Company	Sector
1	Glaxo	Health & household	Rentokil	Business services
2	Unilever	Health & household	Glaxo	Health & household
3	Rentokil	Business services	Marks & Spencer	Retail stores
4	Guinness	Drinks	SmithKline Beecham	Health & household
5	Reuters	Newspapers & publishing	Unilever	Food manufacturers
6	Marks & Spencer	Drapery & stores	Reuters	News & publishers
7	Shell	Oil & gas	Cadbury Schweppes	Food manufacturers
8	J Sainsbury	Food & groceries	Electrocomponents	Electricals
9	SmithKline Beecham	Health & household	Shell Transport & Trading	Oil & gas
10	Redland	Building, timber & roads	Bowthorpe	Electricals

Sources: *The Economist*, 17 October 1992; *Management Today*, December 1994

1995 / 1996

Rank	Company	Sector	Company	Sector
1	Cadbury Schweppes	Food manufacturers	Tesco	Retailers (food)
2	Unilever	Food manufacturers	Burford	Property
3	Smiths Industries	Engineering, auto & aero	Next	Retailers (clothing)
4	Tesco	Food retailers	Marks & Spencer	Retailers (clothing)
5	Whitbread	Drinks	Cadbury Schweppes	Food manufacturers
6	Vodafone	Electricals	Reuters Holdings	News & publishers
7	Marks & Spencer	Retail stores	SmithKline Beecham	Health & household
8	Shell Transport & Trading	Oil, gas & extractive	Siebe	Engineering & metals
9	Sainsbury (J)	Food retailers	Spirax Sarco	Engineering & metals
10	Reuters Holdings	News & publishers	British Petroleum	Oil, gas & extractive

Source: *Management Today*, December 1995; December 1996

1997

Rank	Company	Sector
1	Reuters Holdings	News & publishers
2	Tesco	Food retailers
3	Marks & Spencer	Retailers (clothing)
4	Glaxo Wellcome	Health & household
5	Smiths Industries	Engineering, auto & aero
6	Unilever	Food manufacturers
7	Next	Retailers (clothing)
8	SmithKline Beecham	Health & household
9	Dewhirst Group	Textiles
10	British Petroleum	Oil, gas & extractive

1998

Company	Sector
Tesco	Food retailers
Cadbury Schweppes	Food manufacturers
Schroders	Financial
British Petroleum	Oil, gas & extractive
SmithKline Beecham	Health & household
Glaxo Wellcome	Health & household
Unilever	Food manufacturers
Shell Transport & Trading	Oil, gas & extractive
Lloyds TSB	Banks
Boots	Retailers (general)

Source: *Management Today*, December 1997; December 1998

1999

Rank	Company	Sector
1	Tesco	Food retailers
2	SmithKline Beecham	Health & household
3	Glaxo Wellcome	Health & household
4	Daily Mail & General Trust	News & publishers
5	Cadbury Schweppes	Food manufacturers
6	BP Amoco	Oil, gas & extractive
7	Unilever	Food manufacturers
8	Vodafone AirTouch	Electricals
9	Granada Group	Leisure & hotels
10	AstraZeneca	Health & household

2000

Company	Sector
GlaxoSmithKline	Health & household
BP	Oil, gas & extractive
Shell Transport & Trading	Oil, gas & extractive
Cadbury Schweppes	Food manufacturer
Tesco	Food retailer
Exel	Transport
AstraZeneca	Health & household
Sage Group	Software & computing services
Unilever	Food manufacturer
GKN	Engineering, auto & aero

Source: *Management Today*, December 1999; December 2000

2001   2002

Rank	Company	Sector	Company	Sector
1	Shell Transport & Trading	Oil, gas & extractive	BP	Oil, gas & extractive
2	AstraZeneca	Health & household	Cadbury Schweppes	Food producers & processors
3	BP	Oil, gas & extractive	Tesco	Food retailer
4	Tesco	Food retailer	Unilever	Food producers & processors
5	GlaxoSmithKline	Health & household	GlaxoSmithKline	Health & household
6	Next	Retailers (clothing)	Shell Transport & Trading	Oil, gas & extractive
7	Cadbury Schweppes	Food manufacturer	Next	Retailers (textiles & apparel)
8	Selfridges	Retailers (clothing)	Diageo	Restaurants, pubs & breweries
9	Morrison W	Food retailer	BAA	Transport
10	ARM Holdings	Electrical & IT hardware	W. Morrison	Food retailer

Source: *Management Today*, December 2001; December 2002

2003   2004

Rank	Company	Sector	Company	Sector
1	Tesco	Food retailer	Cadbury Schweppes	Food producers & processors
2	GlaxoSmithKline	Health & household	Unilever	Food producers & processors
3	AstraZeneca	Health & household	BP	Oil, gas & extractive
4	BP	Oil, gas & extractive	Tesco	Retailers (food & personal)
5	Shell Transport & Trading	Oil, gas & extractive	Man Group	Speciality & other financials
6	Unilever	Food producers & processors	Serco Group	Support services
7	Cadbury Schweppes	Food producers & processors	IMI	Engineering & machinery
8	BSkyB	Media	HSBC	Banking
9	Morrison W	Food retailer	Vodafone	Telecommunications
10	Diageo	Restaurants, pubs & breweries	Wolseley	Building materials & merchants

Source: *Management Today*, December 2003; December 2004

2005

Rank	Company	Sector
1	Tesco	Retailers (food & personal)
2	BP	Oil, gas & extractive
3	Cadbury Schweppes	Food producers & processors
4	Unilever	Food producers & processors
5	BSkyB	Media
6	Serco Group	Support services
7	Diageo	Consumer products
8	Vodafone	Telecommunications
9	Mitchells & Butlers	Restaurants, pubs & breweries
10	HBOS	Banking

2006

Company	Sector
Tesco	Retailers (food & personal)
Johnson Matthey	Chemicals
BP	Oil, gas & extractive
GlaxoSmithKline	Health & household
Carphone Warehouse	Retailers (general)
Balfour Beatty	Construction (heavy)
ICAP	Speciality & other financials
Rolls-Royce	Engineering (aero & defence)
Cadbury Schweppes	Food producers & processors
Man Group	Speciality & other financials

Source: *Management Today*, December 2005; December 2006

2007

Rank	Company	Sector
1	Marks & Spencer	Retailers (food & personal)
2	Tesco	Retailers (food & personal)
3	BSkyB	Media
4	Serco Group	Support services
5	Johnson Matthey	Chemicals
6	ICAP	Specialty & other financials
7	Sainsbury (J)	Retailers (food & personal)
8	Capita Group	Support services
9	Diageo	Restaurants, pubs & breweries
10	Rolls-Royce	Engineering (aero & defence)

2008

Company	Sector
Diageo	Restaurants, pubs and breweries
Johnson Matthey	Chemicals
Unilever	Food producers and processors
BSkyB	Media
Tesco	Retailers (food and personal)
Stagecoach	Transport
Rolls-Royce	Engineering (aero and defence)
Man	Speciality and other financials
Kingspan	Building materials and merchants
3i	Speciality and other financials

Source: *Management Today*, December 2007; December 2008

2 America's most admired companies, 1983–2008

1983 — 1984

Rank	Company	Sector	Company	Sector
1	IBM[a]	Office equipment, computers	IBM	Office equipment, computers
2	Hewlett-Packard[a]	Precision instruments	Dow Jones	Publishing & printing
3	Johnson & Johnson	Pharmaceuticals	Hewlett-Packard	Office equipment, computers
4	Eastman Kodak	Precision instruments	Merck	Pharmaceuticals
5	Merck	Pharmaceuticals	Johnson & Johnson	Pharmaceuticals
6	AT&T	Utilities	Time Inc	Publishing & printing
7	Digital Equipment	Office equipment, computers	General Electric	Electronic appliances
8	SmithKline Beecham	Pharmaceuticals	Anheuser-Busch	Beverages
9	General Electric	Electronic appliances	Coca-Cola	Beverages
10	General Mills	Food	Boeing	Aerospace

a Equal first.
Source: *Fortune*, 10 January 1983; 9 January 1984

1985 — 1986

Rank	Company	Sector	Company	Sector
1	IBM	Office equipment, computers	IBM	Office equipment, computers
2	Coca-Cola	Beverages	3M	Precision instruments
3	Dow Jones	Publishing & printing	Dow Jones	Publishing & printing
4	3M	Precision instruments	Coca-Cola	Beverages
5	Hewlett-Packard	Office equipment, computers	Merck	Pharmaceuticals
6	Anheuser-Busch	Beverages	Boeing	Aerospace
7	Boeing	Aerospace	Rubbermaid	Rubber & plastic products
8	General Electric	Electronic appliances	Procter & Gamble	Soaps, cosmetics
9	Eastman Kodak	Precision instruments	Exxon	Petroleum refining
10	Merck	Pharmaceuticals	J.P. Morgan	Commercial banking

Source: *Fortune*, 7 January 1985; 6 January 1986

1987   1988

Rank	Company	Sector	Company	Sector
1	Merck	Pharmaceuticals	Merck	Pharmaceuticals
2	Liz Claiborne	Apparel	Rubbermaid	Rubber products
3	Boeing	Aerospace	Dow Jones	Publishing & printing
4	J.P. Morgan	Commercial banking	Procter & Gamble	Soaps, cosmetics
5	Rubbermaid	Rubber products	Liz Claiborne	Apparel
6	Shell Oil[a]	Petroleum refining	3M	Scientific, photographic & control equipment
7	IBM[a]	Office equipment, computers	Philip Morris	Tobacco
8	Johnson & Johnson	Pharmaceuticals	J.P. Morgan	Commercial banking
9	Dow Jones	Publishing & printing	RJR Nabisco[b]	Tobacco
10	Herman Miller	Furniture	Wal-Mart Stores[b]	Retailing

a Equal sixth.   b Equal ninth.
Source: *Fortune*, 19 January 1987; 18 January 1988

1989   1990

Rank	Company	Sector	Company	Sector
1	Merck	Pharmaceuticals	Merck	Pharmaceuticals
2	Rubbermaid	Rubber products	Philip Morris	Tobacco
3	3M	Scientific/ photographic equipment	Rubbermaid	Rubber products
4	Philip Morris	Tobacco	Procter & Gamble	Soaps, cosmetics
5	Wal-Mart Stores	Retailing	3M	Scientific, photographic & control equipment
6	Exxon	Petroleum refining	PepsiCo[a]	Beverages
7	PepsiCo	Beverages	Wal-Mart[a]	Retailing
8	Boeing	Aerospace	Coca-Cola	Beverages
9	Herman Miller	Furniture	Anheuser-Busch	Beverages
10	Shell Oil	Petroleum refining	Du Pont	Chemicals

a Equal sixth.
Source: *Fortune*, 30 January 1989; 29 January 1990

1991

Rank	Company	Sector
1	Merck	Pharmaceuticals
2	Rubbermaid	Rubber & plastic products
3	Procter & Gamble	Soaps, cosmetics
4	Wal-Mart Stores	Retailing
5	PepsiCo	Beverages
6	Coca-Cola	Beverages
7	3M	Scientific, photographic & control equipment
8	Johnson & Johnson	Pharmaceuticals
9	Boeing	Aerospace
10	Eli Lilly[a]	Pharmaceuticals
	Liz Claiborne[a]	Apparel

1992

Company	Sector
Merck	Pharmaceuticals
Rubbermaid	Rubber & plastic products
Wal-Mart Stores	Retailing
Liz Claiborne	Apparel
Levi Strauss Associates	Apparel
Johnson & Johnson	Pharmaceuticals
Coca-Cola	Beverages
3M	Scientific, photographic & control equipment
PepsiCo	Beverages
Procter & Gamble	Soaps, cosmetics

a Equal tenth.   Source: *Fortune*, 11 February 1991; 10 February 1992

1993

Rank	Company	Sector
1	Merck	Pharmaceuticals
2	Rubbermaid	Rubber & plastic products
3	Wal-Mart Stores	Retailing
4	3M	Scientific, photographic & control equipment
5	Coca-Cola	Beverages
6	Procter & Gamble	Soaps, cosmetics
7	Levi Strauss Associates	Apparel
8	Liz Claiborne	Apparel
9	J.P. Morgan	Commercial banking
10	Boeing	Aerospace

1994

Company	Sector
Rubbermaid	Rubber & plastic products
Home Depot	Specialist retailers
Coca-Cola	Beverages
Microsoft	Computer & data services
3M	Scientific, photographic & control equipment
Walt Disney[a]	Entertainment
Motorola[a]	Electronics, electrical equipment
J.P. Morgan[b]	Commercial banking
Procter & Gamble[b]	Soaps, cosmetics
United Parcel Service	Trucking

a Equal sixth.   b Equal eighth.
Source: *Fortune*, 8 February 1993; 7 February 1994

1995

Rank	Company	Sector
1	Rubbermaid	Rubber & plastic products
2	Microsoft	Computer & data services
3	Coca-Cola	Beverages
4	Motorola	Electronics, electrical equipment
5	Home Depot	Specialist retailers
6	Intel	Electronics
7	Procter & Gamble	Soaps, cosmetics
8	3M	Scientific, photographic & control equipment
9	United Parcel Service	Trucking
10	Hewlett-Packard	Computers, office equipment

1996

Company	Sector
Coca-Cola	Beverages
Procter & Gamble	Soaps, cosmetics
Rubbermaid	Rubber & plastic products
Johnson & Johnson	Pharmaceuticals
Intel	Electronics, electrical equipment
Merck	Pharmaceuticals
Microsoft[a]	Computer & data services
Mirage Resorts[a]	Hotels, casinos, resorts
Hewlett-Packard[b]	Computers, office equipment
Motorola[b]	Electronics, electrical equipment

a Equal seventh.   b Equal ninth.
Source: *Fortune*, 6 March 1995; 4 March 1996

1997

Rank	Company	Sector
1	Coca-Cola	Beverages
2	Mirage Resorts	Hotels, casinos, resorts
3	Merck	Pharmaceuticals
4	United Parcel Service	Mail package & freight delivery
5	Microsoft	Computer & data services
6	Johnson & Johnson[a]	Pharmaceuticals
7	Intel[a]	Electronics
8	Pfizer	Pharmaceuticals
9	Procter & Gamble[b]	Soaps, cosmetics
10	Berkshire Hathaway[b]	Diversified financial

1998

Company	Sector
General Electric	Electronics, electrical equipment
Microsoft	Computer software
Coca-Cola	Beverages
Intel	Electronics, semiconductors
Hewlett-Packard	Computers, office equipment
Southwest Airlines	Airlines
Berkshire Hathaway	Insurance: property, casualty
Disney	Entertainment
Johnson & Johnson	Pharmaceuticals
Merck	Pharmaceuticals

a Equal sixth.   b Equal ninth.   Source: *Fortune*, 3 March 1997; 2 March 1998

1999   2000

Rank	Company	Sector	Company	Sector
1	General Electric	Electronics, electrical equipment	General Electric	Electronics, electrical equipment
2	Coca-Cola	Beverages	Microsoft	Computer software
3	Microsoft	Computer software	Dell Computer	Computers, office equipment
4	Dell Computer	Computers, office equipment	Cisco Systems	Network communications
5	Berkshire Hathaway	Insurance: property, casualty	Wal-Mart Stores	General merchandisers
6	Wal-Mart Stores	General merchandisers	Southwest Airlines	Airlines
7	Southwest Airlines	Airlines	Berkshire Hathaway	Insurance: property, casualty
8	Intel	Electronics, semiconductors	Intel	Semiconductors
9	Merck	Pharmaceuticals	Home Depot	Specialty retailers
10	Walt Disney	Entertainment	Lucent Technologies	Network communications

Source: *Fortune*, 1 March 1999; 21 February 2000

2001   2002

Rank	Company	Sector	Company	Sector
1	General Electric	Electronics, electrical equipment	General Electric	Electronics
2	Cisco Systems	Network communications	Southwest Airlines	Airlines
3	Wal-Mart Stores	General merchandisers	Wal-Mart Stores	General merchandisers
4	Southwest Airlines	Airlines	Microsoft	Computer software
5	Microsoft	Computer software	Berkshire Hathaway	Insurance: property, casualty
6	Home Depot	Specialty retailers	Home Depot	Speciality retailers
7	Berkshire Hathaway	Insurance: property, casualty	Johnson & Johnson	Pharmaceuticals
8	Charles Schwab	Securities	FedEx	Delivery
9	Intel	Semiconductors	Citigroup	Megabanks
10	Dell Computer	Computers, office equipment	Intel	Semiconductors

Source: *Fortune*, 19 February 2001; 4 March 2002

2003 · 2004

Rank	Company	Sector	Company	Sector
1	Wal-Mart Stores	General merchandisers	Wal-Mart Stores	General merchandisers
2	Southwest Airlines	Airlines	Berkshire Hathaway	Insurance: property, casualty
3	Berkshire Hathaway	Insurance: property, casualty	Southwest Airlines	Airlines
4	Dell Computer	Computers	General Electric	Electronics
5	General Electric	Electronics	Dell	Computers
6	Johnson & Johnson	Pharmaceuticals	Microsoft	Computer software
7	Microsoft	Computer software	Johnson & Johnson	Pharmaceuticals
8	FedEx	Delivery	Starbucks	Food services
9	Starbucks	Food services	FedEx	Delivery
10	Procter & Gamble	Household & personal products	IBM	Computers

Source: *Fortune*, 3 March 2003; 8 March 2004

2005 · 2006

Rank	Company	Sector	Company	Sector
1	Dell	Computers	General Electric	Electronics
2	General Electric	Electronics	FedEx	Delivery
3	Starbucks	Food services	Southwest Airlines	Airlines
4	Wal-Mart Stores	General merchandisers	Procter & Gamble	Household & personal products
5	Southwest Airlines	Airlines	Starbucks	Food services
6	FedEx	Delivery	Johnson & Johnson	Pharmaceuticals
7	Berkshire Hathaway	Insurance: property, casualty	Berkshire Hathaway	Insurance: property, casualty
8	Microsoft	Computer software	Dell	Computers
9	Johnson & Johnson	Pharmaceuticals	Toyota Motor	Motor vehicles
10	Procter & Gamble	Household & personal products	Microsoft	Computer software

Source: *Fortune*, 7 March 2005; 6 March 2006

2007 | 2008

Rank	Company	Sector	Company	Sector
1	General Electric	Electronics	Apple	Computers
2	Starbucks	Food services	Berkshire Hathaway	Insurance: property, casualty
3	Toyota Motor	Motor vehicles	General Electric	Electronics
4	Berkshire Hathaway	Insurance: property, casualty	Google	Internet services & retailing
5	Southwest Airlines	Airlines	Toyota Motor	Motor vehicles
6	FedEx	Delivery	Starbucks	Food services
7	Apple Computer	Computers	FedEx	Delivery & logistics
8	Google	Internet services & retailing	Procter & Gamble	Soaps & cosmetics
9	Johnson & Johnson	Pharmaceuticals	Johnson & Johnson	Pharmaceuticals
10	Procter & Gamble	Household & personal products	Goldman Sachs	Securities

Source: *Fortune*, 19 March 2007; 17 March 2008

3 World's most admired companies, 1998–2008

1998 / 1999

Rank	Company	Sector	Company	Sector
1	General Electric	Electronics, electrical equipment	General Electric	Electronics, electrical equipment
2	Coca-Cola	Beverages	Microsoft	Computers
3	Microsoft	Computers	Coca-Cola	Beverages
4	Walt Disney	Entertainment	Intel	Computers
5	Intel	Computers	Berkshire Hathaway	Securities/diversified financials
6	Hewlett-Packard	Computers	IBM	Computers
7	Berkshire Hathaway	Securities/diversified financials	Wal-Mart Stores	Retailers: general & specialist
8	Pfizer	Pharmaceuticals	Cisco Systems	Electronics, electrical equipment
9	Sony	Electronics, electrical equipment	Dell Computer	Computers
10	Dell Computer	Computers	Merck	Pharmaceuticals

Source: *Fortune*, 26 October 1998; 11 October 1999

2000 / 2002

Rank	Company	Sector	Company	Sector
1	General Electric	Electronics, electrical equipment	General Electric	Electronics, electrical equipment
2	Cisco Systems	Electronics, electrical equipment	Wal-Mart Stores	General merchandisers
3	Microsoft	Computers hardware, software	Microsoft	Computers
4	Intel	Computers hardware, software	Berkshire Hathaway	Insurance: property & casualty
5	Wal-Mart Stores	Retailers: general & specialist	Home Depot	Specialist retailer
6	Sony	Electronics, electrical equipment	Johnson & Johnson	Pharmaceuticals
7	Dell Computer	Computers hardware, software	FedEx	Mail, package & freight delivery
8	Nokia	Network communications, internet technology	Citigroup	Megabanks
9	Home Depot	Retail: general, special	Intel	Semiconductors
10	Toyota Motor	Motor vehicles	Cisco Systems	Network communications

Source: *Fortune*, 2 October 2000; 8 March 2002

2003

Rank	Company	Sector
1	Wal-Mart Stores	General merchandisers
2	General Electric	Electronics
3	Microsoft	Computers
4	Dell Computer	Computers
5	Johnson & Johnson	Pharmaceuticals
6	Berkshire Hathaway	Insurance: property, casualty
7	Procter & Gamble	Household & personal products
8	IBM	Computers
9	Coca-Cola	Beverages
10	FedEx	Delivery

2004

Company	Sector
Wal-Mart Stores	General merchandisers
General Electric	Electronics
Microsoft	Computers
Johnson & Johnson	Pharmaceuticals
Berkshire Hathaway	Insurance: property & casualty
Dell	Computers
IBM	Computers
Toyota Motor	Motor vehicles
Procter & Gamble	Household & personal products
FedEx	Delivery

Source: *Fortune*, 3 March 2003; 8 March 2004

2005

Rank	Company	Sector
1	General Electric	Electronics
2	Wal-Mart Stores	General merchandisers
3	Dell	Computers
4	Microsoft	Computers
5	Toyota Motor	Motor vehicles
6	Procter & Gamble	Household & personal products
7	Johnson & Johnson	Pharmaceuticals
8	FedEx	Delivery
9	IBM	Computers
10	Berkshire Hathaway	Insurance: property & casualty

2006

Company	Sector
General Electric	Electronics
Toyota Motor	Motor vehicles
Procter & Gamble	Household & personal products
FedEx	Delivery
Johnson & Johnson	Pharmaceuticals
Microsoft	Computers
Dell	Computers
Berkshire Hathaway	Insurance: property & casualty
Apple Computer	Computers
Wal-Mart Stores	General merchandisers

Source: *Fortune*, 7 March 2005; 6 March 2006

2007

Rank	Company	Sector
1	General Electric	Electronics
2	Toyota Motor	Motor vehicles
3	Procter & Gamble	Household & personal products
4	Johnson & Johnson	Pharmaceuticals
5	Apple	Computers
6	Berkshire Hathaway	Insurance: property & casualty
7	FedEx	Delivery
8	Microsoft	Computers
9	BMW	Motor vehicles
10	PepsiCo	Consumer food products

2008

Company	Sector
Apple	Computers
General Electric	Electronics
Toyota Motor	Motor vehicles
Berkshire Hathaway	Insurance: property & casualty
Procter & Gamble	Household & personal products
FedEx	Delivery
Johnson & Johnson	Pharmaceuticals
Target	General merchandisers
BMW	Motor vehicles
Microsoft	Computers

Source: *Fortune*, 19 March 2007; 7 March 2008

Appendix 3

Britain's most admired companies: rankings by category

1 Quality of management, 1994–2007

1994	1995	1996
1 Vodafone *Telecommunications*	1 Cadbury Schweppes *Food production & processing*	1 Tesco *Retail food & personal*
2 Rentokil *Business services*	2 Smiths Industries *Engineering*	Burford *Property*
3 Marks & Spencer *Retail stores*	3 Tesco *Retail food & personal*	3 Spirax Sarco *Engineering*

1997	1998	1999
1 Smiths Industries *Engineering*	1 Schroders *Other financials*	1 Tesco *Retail food & personal*
2 Next *Retail stores*	2 British Petroleum *Oil, gas & extractive*	BP Amoco *Oil, gas & extractive*
3 Rentokil Initial *Business services*	3 Tesco *Retail food & personal*	3 Granada Group *Leisure & hotels*

2000	2001	2002
1 BP *Oil, gas & extractive*	1 AstraZeneca *Health & household*	1 Tesco *Retail food & personal*
2 Vodafone *Telecommunications*	2 BP *Oil, gas & extractive*	2 BP *Oil, gas & extractive*
Sage Group *Software & computers*	3 Tesco *Retail food & personal*	3 Morrison W *Retail food & personal*
Exel *Transport*		

2003	2004	2005
1 Tesco *Retail food & personal*	1 Royal Bank of Scotland *Banking*	1 Cadbury Schweppes *Food production & processing*
2 BSkyB *Media*	2 BP *Oil, gas & extractive*	Tesco *Retail food & personal*
3 BP *Oil, gas & extractive*	3 Tesco *Retail food & personal*	3 BP *Oil, gas & extractive*

2006	2007
1 Tesco *Retail food & personal*	1 Persimmon *Construction (home)*
2 ICAP *Other financials*	2 Berkeley Group *Construction*
3 BP *Oil, gas & extractive*	3 ICAP *Other financials*

2 Financial soundness, 1994–2007

	1994		1995		1996
1	GEC *Electricals*	1	Land Securities *Property*	1	Marks & Spencer *Retail food & personal*
2	Land Securities *Property*	2	Marks & Spencer *Retail food & personal*	2	Shell Transport & Trading *Oil, gas & extractive*
3	Glaxo Holdings *Health & household*	3	Smiths Industries *Engineering aero & defence*	3	BT *Telecommunications*

	1997		1998		1999
1	Shell Transport & Trading *Oil, gas & extractive*	1	Shell Transport & Trading *Oil, gas & extractive*	1	Land Securities *Property*
2	Associated British Foods *Food manufacturing*	2	Unilever *Food production & processing*	2	Glaxo Wellcome *Health & household*
3	Marks & Spencer *Retail food & personal*	3	British Telecom *Telecommunications*	3	Shell Transport & Trading *Oil, gas & extractive*

	2000		2001		2002
1	Land Securities *Property*	1	Shell Transport & Trading *Oil, gas & extractive*	1	Shell Transport & Trading *Oil, gas & extractive*
2	GlaxoSmithKline *Health & household*	2	HSBC *Banking*	2	Morrison W *Retail food & personal*
	Shell Transport & Trading *Oil, gas & extractive*	3	Morrison W *Retail food & personal*	3	Six Continents *Leisure, entertainment & hotels*

	2003		2004		2005
1	Morrison W *Retail food & personal*	1	HSBC *Banking*	1	HSBC *Banking*
2	Tesco *Retail food & personal*	2	AstraZeneca *Health & household*		Vodafone *Telecommunications*
	Shell Transport & Trading *Oil, gas & extractive*	3	Greene King *Drinks, pubs & breweries*	3	BP *Oil, gas & extractive*

2006		2007	
1	Tesco *Retail food & personal*	1	Tesco *Retail food & personal*
2	Vodafone *Telecommunications*	2	Marks & Spencer *Retail food & personal*
3	HSBC *Banking*	3	AstraZeneca *Health & household*

3 Quality of goods and services, 1994–2007

1994		1995		1996	
1	Glaxo Holdings *Health & household*	1	Whitbread *Drinks*	1	Tesco *Retail food*
2	Electrocomponents *Electricals*	2	Cadbury Schweppes *Food production &* *processing*	2	Cadbury Schweppes *Food production &* *processing*
3	Siebe *Engineering*	3	Vodafone *Telecommunications*	3	British Airways *Transport*

1997		1998		1999	
1	Reuters Holdings *Media*	1	Cadbury Schweppes *Food production &* *processing*	1	Daily Mail & General Trust *Media*
2	Marks & Spencer *Retail food & personal*	2	Schroders *Financials*	2	Rolls-Royce *Engineering*
3	British Telecom *Telecommunications*	3	SmithKline Beecham *Health & household*	3	Glaxo Wellcome *Health & household*

2000		2001		2002
1 Cadbury Schweppes *Food production &* *processing*	1	AstraZeneca *Health & household*	1	Cadbury Schweppes *Food production &* *processing*
2 Shell Transport & Trading *Oil, gas & extractive*	2	GlaxoSmithKline *Health & household*	2	Canary Warf *Property*
3 Rolls-Royce *Engineering*	3	Shell Transport & Trading *Oil, gas & extractive*	3	Selfridges *Retail food & personal*

2003		2004		2005
1 Tesco *Retail food & personal*	1	Cadbury Schweppes *Food production &* *processing*	1	Diageo *Consumer Products*
2 AstraZeneca *Health & household*	2	Man Group *Financials*	2	Man Group *Financials*
				Cadbury Schweppes *Food production &* *processing*
				BSkyB *Media*
				Boots *Retail food & personal*
				Burberry Group *Retail food & personal*
3 GlaxoSmithKline *Health & household*	3	Rotork *Engineering*		

2006		2007
1 GlaxoSmithKline *Health & household*	1	Marks & Spencer *Retail food & personal*
2 Rolls-Royce *Engineering*	2	Johnson Matthey *Chemicals*
3 Johnson Matthey *Chemicals*	3	Tesco *Retail food & personal*

4 People management, 1994–2007

	1994		1995		1996
1	Glaxo Holdings *Health & household*	1	Vodafone *Telecommunications*	1	Mercury Asset Management *Other financials*
2	Unilever *Food production & processing*	2	Unilever *Food production & processing*	2	Tesco *Retail food & personal*
3	SmithKline Beecham *Health & household*	3	Cadbury Schweppes *Food production & processing*	3	Cadbury Schweppes *Food production & processing*

	1997		1998		1999
1	Tesco *Retail food & personal*	1	Tesco *Retail food & personal*	1	Tesco *Retail food & personal*
2	Reuters Holdings *Media*	2	Schroders *Other financials*	2	SmithKline Beecham *Health & household*
3	SmithKline Beecham *Health & household*	3	Siebe *Engineering*	3	Glaxo Wellcome *Health & household*

	2000		2001		2002
1	GlaxoSmithKline *Health & household*	1	BP *Oil, gas & extractive*	1	BP *Oil, gas & extractive*
2	BP Amoco *Oil, gas & extractive*	2	Shell Transport & Trading *Oil, gas & extractive*	2	Unilever *Food production & processing*
3	BSkyB *Media*	3	Tesco *Retail food & personal*	3	Cadbury Schweppes *Food production & processing*

	2003		2004		2005
1	Tesco *Retail food & personal*	1	Vodafone *Telecommunications*	1	Unilever *Food production & processing*
2	BSkyB *Media*	2	BP *Oil, gas & extractive*	2	BP *Oil, gas & extractive*
3	BP *Oil, gas & extractive*	3	Tesco *Retail food & personal*		Tesco *Retail food & personal*

2006		2007	
1	Virgin Mobile *Telecommunications*	1	Marks & Spencer *Retail food & personal*
2	Cadbury Schweppes *Food production & processing*	2	Tesco *Retail food & personal*
3	Johnson Matthey *Chemicals*	3	GlaxoSmithKline *Health & household*

5 Value as a long-term investment, 1994–2007

1994		1995		1996	
1	Rentokil *Business services*	1	Unilever *Food production & processing*	1	Smiths Industries *Engineering*
2	Marks & Spencer *Retail stores*	2	Marks & Spencer *Retail stores*	2	Reuters Holdings *News & publishers*
3	Electrocomponents *Electricals*	3	Smiths Industries *Engineering*	3	Mercury Asset Management *Other financials*

1997		1998		1999	
1	Reuters Holdings *News & publishers*	1	Cadbury Schweppes *Food production & processing*	1	SmithKline Beecham *Health & household*
2	Lloyds TSB *Banking*	2	Unilever *Food production & processing*		Granada Group *Leisure & hotels*
3	Shell Transport & Trading *Oil, gas & extractive*	3	Tesco *Retail food & personal*	3	Cadbury Schweppes *Food production & processing*

2000		2001		2002	
1	GlaxoSmithKline *Health & household*	1	Shell Transport & Trading *Oil, gas & extractive*	1	BAA *Transport*
2	Shell Transport & Trading *Oil, gas & extractive*	2	BP *Oil, gas & extractive*	2	Shell Transport & Trading *Oil, gas & extractive*
3	National Grid *Electricity*	3	Tesco *Retail food & personal*	3	Morrison W *Retail food & personal*

2003		2004		2005	
1	Tesco *Retail food & personal*	1	Wolseley *Building materials & merchants*	1	Wolseley *Building materials & merchants*
2	Morrison W *Retail food & personal*	2	Tesco *Retail food & personal*	2	Tesco *Retail food & personal*
3	Royal Bank of Scotland *Banking*	3	Weir Group *Engineering*	3	Serco Group *Support services*
					BP *Oil, gas & extractive*

2006		2007	
1	Tesco *Retail food & personal*	1	Marks & Spencer *Retail food & personal*
2	GlaxoSmithKline *Health & household*	2	Tesco *Retail food & personal*
3	BP *Oil, gas & extractive*	3	Serco Group *Support services*

6 Capacity to innovate, 1994–2007

1994		1995		1996	
1	Glaxo Holdings *Health & household*	1	The British Land Co *Property*	1	Burford *Property*
2	Dorling Kindersley *News & publishers*	2	Tesco *Retail food & personal*	2	Tesco *Retail food & personal*
3	The British Land Co *Property*	3	Burford *Property*	3	The British Land Co *Property*

1997	1998	1999
1 Burford *Property*	1 Tesco *Retail food & personal*	1 BSkyB *Media*
2 Tesco *Retail food & personal*	2 Glaxo Wellcome *Health & household*	2 SmithKline Beecham *Health & household*
3 The British Land Co *Property*	3 BSkyB *Media*	3 Tesco *Retail food & personal*

2000	2001	2002
1 BSkyB *Media*	1 BSkyB *Media*	1 Tesco *Retail food & personal*
2 Iceland *Retail food & personal*	2 ARM Holdings *Electronic & electricals*	2 BP *Oil, gas & extractive*
3 Celltech *Health & household* Exel *Transport*	3 AstraZeneca *Health & household*	3 BSkyB *Media*

2003	2004	2005
1 BSkyB *Media*	1 Man *Other financials*	1 Tesco *Retail food & personal*
2 Tesco *Retail food & personal*	2 Carphone Warehouse *Retail general*	2 Man *Other financials*
3 Autonomy *Software & computers*	3 Rolls-Royce *Engineering*	3 Pilkington *Building materials &* *merchants*

2006	2007
1 ARM Holdings *Electronic & electricals*	1 BSkyB *Media*
2 Carphone Warehouse *Retail general*	2 Johnson Matthey *Chemicals*
3 Johnson Matthey *Chemicals*	3 Marks & Spencer *Retail food & personal*

7 Quality of marketing, 1994–2007

1994		1995		1996	
1	British Airways *Transport*	1	Cadbury Schweppes *Food production & processing*	1	Cadbury Schweppes *Food production & processing*
2	Glaxo Holdings *Health & household*	2	Vodafone *Telecommunications*	2	Burford *Property*
3	Cadbury Schweppes *Food production & processing*	3	Whitbread *Leisure & hotels*	3	Tesco *Retail food & personal*

1997		1998		1999	
1	Tesco *Retail food & personal*	1	Orange *Telecommunications*	1	SmithKline Beecham *Health & household*
2	British Airways *Transport*	2	Tesco *Retail food & personal*	2	Tesco *Retail food & personal*
3	BSkyB *Media*	3	Gallaher *Tobacco*	3	BSkyB *Media*

2000		2001		2002	
1	GlaxoSmithKline *Health & household*	1	BSkyB *Media*	1	GlaxoSmithKline *Health & household*
2	Cadbury Schweppes *Food production & processing*	2	GlaxoSmithKline *Health & household*	2	Diageo *Drinks, pubs & breweries*
	Tesco *Retail food & personal*	3	easyJet *Transport*	3	easyJet *Transport*

2003		2004		2005	
1	Tesco *Retail food & personal*	1	BSkyB *Media*	1	BSkyB *Media*
2	GlaxoSmithKline *Health & household*	2	Cadbury Schweppes *Food production & processing*	2	Tesco *Retail food & personal*
3	Cadbury Schweppes *Food production & processing*	3	Vodafone *Telecommunications*	3	Cadbury Schweppes *Food production & processing*

2006		2007	
1	Cadbury Schweppes *Food production & processing*	1	Marks & Spencer *Retail food & personal*
2	Carphone Warehouse *Retail general*	2	British Airways *Transport*
3	British Airways *Transport*	3	Tesco *Retail food & personal*

8 Community, social and environmental responsibility, 1994–2007

1994		1995		1996	
1	Rentokil *Business services*	1	BT *Telecommunications*	1	Argyll Group *Food retailers*
2	BT *Telecommunications*	2	ICI *Chemicals & plastics*	2	ICI *Chemicals & plastics*
3	Whitbread *Drinks*	3	Sainsbury (J) *Retail food & personal*	3	Smith D.S. *Paper & printing*

1997		1998		1999	
1	Body Shop *General retailers*	1	Body Shop *General retailers*	1	Body Shop *General retailers*
2	Unilever *Food production & processing*	2	Cadbury Schweppes *Food production & processing*	2	Iceland *Retail food & personal*
3	Anglian Water *Utilities*	3	Marks & Spencer *Retail food & personal*	3	Daily Mail & General Trust *News & publishing*

2000	2001	2002
1 Iceland *Retail food & personal*	1 Shell Transport & Trading *Oil, gas & extractive*	1 Cadbury Schweppes *Food production & processing*
2 Exel *Transport*	2 BP *Oil, gas & extractive*	2 BP *Oil, gas & extractive*
3 Anglian Water *Utilities*	3 GlaxoSmithKline *Health & household*	3 GlaxoSmithKline *Health & household*

2003	2004	2005
1 BOC *Chemicals*	1 Unilever *Food production & processing*	1 BT Group *Telecommunications*
2 BT Group *Telecommunications*	2 Serco Group *Support services*	2 IMI *Engineering & machinery*
Cadbury Schweppes *Food production & processing*	3 IMI *Engineering & machinery*	3 BP *Oil, gas & extractive*

2006	2007
1 BT Group *Telecommunications*	1 BSkyB *Media*
2 AstraZeneca *Health & household*	2 Marks & Spencer *Retail food & personal*
GlaxoSmithKline *Health & household*	3 Marshalls *Building materials & merchants*
BHP Billiton *Oil, gas & extractive*	

9 Use of corporate assets, 1994–2007

1994	**1995**	**1996**
1 Rentokil *Business services*	1 Smiths Industries *Engineering*	1 Burford *Property*
2 Caledonia Investments *Financials*	2 BTR *Conglomerates*	2 The British Land Co *Property*
3 The British Land Co *Property*	3 Hanson *Conglomerates*	Siebe *Engineering*

1997	**1998**	**1999**
1 Lloyds TSB *Banking*	1 Tesco *Retail food & personal*	1 BP Amoco *Oil, gas & extractive*
2 Rentokil Initial *Business services*	2 The British Land Co *Property*	2 Airtours *Leisure & hotels*
3 Reuters Holdings *News & publishers*	3 Dewhirst Group *Textiles*	3 Tesco *Retail food & personal*

2000	**2001**	**2002**
1 BP Amoco *Oil, gas & extractive*	1 BP *Oil, gas & extractive*	1 Rentokil Initial *Support services*
2 National Grid *Electricity*	2 Shell Transport & Trading *Oil, gas & extractive*	Diageo *Restaurants, pubs & breweries*
3 Pearson *Media*	3 Tesco *Retail food & personal*	3 Morrison W *Retail food & personal*

2003	**2004**	**2005**
1 Tesco *Retail food & personal*	1 Enterprise Inns *Restaurants, pubs & breweries*	1 Tesco *Retail food & personal*
2 Morrison W *Retail food & personal*	2 Man Group *Financials*	2 Punch Taverns *Restaurants, pubs & breweries*
3 Capita Group *Support services*	3 IMI *Engineering*	3 Vodafone *Telecommunications*
	Tesco *Retail, food & personal*	

2006		2007	
1	Barratt Developments *Construction (home)*	1	Marks & Spencer *Retail food & personal*
2	Rotork *Engineering*	2	Aggreko *Support services*
3	Tesco *Retail food & personal*	3	Tesco *Retail food & personal*
	Persimmon *Construction (home)*		

Sources

All category rankings in the British most admired surveys come from *Management Today* and were published in December of the relevant year.

Appendix 4

America's most admired companies: rankings by category

1 Quality of management, 1983–2007

1983		1984		1985	
1	IBM *Office equipment, computers*	1	IBM *Office equipment, computers*	1	IBM *Office equipment, computers*
2	Hewlett-Packard *Computers*	2	Hewlett-Packard *Computers*	2	Dow Jones *Publishing, printing*
3	Johnson & Johnson *Pharmaceuticals*	3	Dow Jones *Publishing, printing*	3	Anheuser-Busch *Beverages*

1986		1987		1988	
1	IBM *Office equipment, computers*	1	Liz Claiborne *Apparel*	1	Merck *Pharmaceuticals*
2	J.P. Morgan *Commercial banking*	2	J.P. Morgan *Commercial banking*	2	Liz Claiborne *Apparel*
3	Boeing *Aerospace*	3	Rubbermaid *Rubber & plastic products*	3	J.P. Morgan *Commercial banking*

1989	1990	1991
1 Merck *Pharmaceuticals*	1 Philip Morris *Tobacco*	1 Wal-Mart Stores *Retailing*
2 Wal-Mart Stores *Retailing*	2 Wal-Mart Stores *Retailing*	2 Rubbermaid *Rubber & plastic products*
3 Rubbermaid *Rubber & plastic products*	3 Merck *Pharmaceuticals*	3 Merck *Pharmaceuticals*

1992	1993	1994
1 Wal-Mart Stores *Retailing*	1 Wal-Mart Stores *Retailing*	1 Home Depot *Specialist retailers*
2 Rubbermaid *Rubber & plastic products*	2 Merck *Pharmaceuticals*	2 Rubbermaid *Rubber & plastic products*
3 Merck *Pharmaceuticals*	3 Rubbermaid *Rubber & plastic products*	3 J.P. Morgan *Commercial banking*

1995	1996	1997
1 Rubbermaid *Rubber & plastic products*	1 Coca-Cola *Beverages*	1 Coca-Cola *Beverages*
2 Home Depot *Specialist retailers*	2 Procter & Gamble *Soaps, cosmetics*	2 Berkshire Hathaway *Diversified financials*
3 Microsoft *Computer & data services*	3 Berkshire Hathaway *Diversified financials*	3 Microsoft *Computer & data services*

1998	1999	2000
1 Coca-Cola *Beverages*	1 Philip Morris *Tobacco*	1 Enron *Pipelines*
2 Intel *Electronics, semiconductors*	2 General Electric *Electronics & electrical equipment*	2 General Electric *Electronics & electrical equipment*
3 General Electric *Electronics & electrical equipment*	3 Cisco Systems *Electronics, networks*	3 Omnicom Group *Advertising & marketing*

2001	2002	2003
1 Omnicom Group *Advertising & marketing*	1 General Electric *Electronics*	1 Philip Morris *Tobacco*
2 Enron *Pipelines*	2 Walgreen *Food & drug stores*	2 Berkshire Hathaway *Insurance: property, casualty*
3 Citigroup *Money center banks*	3 Citigroup *Money center banks*	3 General Electric *Electronics*

2004	2005	2006
1 United Parcel Service *Delivery*	1 Kinder Morgan Energy Partners *Pipelines*	1 UnitedHealth Group *Health care: insurance*
2 Liz Claiborne *Apparel*	2 Altria Group *Tobacco*	2 General Electric *Electronics*
3 Procter & Gamble *Household & personal products*	3 Berkshire Hathaway *Insurance: property, casualty*	3 Procter & Gamble *Household & personal products*

2007
1 Procter & Gamble *Household & personal products*
2 General Electric *Electronics*
Kinder Morgan Energy Partners *Pipelines*

2 Financial soundness, 1983–2007

1983	1984	1985
1 IBM *Office equipment, computers*	1 IBM *Office equipment, computers*	1 IBM *Office equipment, computers*
2 American Home Products *Pharmaceuticals*	2 General Electric *Electronics, appliances*	2 Coca-Cola *Beverages*
3 Johnson & Johnson *Pharmaceuticals*	3 Dow Jones *Publishing, printing*	3 Dow Jones *Publishing, printing*

1986	1987	1988
1 IBM *Office equipment, computers*	1 Exxon *Petroleum refining*	1 Merck *Pharmaceuticals*
2 Exxon *Petroleum refining*	2 IBM *Office equipment, computers*	2 Exxon *Petroleum refining*
3 Dow Jones *Publishing, printing*	3 Merck *Pharmaceuticals*	3 Philip Morris *Tobacco*

1989	1990	1991
1 Exxon *Petroleum refining*	1 Merck *Pharmaceuticals*	1 Merck *Pharmaceuticals*
2 Merck *Pharmaceuticals*	2 Coca-Cola *Beverages*	2 Coca-Cola *Beverages*
3 Philip Morris *Tobacco*	3 IBM *Computers*	3 Shell Oil *Petroleum refining*

1992	1993	1994
1 Merck *Pharmaceuticals*	1 Merck *Pharmaceuticals*	1 J.P. Morgan *Commercial banking*
2 Wal-Mart Stores *Retailing*	2 Coca-Cola *Beverages*	2 Coca-Cola *Beverages*
3 Coca-Cola *Beverages*	3 J.P. Morgan *Commercial banking*	3 Microsoft *Computer & data services*

1995	1996	1997
1 Microsoft *Computer & data services*	1 Microsoft *Computer & data services*	1 Coca-Cola *Beverages*
2 Coca-Cola *Beverages*	2 Coca-Cola *Beverages*	2 Microsoft *Computer & data services*
3 Rubbermaid *Rubber & plastic products*	3 Berkshire Hathaway *Publishing & printing*	3 United Parcel Service *Delivery*

1998	1999	2000
1 Microsoft *Computer software*	1 Microsoft *Computer software*	1 Microsoft *Computer software*
2 Intel *Electronics, semiconductors*	2 Intel *Electronics, semiconductors*	2 Intel *Electronics, semiconductors*
3 Cisco Systems *Electronics, networks*	3 Cisco Systems *Electronics, networks*	3 Cisco Systems *Electronics, networks*

2001	2002	2003
1 Exxon Mobil *Petroleum refining*	1 Exxon Mobil *Petroleum refining*	1 Microsoft *Computer software*
2 Citigroup *Money center banks*	2 Wal-Mart Stores *General merchandisers*	2 Berkshire Hathaway *Insurance: property, casualty*
United Parcel Service *Delivery*	3 Intel *Electronics, semiconductors*	3 Philip Morris (Altria) *Tobacco*
Omnicom Group *Advertising & marketing*		
Intel *Electronics, semiconductors*		

2004	2005	2006
1 United Parcel Service *Delivery*	1 Kinder Morgan Energy Partners *Pipeline, energy*	1 Exxon Mobil *Petroleum refining*
2 Microsoft *Computer software*	2 Intel *Semiconductors*	2 Microsoft *Computer software*
3 Anheuser-Busch *Beverages*	3 Exxon Mobil *Petroleum refining*	3 United Parcel Service *Delivery*

2007
1 Exxon Mobil *Petroleum refining*
2 CHS *Wholesalers: food & grocery*
3 Berkshire Hathaway *Insurance: property, casualty*

3 Quality of goods and services, 1983–2007

1983	1984	1985
1 Boeing *Aerospace*	1 Dow Jones *Publishing, printing*	1 Dow Jones *Publishing, printing*
2 Caterpillar Tractor *Industrial farm equipment*	2 Boeing *Aerospace*	2 Boeing *Aerospace*
3 Hewlett-Packard *Computers*	3 Anheuser-Busch *Beverages*	3 Coca-Cola *Beverages*

1986	1987	1988
1 Dow Jones *Publishing, printing*	1 Dow Jones *Publishing, printing*	1 Merck *Pharmaceuticals*
2 Boeing *Aerospace*	2 Merck *Pharmaceuticals*	2 Dow Jones *Publishing, printing*
3 Eastman Kodak *Precision instruments*	3 Boeing *Aerospace*	3 Rubbermaid *Rubber & plastic products*

1989	1990	1991
1 Merck *Pharmaceuticals*	1 Merck *Pharmaceuticals*	1 Merck *Pharmaceuticals*
2 Rubbermaid *Rubber & plastic products*	2 Rubbermaid *Rubber & plastic products*	2 Rubbermaid *Rubber & plastic products*
3 Boeing *Aerospace*	3 Philip Morris *Tobacco*	3 Procter & Gamble *Soaps, cosmetics*

1992	1993	1994
1 Merck *Pharmaceuticals*	1 Merck *Pharmaceuticals*	1 Rubbermaid *Rubber & plastic products*
2 Rubbermaid *Rubber & plastic products*	2 Rubbermaid *Rubber & plastic products*	2 Procter & Gamble *Soaps, cosmetics*
3 Procter & Gamble *Soaps, cosmetics*	3 Boeing *Aerospace*	3 Walt Disney *Entertainment*

1995	1996	1997
1 Rubbermaid *Rubber & plastic products*	1 Mirage Resorts *Hotels, casinos, resorts*	1 Coca-Cola *Beverages*
2 Motorola *Electronics, electrical equipment*	2 Rubbermaid *Rubber & plastic products*	2 Mirage Resorts *Hotels, casinos, resorts*
3 Procter & Gamble *Soaps, cosmetics*	3 Coca-Cola *Beverages*	3 Walt Disney *Entertainment*

1998	1999	2000
1 Toyota Motor Sales USA *Motor vehicles & parts*	1 Mirage Resorts *Hotels, casinos, resorts*	1 Omnicom Group *Advertising & marketing*
2 Coca-Cola *Beverages*	2 Corning *Building materials, glass*	2 Philip Morris *Tobacco*
3 Gillette *Soaps, cosmetics*	3 Toyota Motor Sales USA *Motor vehicles & parts*	3 United Parcel Service *Delivery*

2001		**2002**		**2003**	
1	Toyota Motor Sales USA *Motor vehicles*	1	New York Times *Publishing*	1	Philip Morris *Tobacco*
2	Omnicom Group *Advertising & marketing*	2	Intel *Electronics, semiconductors*	2	Medtronic *Medical products, equipment*
3	New York Times *Publishing*	3	Philip Morris *Tobacco*	3	Procter & Gamble *Household & personal products*

2004		**2005**		**2006**	
1	Anheuser-Busch *Beverages*	1	Kinder Morgan Energy Partners *Pipelines*	1	Nordstrom *General merchandisers*
2	United Parcel Service *Delivery*	2	FedEx *Delivery*	2	United Parcel Service *Delivery*
3	Procter & Gamble *Household & personal products*	3	American Express *Consumer credit*	3	Walt Disney *Media & entertainment*

2007	
1	FedEx *Delivery*
2	Walt Disney *Media & entertainment*
3	Procter & Gamble *Household & personal products*

4 People management, 1983–2007

1983	**1984**	**1985**
1 Hewlett-Packard *Computers*	1 Hewlett-Packard *Computers*	1 Hewlett-Packard *Computers*
2 IBM *Office equipment, computers*	2 IBM *Office equipment, computers*	2 IBM *Office equipment, computers*
Merck *Pharmaceuticals*	3 Merck *Pharmaceuticals*	3 Dow Jones *Publishing, printing*

1986	**1987**	**1988**
1 IBM *Office equipment, computers*	1 Merck *Pharmaceuticals*	1 Merck *Pharmaceuticals*
2 J.P. Morgan *Commercial banking*	2 J.P. Morgan *Commercial banking*	2 Philip Morris *Tobacco*
3 Merck *Pharmaceuticals*	3 Boeing *Aerospace*	3 J.P. Morgan *Commercial banking*

1989	**1990**	**1991**
1 Merck *Pharmaceuticals*	1 Merck *Pharmaceuticals*	1 Merck *Pharmaceuticals*
2 Philip Morris *Tobacco*	2 Philip Morris *Tobacco*	2 Wal-Mart Stores *Retailing*
3 Wal-Mart Stores *Retailing*	3 3M *Scientific, photographic & control equipment*	3 Rubbermaid *Rubber & plastics products*

1992	**1993**	**1994**
1 Merck *Pharmaceuticals*	1 Merck *Pharmaceuticals*	1 Microsoft *Computer & data services*
2 Wal-Mart Stores *Retailing*	2 Wal-Mart Stores *Retailing*	2 J.P. Morgan *Commercial banking*
3 Liz Claiborne *Apparel*	3 3M *Scientific, photographic & control equipment*	3 Home Depot *Specialist retailers*

* The admirable company

1995	1996	1997
1 Microsoft *Computer & data services*	1 Microsoft *Computer & data services*	1 Microsoft *Computer & data services*
2 Coca-Cola *Beverages*	2 Procter & Gamble *Soaps, cosmetics*	2 Coca-Cola *Beverages*
3 Motorola *Electronics, electrical equipment*	3 Intel *Electronics, electrical equipment*	3 Mirage Resorts *Hotels, casinos, resorts*

1998	1999	2000
1 Microsoft *Computer & data services*	1 Microsoft *Computer & data services*	1 Goldman Sachs *Securities*
2 J.P. Morgan *Commercial banking*	2 Cisco Systems *Electronics, networks*	2 Enron *Pipelines*
3 Intel *Electronics, semiconductors*	3 Coca-Cola *Beverages*	3 Cisco Systems *Electronics, networks*

2001	2002	2003
1 Omnicom Group *Advertising & marketing*	1 Intel *Electronics, semiconductors*	1 General Electric *Electronics*
2 Goldman Sachs *Securities*	2 General Electric *Electronics*	2 American Express *Consumer credit*
3 Citigroup *Money center banks*	3 Walgreen *Food & drug stores*	3 Philip Morris *Tobacco*

2004	2005	2006
1 Procter & Gamble *Household & personal products*	1 Kinder Morgan Energy Partners *Pipelines*	1 Procter & Gamble *Household & personal products*
2 American Express *Consumer credit*	2 General Electric *Electronics*	2 General Electric *Electronics*
3 Walgreen *Food & drug stores*	3 American Express *Consumer credit*	3 Google *Computers & communications*

2007

1 FedEx
Delivery

2 Procter & Gamble
Household & personal products

3 Google
Computers & communications

5 Value as a long-term investment, 1983–2007

1983	**1984**	**1985**
1 IBM *Office equipment, computers*	1 IBM *Office equipment, computers*	1 IBM *Office equipment, computers*
2 Hewlett-Packard *Computers*	2 Dow Jones *Publishing, printing*	2 Dow Jones *Publishing, printing*
3 Johnson & Johnson *Pharmaceuticals*	3 Hewlett-Packard *Computers*	3 Coca-Cola *Beverages*

1986	**1987**	**1988**
1 IBM *Office equipment, computers*	1 Merck *Pharmaceuticals*	1 Merck *Pharmaceuticals*
2 Coca-Cola *Beverages*	2 RJR Nabisco *Tobacco*	2 Philip Morris *Tobacco*
3 Dow Jones *Publishing, printing*	3 Philip Morris *Tobacco*	3 Dow Jones *Publishing, printing*

1989	**1990**	**1991**
1 Merck *Pharmaceuticals*	1 Philip Morris *Tobacco*	1 Merck *Pharmaceuticals*
2 Philip Morris *Tobacco*	2 Merck *Pharmaceuticals*	2 Procter & Gamble *Soaps, cosmetics*
3 Rubbermaid *Rubber & plastic products*	3 Berkshire Hathaway *Publishing, printing*	3 Rubbermaid *Rubber & plastic products*

1992	1993	1994
1 Merck *Pharmaceuticals*	1 Coca-Cola *Beverages*	1 Coca-Cola *Beverages*
2 Coca-Cola *Beverages*	2 Wal-Mart Stores *Retailing*	2 United Parcel Service *Trucking*
3 Wal-Mart Stores *Retailing*	3 Merck *Pharmaceuticals*	3 Rubbermaid *Rubber & plastic products*

1995	1996	1997
1 Coca-Cola *Beverages*	1 Coca-Cola *Beverages*	1 Coca-Cola *Beverages*
2 Motorola *Electronics, electrical equipment*	2 Berkshire Hathaway *Publishing, printing*	2 Berkshire Hathaway *Publishing, printing*
3 Microsoft *Computers & data services*	3 Procter & Gamble *Soaps, cosmetics*	3 Microsoft *Computers & data services*

1998	1999	2000
1 Cisco Systems *Electronics, networks*	1 General Electric *Electronics & electrical equipment*	1 Microsoft *Computers & data services*
2 Intel *Electronics, semiconductors*	2 Coca-Cola *Beverages*	2 Home Depot *Specialty retailers*
3 Microsoft *Computers & data services*	3 Cisco Systems *Electronics, networks*	3 Cisco Systems *Electronics, networks*

2001	2002	2003
1 Citigroup *Money center banks*	1 Citigroup *Money center banks*	1 Medtronic *Medical products, equipment*
2 ExxonMobil *Petroleum refining*	2 ExxonMobil *Petroleum refining*	2 Cardinal Health *Wholesalers: health care*
3 Omnicom Group *Advertising & marketing*	3 Berkshire Hathaway *Insurance: property, casualty*	3 Cintas *Diversified outsourcing*

2004	2005	2006
1 ExxonMobil *Petroleum refining*	1 Berkshire Hathaway *Insurance: property, casualty*	1 Exxon Mobil *Petroleum refining*
2 United Parcel Service *Delivery*	2 Kinder Morgan Energy Partners *Pipelines*	2 UnitedHealth Group *Health care*
3 Berkshire Hathaway *Insurance: property, casualty*	3 CHS *Wholesalers: food & grocery*	3 Altria Group *Tobacco*

2007
1 CHS *Wholesalers: food & grocery*
2 Berkshire Hathaway *Insurance: property, casualty*
3 ExxonMobil *Petroleum refining*

6 Capacity to innovate, 1983–2007

1983	1984	1985
1 Citicorp *Commercial banking*	1 Citicorp *Commercial banking*	1 Citicorp *Commercial banking*
2 Merrill Lynch *Diversified financial*	2 Merrill Lynch *Diversified financial*	2 Gannett *Publishing, printing*
3 Hewlett-Packard *Computers*	3 Time Inc. *Publishing, printing*	3 3M *Precision instruments*

1986	1987	1988
1 Citicorp *Commercial banking*	1 Liz Claiborne *Apparel*	1 Merck *Pharmaceuticals*
2 Gannett *Publishing, printing*	2 Gannett *Publishing, printing*	2 Liz Claiborne *Apparel*
3 3M *Scientific, photographic & control equipment*	3 Herman Miller *Furniture*	3 Rubbermaid *Rubber & plastic products*

1989	1990	1991
1 Merck *Pharmaceuticals*	1 Merck *Pharmaceuticals*	1 Merck *Pharmaceuticals*
2 Rubbermaid *Rubber & plastic products*	2 3M *Scientific, photographic & control equipment*	2 Rubbermaid *Rubber & plastic products*
3 3M *Scientific, photographic & control equipment*	3 Rubbermaid *Rubber & plastic products*	3 3M *Scientific, photographic & control equipment*

1992	1993	1994
1 Merck *Pharmaceuticals*	1 Rubbermaid *Rubber & plastic products*	1 Rubbermaid *Rubber & plastic products*
2 Wall-Mart Stores *Retailing*	2 Merck *Pharmaceuticals*	2 3M *Scientific, photographic & control equipment*
3 Rubbermaid *Rubber & plastic products*	3 3M *Scientific, photographic & control equipment*	3 Motorola *Electronics, electrical equipment*

1995	1996	1997
1 Rubbermaid *Rubber & plastic products*	1 Enron *Pipelines*	1 Enron *Pipelines*
2 Intel *Electronics, electrical equipment*	2 Rubbermaid *Rubber & plastic products*	2 Mirage Resorts *Hotels, casinos, resorts*
3 Motorola *Electronics, electrical equipment*	3 Intel *Electronics, electrical equipment*	3 Intel *Electronics, electrical equipment*

1998	1999	2000
1 Enron *Pipelines*	1 Enron *Pipelines*	1 Enron *Pipelines*
2 Intel *Electronics, electrical equipment*	2 Mirage Resorts *Hotels, casinos, resorts*	2 Charles Schwab *Securities*
3 Nike *Apparel*	3 Herman Miller *Furniture*	3 Herman Miller *Furniture*

2001	2002	2003
1 Enron *Pipelines, energy*	1 Minnesota Mining & Mfg. *Precision equipment*	1 PepsiCo *Beverages*
2 Charles Schwab *Securities*	2 Intel *Electronics, electrical equipment*	2 Nike *Apparel*
3 Citigroup *Money center banks*	3 Charles Schwab *Securities*	3 Medtronic *Medical products, equipment*

2004	2005	2006
1 Washington Mutual *Mortgage Services*	1 Kinder Morgan Energy Partners *Pipelines*	1 Apple Computer *Computers & communications*
2 Starbucks *Food services*	2 FedEx *Delivery*	2 Google *Computers & communications*
3 Procter & Gamble *Household, personal products*	3 Apple Computer *Computers & communications*	3 UnitedHealth Group *Health care*

2007
1 Apple *Computers & communications*
2 Google *Computers & communications*
3 Fed Ex *Delivery*

7 Community, social and environmental responsibility, 1983–2007

1983	1984	1985
1 Eastman Kodak *Precision instruments*	1 Johnson & Johnson *Pharmaceuticals*	1 Eastman Kodak *Precision instruments*
2 IBM *Office equipment, computers*	2 Eastman Kodak *Precision instruments*	2 Johnson & Johnson *Pharmaceuticals*
3 Johnson & Johnson *Pharmaceuticals*	3 IBM *Office equipment, computers*	3 IBM *Office equipment*
		3M *Precision instruments*

1986	1987	1988
1 Eastman Kodak *Precision instruments*	1 Johnson & Johnson *Pharmaceuticals*	1 Johnson & Johnson *Pharmaceuticals*
2 3M *Precision instruments*	2 IBM *Office equipment, computers*	2 Eastman Kodak *Precision instruments*
3 Coca-Cola *Beverages*	3 Merck *Pharmaceuticals*	3 Procter & Gamble *Soaps & cosmetics*
Johnson & Johnson *Pharmaceuticals*		

1989	1990	1991
1 Johnson & Johnson *Pharmaceuticals*	1 Johnson & Johnson *Pharmaceuticals*	1 Merck *Pharmaceuticals*
2 E.I. du Pont de Nemours *Chemicals*	2 Merck *Pharmaceuticals*	2 Johnson & Johnson *Pharmaceuticals*
3 Merck *Pharmaceuticals*	3 Du Pont *Chemicals*	3 Du Pont *Chemicals*

1992	1993	1994
1 Merck *Pharmaceuticals*	1 3M *Scientific, photographic & control equipment*	1 Rubbermaid *Rubber & plastic products*
2 Johnson & Johnson *Pharmaceuticals*	2 Rubbermaid *Rubber & plastic products*	2 Corning *Building materials, glass*
3 Rubbermaid *Rubber & plastic products*	3 Merck *Pharmaceuticals*	3 Johnson & Johnson *Pharmaceuticals*

1995	1996	1997
1 Rubbermaid *Rubber & plastic products*	1 Levi Strauss Associates *Apparel*	1 Coca-Cola *Beverages*
2 Coca-Cola *Beverages*	2 Johnson & Johnson *Pharmaceuticals*	2 Herman Miller *Furniture*
3 3M *Scientific, photographic & control equipment*	3 3M *Scientific, photographic & control equipment*	3 Corning *Building materials, glass*

1998	1999	2000
1 Herman Miller *Furniture*	1 Corning *Building materials, glass*	1 McDonald's *Food services*
2 Coca-Cola *Beverages*	2 Du Pont *Chemicals*	2 Du Pont *Chemicals*
3 Du Pont *Chemicals*	3 Herman Miller *Furniture*	3 Herman Miller *Furniture*

2001	2002	2003
1 Du Pont *Chemicals*	1 New York Times *Publishing*	1 Alexander & Baldwin *Transportation, logistics*
2 McDonald's *Food services*	2 Target *General merchandisers*	2 Johnson & Johnson *Pharmaceuticals*
3 Waste Management *Waste management*	3 Procter & Gamble *Soaps & cosmetics*	3 American Express *Consumer credit*

2004	2005	2006
1 United Parcel Service *Delivery*	1 United Parcel Service *Delivery*	1 United Parcel Service *Delivery*
2 Alcoa *Metals*	2 CHS *Wholesalers: food & grocery*	2 International Paper *Forest & paper products*
3 Washington Mutual *Mortgage services*	3 Kinder Morgan Energy Partners *Pipelines*	3 Exelon *Electric & gas utilities*

2007
1 CHS *Wholesalers: food & grocery*
2 United Parcel Service *Delivery*
3 Whole Foods Market *Food & drug stores*

8 Use of corporate assets, 1983–2007

1983	1984	1985
1 Johnson & Johnson *Pharmaceuticals*	1 IBM *Office equipment, computers*	1 IBM *Office equipment, computers*
2 IBM *Office equipment, computers*	2 Dow Jones *Publishing, printing*	2 Dow Jones *Publishing, printing*
3 Abbott Laboratories *Pharmaceuticals*	3 Hewlett-Packard *Computers*	3 Coca-Cola *Beverages*

1986	1987	1988
1 IBM *Office equipment, computers*	1 RJR Nabisco *Tobacco*	1 Merck *Pharmaceuticals*
2 3M *Precision instruments*	2 Merck *Pharmaceuticals*	2 J.P. Morgan *Commercial banking*
3 Amoco *Petroleum refining*	3 Liz Claiborne *Apparel*	3 Wal-Mart Stores *Retailing*

1989	1990	1991
1 Merck *Pharmaceuticals*	1 Berkshire Hathaway *Publishing, printing*	1 Wal-Mart Stores *Retailing*
Wal-Mart Stores *Retailing*	2 Merck *Pharmaceuticals*	2 Rubbermaid *Rubber & plastic products*
3 Rubbermaid *Rubber & plastic products*	3 Wal-Mart Stores *Retailing*	3 Merck *Pharmaceuticals*

1992	1993	1994
1 Merck *Pharmaceuticals*	1 Wal-Mart Stores *Retailing*	1 Rubbermaid *Rubber & plastic products*
2 Wal-Mart Stores *Retailing*	2 Golden West Financial *Savings institutions*	2 Berkshire Hathaway *Publishing, printing*
3 Rubbermaid *Rubber & plastic products*	3 Rubbermaid *Rubber & plastic products*	3 Microsoft *Computer & data services*

1995	1996	1997
1 Rubbermaid *Rubber & plastic products*	1 Berkshire Hathaway *Publishing, printing*	1 Berkshire Hathaway *Insurance: property, casualty*
2 Coca-Cola *Beverages*	2 Coca-Cola *Beverages*	2 Coca-Cola *Beverages*
3 Motorola *Electronics, electrical equipment*	3 Johnson & Johnson *Pharmaceuticals*	3 McDonald's *Food services*

1998	1999	2000
1 Coca-Cola *Beverages*	1 Cisco Systems *Electronics, networks*	1 Berkshire Hathaway *Insurance: property, casualty*
2 Intel *Electronics, semiconductors*	2 Berkshire Hathaway *Insurance: property, casualty*	2 Cisco Systems *Electronics, networks*
3 Berkshire Hathaway *Insurance: property, casualty*	3 Coca-Cola *Beverages*	3 General Electric *Electronics, electrical equipment*

2001		2002		2003	
1	Citigroup *Megabanks*	1	Berkshire Hathaway *Insurance: property, casualty*	1	Berkshire Hathaway *Insurance: property, casualty*
2	Omnicom Group *Advertising & marketing*	2	Walgreen *Food & drug stores*	2	Cintas *Diversified outsourcing*
3	Exxon Mobil *Petroleum refining*	3	Fifth Third Bancorp *Commercial banks*	3	Philip Morris *Tobacco*

2004		2005		2006	
1	United Parcel Service *Delivery*	1	Kinder Morgan Energy Partners *Pipelines*	1	Exxon Mobil *Petroleum refining*
2	Procter & Gamble *Household & personal products*	2	Berkshire Hathaway *Insurance: property, casualty*	2	UnitedHealth Group *Health care*
3	Berkshire Hathaway *Insurance: property, casualty*	3	Wal-Mart Stores *General merchandisers*	3	United Parcel Service *Delivery*

2007	
1	Kinder Morgan *Pipelines*
2	CHS *Wholesalers: food & grocery*
3	Exxon Mobil *Petroleum refining*

Sources

All category rankings in the American most admired surveys come from *Fortune* and were published as follows: 1983–90 January; 1991–94 February; 1995–99 March; 2000–01 February; 2001–07 March.

Appendix 5

World's most admired companies: rankings by category

1 Quality of management, 1999–2007

	1999		2000		2002
1	General Electric *Electronics, electrical equipment*	1	General Electric *Electronics, electrical equipment*	1	General Electric *Electronics*
2	Intel *Computers*	2	Home Depot *Retailers: general & specialist*	2	Nokia *Network communications*
3	Dell Computer *Computers*	3	Wal-Mart Stores *Retailers: general & specialist*	3	Walgreen *Food & drug stores*

	2003		2004		2005
1	Berkshire Hathaway *Insurance: property, casualty*	1	Procter & Gamble *Household & personal products*	1	Berkshire Hathaway *Insurance: property, casualty*
2	General Electric *Electronics*	2	Berkshire Hathaway *Insurance: property, casualty*	2	General Electric *Electronics*
3	Microsoft *Computers*	3	United Parcel Service *Delivery*	3	Texas Instruments *Semiconductors*

2006		2007	
1	Procter & Gamble *Household & personal products*	1	General Electric *Electronics*
2	General Electric *Electronics*	2	Walt Disney *Entertainment*
3	Walgreen *Food & drug stores*	3	ExxonMobil *Petroleum refining*

2 Financial soundness, 1999–2007

1999		2000		2002	
1	Microsoft *Computers*	1	Fuji Photo Film *Imaging, office equipment*	1	ExxonMobil *Petroleum refining*
2	Intel *Computers*	2	General Electric *Electronics, electrical equipment*	2	Wal-Mart Stores *Retailers: general, speciality*
3	General Electric *Electronics, electrical equipment*	3	United Parcel Service *Delivery*	3	Intel *Computers*

2003		2004		2005	
1	Microsoft *Computers*	1	United Parcel Service *Delivery*	1	Intel *Semiconductors*
2	Berkshire Hathaway *Insurance: property & casualty*	2	Procter & Gamble *Household & personal products*	2	Texas Instruments *Semiconductors*
3	ExxonMobil *Petroleum refining*	3	Exxon Mobil *Petroleum refining*	3	Exxon Mobil *Petroleum refining*

2006		2007	
1	Exxon Mobil *Petroleum refining*	1	Exxon Mobil *Petroleum refining*
2	United Parcel Service *Delivery*	2	Berkshire Hathaway *Insurance: property & casualty*
3	Intel *Semiconductors*	3	Walt Disney *Entertainment*

3 Quality of goods and services, 1999–2007

1999	2000	2002
1 Intel *Computers*	1 New York Times *Publishing*	1 Toyota Motor *Motor vehicles*
2 Procter & Gamble *Household & personal products*	2 Singapore Airlines *Airlines*	2 Intel *Semiconductors*
3 EMC *Computers*	3 Target *Retailers: general, specialty*	3 United Parcel Service *Delivery*

2003	2004	2005
1 PepsiCo *Beverages*	1 Tesco *Food & drug stores*	1 Texas Instruments *Semiconductors*
2 United Parcel Service *Delivery*	2 Procter & Gamble *Household & personal products*	2 Alcoa *Metals*
3 Procter & Gamble *Household & personal products*	3 United Parcel Service *Delivery*	3 FedEx *Delivery*

2006	2007
1 Walt Disney *Entertainment*	1 Walt Disney *Entertainment*
2 Procter & Gamble *Household & personal products*	2 FedEx *Delivery*
3 Tesco *Food & drug stores*	3 Anheuser-Busch *Beverages*

4 People management, 1999–2007

1999	2000	2002
1 Microsoft *Computers*	1 General Electric *Electronics*	1 Intel *Semiconductors*
2 Home Depot *Specialist retailers*	2 Enron *Energy transmission, providers*	2 General Electric *Electronics*
3 Intel *Semiconductors*	3 Merck *Pharmaceuticals*	3 Walgreen *Food & drug stores*

2003	2004	2005
1 General Electric *Electronics*	1 Procter & Gamble *Household & personal products*	1 General Electric *Electronics*
2 Procter & Gamble *Household & personal products*	2 Walgreen *Food & drug stores*	2 Procter & Gamble *Household & personal products*
3 PepsiCo *Consumer food products*	3 Johnson & Johnson *Pharmaceuticals*	3 Intel *Semiconductors*

2006	2007
1 Procter & Gamble *Household & personal products*	1 Procter & Gamble *Household & personal products*
2 General Electric *Electronics*	2 FedEx *Delivery*
3 Walgreen *Food & drug stores*	3 General Electric *Electronics*

5 Value as a long-term investment, 1999–2007

1999		2000		2002	
1	Berkshire Hathaway *Insurance: property, casualty*	1	Home Depot *Retailers: general, specialty*	1	Citigroup *Megabanks*
2	Home Depot *Retailers: general, specialty*	2	Wal-Mart Stores *Retailers: general, speciality*	2	Exxon Mobil *Petroleum refining*
3	Intel *Computers*	3	General Electric *Electronics, electrical equipment*	3	Berkshire Hathaway *Insurance: property, casualty*

2003		2004		2005	
1	Procter & Gamble *Household & personal products*	1	Exxon Mobil *Petroleum refining*	1	Berkshire Hathaway *Insurance: property, casualty*
2	Berkshire Hathaway *Insurance: property, casualty*	2	United Parcel Service *Delivery*	2	Procter & Gamble *Household & personal products*
3	Caterpillar *Industrial & farm equipment*	3	Berkshire Hathaway *Insurance: property, casualty*	3	Exxon Mobil *Petroleum refining*

2006		2007	
1	Exxon Mobil *Petroleum refining*	1	Berkshire Hathaway *Insurance: property, casualty*
2	Walgreen *Food & drug stores*	2	Exxon Mobil *Petroleum refining*
3	General Electric *Electronics*	3	Walt Disney *Entertainment*

6 Capacity to innovate, 1999–2007

	1999		2000		2002
1	Home Depot *Retailers: general, specialist*	1	Enron *Energy transmission, providers*	1	Intel *Semiconductors*
2	Intel *Computers*	2	Nokia *Network communications, internet technology*	2	Texas Instruments *Semiconductors*
3	Fortune Brands *Metals, metal products*	3	Home Depot *Retailers: general, specialist*	3	AOL Time Warner *Entertainment*

	2003		2004		2005
1	PepsiCo *Beverages*	1	Procter & Gamble *Household & personal products*	1	FedEx *Delivery*
2	Procter & Gamble *Household & personal products*	2	Tesco *Food & drug stores*		Procter & Gamble *Household & personal products*
3	Citigroup *Megabanks*	3	Citigroup *Megabanks*	3	Alcoa *Metals*

	2006		2007
1	Apple Computer *Computers*	1	Apple *Computers*
2	Procter & Gamble *Household & personal products*	2	FedEx *Delivery*
3	Walt Disney *Entertainment*	3	Walt Disney *Entertainment*

7 Globalness, 1999–2007

1999	2000	2002
1 IBM *Computers*	1 Nestlé *Food production, processing*	1 Citigroup *Megabanks*
2 McDonald's *Food services*	2 News Corporation *Entertainment*	2 Caterpillar *Industrial & farm equipment*
3 General Electric *Electronics, electrical equipment*	3 Coca-Cola *Beverages*	3 Procter & Gamble *Household & personal products* Texas Instruments *Semiconductors*

2003	2004	2005
1 Caterpillar *Industrial & farm equipment*	1 Procter & Gamble *Household & personal products*	1 Alcoa *Metals*
2 Citigroup *Megabanks*	2 Citigroup *Megabanks*	2 Nestlé *Food production, processing*
3 Procter & Gamble *Household & personal products*	3 Nestlé *Food production, processing*	3 FedEx *Delivery*

2006	2007
1 Nestlé *Food production, processing*	1 Procter & Gamble *Household & personal products*
2 Procter & Gamble *Household & personal products*	2 Nestlé *Food production, processing*
3 General Electric *Electronics*	3 FedEx *Delivery*

8 Community, social and environmental responsibility, 1999–2007

1999	2000	2002
1 IBM *Computers*	1 Target *General merchandisers*	1 Target *General merchandisers*
2 Procter & Gamble *Household & personal products*	2 New York Times *Publishing*	2 Procter & Gamble *Household & personal products*
3 Home Depot *Retailers: general & specialist*	3 Merck *Pharmaceuticals*	3 United Parcel Service *Delivery*

2003	2004	2005
1 United Parcel Service *Delivery*	1 BP *Petroleum refining*	1 United Parcel Service *Delivery*
2 Johnson & Johnson *Pharmaceuticals*	2 Procter & Gamble *Household & personal products*	2 Alcoa *Metals*
3 BP *Petroleum refining*	3 United Parcel Service *Delivery*	3 Anheuser-Busch *Beverages*

2006	2007
1 Tesco *Food & drug stores*	1 United Parcel Service *Delivery*
2 International Paper *Forest & paper products*	2 Alcan *Metals*
3 Anheuser-Busch *Beverages*	3 Walt Disney *Entertainment*

9 Use of corporate assets, 1999–2007

1999	2000	2002
1 Home Depot *Retailers: general, specialist*	1 Home Depot *Retailers: general, specialist*	1 Berkshire Hathaway *Insurance: property & casualty*
2 General Electric *Electronics, electrical equipment*	2 General Electric *Electronics, electrical equipment*	2 Walgreen *Food & drug stores*
3 Procter & Gamble *Household & personal products*	3 Wal-Mart *Retailers: general, speciality*	3 Citigroup *Megabanks*

2003	2004	2005
1 Berkshire Hathaway *Insurance: property, casualty*	1 Procter & Gamble *Household & personal products*	1 Berkshire Hathaway *Insurance: property, casualty*
2 Procter & Gamble *Household & personal products*	2 United Parcel Service *Delivery*	2 General Electric *Electronics, electrical equipment*
3 BP *Petroleum refining*	3 Berkshire Hathaway *Insurance: property, casualty*	3 Exxon Mobil *Petroleum refining*

2006	2007	
1 Exxon Mobil *Petroleum refining*	1 Exxon Mobil *Petroleum refining*	
2 Walgreen *Food & drug stores*	2 Berkshire Hathaway *Insurance: property, casualty*	
3 Tesco *Food & drug stores*	3 Walt Disney *Entertainment*	

Sources

All category rankings in the world's most admired surveys come from *Fortune* and were published as follows: 1999–2002 October (US edition); 2003–07 March (European edition).

Appendix 6

Britain's most admired companies: examples of correlations between categories

The correlation coefficient is a statistical value that exists between +1 and −1 for two sets of data. It is a single number that describes the degree of relationship between two variables, in this case the quality of management and each of the other categories. The closer the figure is to +1, the greater is the correlation between two categories.

These figures have been calculated over a 13-year period (1994–2006) and illustrate the nature of the correlations between some of the categories in Britain's most admired company surveys.

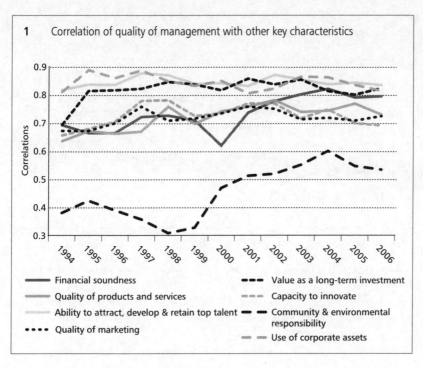

1   Correlation of quality of management with other key characteristics

Legend:
- Financial soundness
- Quality of products and services
- Ability to attract, develop & retain top talent
- Quality of marketing
- Value as a long-term investment
- Capacity to innovate
- Community & environmental responsibility
- Use of corporate assets

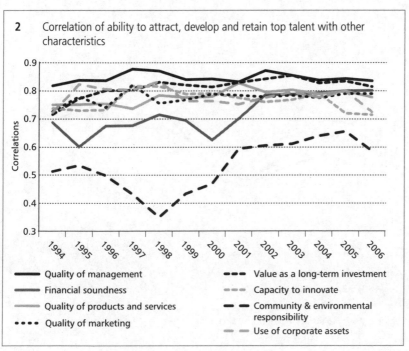

2   Correlation of ability to attract, develop and retain top talent with other characteristics

Legend:
- Quality of management
- Financial soundness
- Quality of products and services
- Quality of marketing
- Value as a long-term investment
- Capacity to innovate
- Community & environmental responsibility
- Use of corporate assets

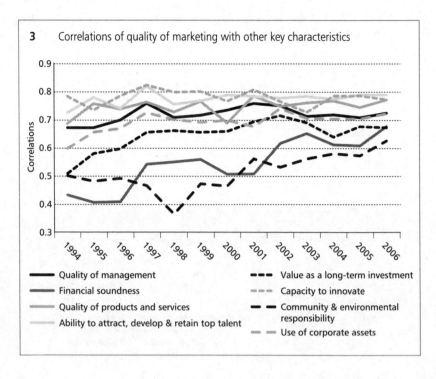

3   Correlations of quality of marketing with other key characteristics

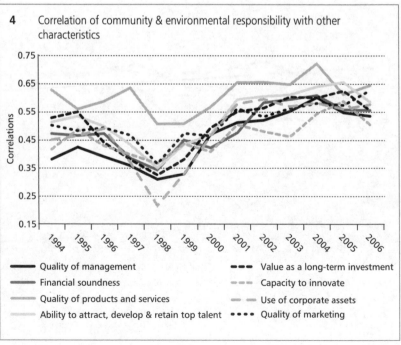

4   Correlation of community & environmental responsibility with other characteristics

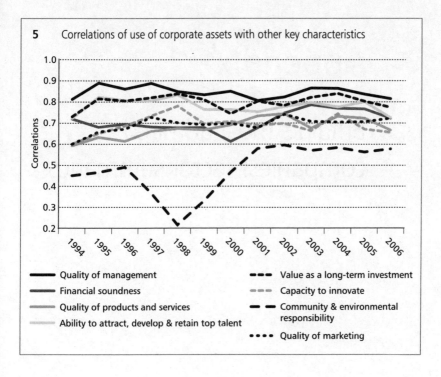

5 Correlations of use of corporate assets with other key characteristics

Legend:
- Quality of management
- Financial soundness
- Quality of products and services
- Ability to attract, develop & retain top talent
- Value as a long-term investment
- Capacity to innovate
- Community & environmental responsibility
- Quality of marketing

Appendix 7

Britain's most admired companies: sector summaries

1 Building materials and merchants, 2007

	QMan	Rank	FS	Rank	QG&S	Rank	AAT	Rank	VLTI	Rank	CI	Rank	QMar	Rank	C&ER	Rank	UCA	Rank	TOTAL	Rank
1 BSS	7.7	3	7.3	4	7.2	3	6.4	2	6.5	3	6.2	5	5.7	7	5.6	7	6.6	3	59.2	4
2 Electrocomponents	5.3	10	5.8	9	6.8	5	5.5	7	5.2	10	5.8	8	5.8	5	4.6	9	5.4	8	50.2	9
3 Galiform	5.8	8	5.7	10	5.8	10	5.3	9	5.4	8	5.9	7	5.7	7	4.6	9	5.1	10	49.2	10
4 Hanson[a]	5.8	7	8.0	1	6.6	6	5.7	6	6.2	5	5.5	10	5.6	9	6.5	3	6.1	6	55.9	5
5 Headlam	6.3	6	6.5	6	6.4	9	5.1	10	5.6	7	6.4	3	5.8	3	5.3	8	6.0	7	53.3	7
6 Marshalls	7.8	1	6.9	5	7.9	1	6.8	1	6.0	6	7.6	1	7.8	1	7.4	1	6.8	2	65.1	1
7 Premier Farnell	5.5	9	6.3	8	6.5	8	5.4	8	5.4	9	6.0	6	5.8	5	5.9	5	5.4	9	52.0	8
8 SIG	7.7	2	7.7	2	7.4	2	6.3	4	7.9	1	6.7	2	6.0	2	6.1	4	6.9	1	62.7	2
9 Travis Perkins	7.2	4	7.3	3	6.9	4	6.3	3	6.7	2	6.3	4	5.8	3	6.7	2	6.6	4	59.9	3
10 Wolseley	7.0	5	6.4	7	6.6	6	6.1	5	6.2	4	5.6	9	5.3	10	5.8	6	6.4	5	55.4	6

a Merged, acquired or name change

QMan = Quality of management, FS = Financial soundness, QG&S = Quality of goods & services, AAT = Ability to attract, develop and retain top talent, VLTI = Value as a long-term investment, CI = Capacity to innovate, Mar = Quality of marketing, C&ER = Community and environmental responsibility, UCA = Use of corporate assets

2 Engineering: aero and defence, 2007

	QMan	Rank	FS	Rank	QG&S	Rank	AAT	Rank	VLTI	Rank	CI	Rank	QMar	Rank	C&ER	Rank	UCA	Rank	TOTAL	Rank
1 BAE Systems	6.9	4	8.0	1	7.6	3	7.3	2	7.2	2	6.5	4	6.5	2	5.3	5	5.9	8	61.2	3
2 Chemring Group	6.1	7	6.2	8	7.1	4	6.0	7	6.8	4	5.8	9	5.7	7	5.5	4	6.4	4	55.4	6
3 Cobham	6.9	3	7.5	3	7.7	2	7.3	2	6.9	3	7.1	3	6.4	3	5.8	3	7.1	1	62.8	2
4 GKN	7.1	1	6.6	6	7.0	6	6.4	5	6.3	6	6.2	7	6.3	5	6.2	2	6.1	5	58.0	4
5 Meggitt	6.5	5	6.6	5	6.8	8	6.0	6	6.4	5	6.4	5	5.5	8	5.0	9	6.8	3	56.0	5
6 QinetiQ Group	5.5	9	6.5	7	6.8	7	6.9	4	5.4	9	7.8	2	4.7	10	5.2	6	5.4	9	54.2	8
7 Rolls-Royce	7.0	2	7.9	2	8.1	1	7.3	1	8.0	1	7.8	1	6.8	1	6.7	1	6.9	2	66.3	1
8 Smiths Group	5.7	8	7.0	4	6.5	10	5.9	8	5.9	8	5.9	8	6.0	6	5.1	7	6.0	7	54.0	9
9 UMECO	5.0	10	5.8	10	6.6	9	5.0	10	5.0	10	4.6	10	5.0	9	4.4	10	4.8	10	46.2	10
10 VT Group	6.3	6	6.2	9	7.0	5	5.1	9	6.0	7	6.3	6	6.3	4	5.0	8	6.1	6	54.4	7
																			568.4	

QMan = Quality of management, FS = Financial soundness, QG&S = Quality of goods & services, AAT = Ability to attract, develop and retain top talent, VLTI = Value as a long-term investment, CI = Capacity to innovate, Mar = Quality of marketing, C&ER = Community and environmental responsibility, UCA = Use of corporate assets

3 Media, 2007

	QMan	Rank	FS	Rank	QG&S	Rank	AAT	Rank	VLTI	Rank	CI	Rank	QMar	Rank	C&ER	Rank	UCA	Rank	TOTAL	Rank
1 BSkyB	8.2	1	8.2	1	8.2	1	7.7	1	7.4	1	8.4	1	8.1	1	8.2	1	7.6	1	72.0	1
2 Daily Mail & General Trust	7.0	7	7.2	5	7.1	5	6.7	5	6.6	6	6.6	6	6.6	5	5.9	10	6.2	9	59.6	7
3 ITV	6.5	9	5.7	10	6.2	10	5.7	10	5.5	10	5.7	10	5.9	10	6.0	8	5.6	10	52.6	10
4 Pearson	7.0	5	7.4	2	7.8	2	7.5	2	6.9	4	7.0	4	6.3	8	6.7	4	6.6	5	63.1	3
5 Reed Elsevier	6.5	10	7.3	4	7.2	3	6.3	9	5.9	9	5.7	9	6.6	4	6.3	7	6.4	8	58.1	9
6 Reuters	7.0	5	6.9	6	6.9	6	6.5	7	7.1	2	7.1	2	6.2	9	6.8	3	6.7	2	61.3	4
7 Informa	7.4	3	6.8	8	6.9	6	6.9	4	6.4	7	6.4	7	6.4	6	6.6	5	6.6	3	60.6	5
8 United Business Media	6.8	8	6.9	7	6.6	9	6.5	7	6.7	5	6.2	8	6.4	6	5.9	9	6.6	6	58.5	8
9 WPP Group	7.6	2	7.3	3	7.2	4	7.1	3	7.0	3	7.1	2	6.9	3	7.1	2	6.6	3	64.0	2
10 Yell Group	7.2	4	6.7	9	6.9	8	6.7	6	5.9	8	6.7	5	7.3	2	6.4	6	6.5	7	60.2	6
																			609.9	

QMan = Quality of management, FS = Financial soundness, QG&S = Quality of goods & services, AAT = Ability to attract, develop and retain top talent, VLTI = Value as a long-term investment, CI = Capacity to innovate, C&ER = Community and environmental responsibility, UCA = Use of corporate assets

4 Retailers (food and personal), 2007

	QMan	Rank	FS	Rank	QG&S	Rank	AAT	Rank	VLTI	Rank	CI	Rank	QMar	Rank	C&ER	Rank	UCA	Rank	TOTAL	Rank
1 Burberry Group	5.6	6	6.1	7	7.8	4	6.5	5	6.8	4	6.8	4	7.4	4	3.8	8	6.5	4	57.3	5
2 Debenhams	5.5	7	5.7	8	5.6	7	5.3	8	4.8	9	5.4	7	6.4	5	4.2	6	5.6	7	48.3	6
3 Marks & Spencer	8.3	1	8.8	2	8.5	1	8.3	1	8.8	1	8.0	1	9.2	1	8.0	1	8.3	1	76.3	1
4 Monsoon	4.4	9	5.5	9	6.4	6	5.3	7	5.3	8	4.9	8	5.3	7	4.5	5	5.3	8	47.1	8
5 Morrison (Wm)	5.1	8	6.3	5	5.3	8	5.1	9	5.7	6	4.9	8	4.7	9	3.8	9	5.7	6	46.4	9
6 Next	7.4	3	7.6	4	6.6	5	7.0	4	6.7	5	6.3	5	6.0	6	4.6	4	6.5	4	58.7	4
7 Sainsbury (J)	7.4	3	7.8	3	7.9	3	7.3	3	7.6	3	7.7	3	7.6	3	6.9	2	6.9	3	67.1	3
8 Signet	5.8	5	6.3	5	5.3	8	5.6	6	5.7	6	5.6	6	4.8	8	4.1	7	4.8	9	47.9	7
9 Sports Direct	3.9	10	4.2	10	3.6	10	3.6	10	4.1	10	3.6	10	3.5	10	2.4	10	3.6	10	32.5	10
10 Tesco	8.2	2	8.9	1	8.3	2	8.3	2	8.7	2	7.8	2	8.2	2	6.6	3	7.8	2	72.9	2
																			554.6	

QMan = Quality of management, FS = Financial soundness, QG&S = Quality of goods & services, AAT = Ability to attract, develop and retain top talent, VLTI = Value as a long-term investment, CI = Capacity to innovate, Mar = Quality of marketing, C&ER = Community and environmental responsibility, UCA = Use of corporate assets

5 Utilities, 2007

	QMan	Rank	FS	Rank	QG&S	Rank	AAT	Rank	VLTI	Rank	CI	Rank	QMar	Rank	C&ER	Rank	UCA	Rank	TOTAL	Rank
1 British Energy	5.3	7	4.0	10	4.6	10	4.2	9	5.1	7	3.3	10	3.2	9	3.9	9	4.5	9	38.2	10
2 Centrica	6.0	4	6.4	3	4.9	8	6.0	1	5.6	4	5.2	4	5.9	2	4.9	7	5.2	6	50.1	4
3 Drax	5.6	5	5.2	9	5.0	7	4.5	6	4.0	10	3.9	9	3.1	10	3.5	10	6.5	3	41.4	9
4 International Power	6.4	3	6.0	5	5.7	3	6.0	3	5.9	3	5.6	3	3.9	8	4.5	8	6.3	4	50.1	3
5 Kelda	5.4	6	6.2	4	5.2	4	4.7	5	5.5	5	4.8	5	4.4	6	5.6	3	5.4	5	47.2	5
6 National Grid	6.6	2	7.5	1	6.4	2	5.9	4	6.6	1	5.9	2	4.7	4	5.5	4	6.5	2	55.5	2
7 Scottish Power[a]	4.8	9	5.4	7	5.2	5	4.3	8	4.4	9	4.7	6	4.8	3	5.5	4	5.2	7	44.3	6
8 Scottish & Southern Energy	7.5	1	7.3	2	7.3	1	6.0	2	6.5	2	6.0	1	6.2	1	5.7	1	6.6	1	59.1	1
9 Seven Trent	4.2	10	5.5	6	4.7	9	3.9	10	4.6	8	4.4	7	4.5	5	5.3	6	4.4	10	41.5	8
10 United Utilities	4.8	8	5.3	8	5.1	6	4.5	7	5.2	6	4.3	8	4.2	7	5.7	1	4.7	8	43.7	7
																			471.2	

a Merged, acquired or name change

QMan = Quality of management, FS = Financial soundness, QG&S = Quality of goods & services, AAT = Ability to attract, develop and retain top talent, VLTI = Value as a long-term investment, CI = Capacity to innovate, Mar = Quality of marketing, C&ER = Community and environmental responsibility, UCA = Use of corporate assets

Appendix 8

Britain's most admired companies: company profiles

1 Diageo (Guinness), 1990–2007

ECONOMIST	QMan	Rank	FS	Rank	QG&S	Rank	AAT	Rank	VLTI	Rank	CI	Rank	QMar	Rank	C&ER	Rank	UCA	Rank	TOTAL	Rank	TOTAL
1990 Guinness	7.3	2	6.9	7	7.5	2	7.1	2	6.8	4	6.7	1	7.6	1	5.7	7			55.7	2	500.2
1991 Guinness	7.3	2	8.0	1	7.3	2	7.4	1	7.9	1	6.7	1	8.0	1	5.4	3			58.1	2	480.7
1992 Guinness	8.2	1	8.3	1	8.4	1	8.3	1	8.3	1	7.5	1	8.2	1	6.0	3	7.5	1	70.7	1	530.5
MANAGEMENT TODAY																					
1994 Guinness	7.1	1	7.4	3	7.6	1	7.2	1	7.9	1	7.0	2	7.6	1	6.5	4	7.3	1	65.7	1	568.1
1995 Guinness	6.8	3	7.8	2	8.0	2	7.1	2	7.4	2	5.9	3	7.7	2	5.9	2	6.9	2	63.5	2	543.5
1996 Guinness	6.6	5	7.1	3	7.5	1	7.1	1	6.7	4	6.2	4	7.5	1	5.6	7	6.3	4	60.8	3	542.9
1997 Guinness	6.0	5	7.5	1	7.6	1	7.2	1	6.8	2	6.0	2	6.8	2	5.7	1	6.4	1	59.8	1	485.5
1998 Diageo	7.4	1	8.4	1	7.6	1	7.8	1	7.2	1	6.6	2	7.4	1	5.8	2	7.1	1	65.2	1	521.0
1999 Diageo	7.0	5	6.2	5	7.2	3	7.8	1	7.0	5	6.0	4	7.8	1	5.9	5	6.6	4	61.4	4	555.9
2000 Diageo	6.7	6	7.1	2	7.6	2	6.9	2	6.8	4	5.8	4	6.8	3	5.4	7	6.5	2	59.6	2	550.1
2001 Diageo	6.3	4	7.1	2	7.1	1	6.4	1	6.8	1	6.3	2	6.3	1	4.9	6	6.3	5	57.5	1	492.6
2002 Diageo	7.3	1	8.0	1	7.7	1	7.0	1	7.7	1	7.7	1	8.0	1	5.7	1	8.0	1	67.0	1	488.9
2003 Diageo	7.3	1	8.0	1	7.8	1	7.8	1	7.3	1	7.2	1	7.6	1	6.6	1	7.1	1	66.7	1	498.0
2004 Diageo	6.4	4	7.0	1	7.0	1	6.8	1	7.5	1	6.4	1	6.8	1	6.4	1	6.8	2	61.1	2	498.0
2005 Diageo	7.2	3	8.4	1	8.1	1	7.8	2	7.6	1	6.0	2	7.4	1	6.4	1	7.2	1	66.1	1	550.5
2006 Diageo	6.3	9	7.9	1	8.0	1	7.1	1	7.1	2	7.1	1	8.0	1	6.7	1	6.6	3	64.7	3	561.8
2007 Diageo	7.0	5	8.1	1	7.9	1	7.9	1	7.3	1	6.7	1	7.6	1	7.0	1	7.0	1	66.5	1	569.8

QMan = Quality of management, FS = Financial soundness, QG&S = Quality of goods & services, AAT = Ability to attract, develop and retain top talent, VLTI = Value as a long-term investment, CI = Capacity to innovate, Mar = Quality of marketing, C&ER = Community and environmental responsibility, UCA = Use of corporate assets

2 Marks & Spencer, 1990–2007

ECONOMIST	QMan	Rank	FS	Rank	QG&S	Rank	AAT	Rank	VLTI	Rank	CI	Rank	QMar	Rank	C&ER	Rank	UCA	Rank	TOTAL	Rank	TOTAL
1990 Marks & Spencer	8.2	1	8.9	1	8.3	1	7.7	1	7.6	1	6.3	4	6.1	4	8.6	1		1	61.71	1	463.13
1991 Marks & Spencer	8.6	1	9.1	1	8.9	1	8.1	1	8.4	1	7.5	2	7.6	2	8.4	1		1	66.51	1	476.83
1992 Marks & Spencer	8.1	1	9.0	1	8.5	1	7.8	1	8.1	1	6.8	2	7.1	2	7.5	2	6.9	1	69.80	1	550.06
MANAGEMENT TODAY																					
1994 Marks & Spencer	8.5	1	9.2	1	8.3	1	8.0	1	8.6	1	7.5	1	7.2	2	7.3	1	7.7	1	72.26	1	538.90
1995 Marks & Spencer	8.3	1	9.1	1	7.9	1	7.7	1	8.2	1	6.8	2	6.8	3	6.2	2	6.9	2	67.89	1	529.03
1996 Marks & Spencer	8.1	1	9.4	1	8.2	1	7.3	2	8.1	1	6.6	2	6.9	2	7.5	1	7.2	2	69.14	2	521.66
1997 Marks & Spencer	8.4	2	9.0	1	8.3	1	8.0	2	8.2	1	6.9	2	7.0	3	6.9	1	7.3	2	70.09	1	520.76
1998 Marks & Spencer	8.3	1	9.0	1	8.4	1	7.9	1	6.9	1	6.5	1	6.1	4	7.7	1	6.5	1	67.24	1	483.26
1999 Marks & Spencer	5.5	4	7.3	2	5.8	5	5.8	3	5.8	4	4.3	7	4.2	8	6.4	1	4.9	6	50.00	4	467.17
2000 Marks & Spencer	4.2	10	6.5	2	6.5	2	4.7	9	5.0	10	3.5	10	4.3	9	5.0	2	4.2	10	43.83	10	502.10
2001 Marks & Spencer	3.6	10	6.0	9	4.4	10	3.6	10	4.4	10	2.9	10	2.6	10	5.7	3	3.3	10	36.44	10	536.00
2002 Marks & Spencer	6.8	6	6.8	4	7.1	3	6.8	3	7.0	3	6.6	4	6.3	6	6.9	1	5.6	9	59.75	3	573.36
2003 Marks & Spencer	7.0	2	7.0	2	8.2	2	7.2	3	6.8	2	6.0	5	7.0	2	5.5	4	6.5	2	61.17	3	547.10
2004 Marks & Spencer	5.6	6	6.2	5	6.8	6	5.9	3	5.2	5	4.8	7	4.8	7	6.7	1	5.0	7	51.00	5	513.17
2005 Marks & Spencer	5.9	6	5.5	7	6.9	5	5.9	6	4.2	10	5.1	8	6.4	3	6.2	1	6.1	5	52.14	6	538.57
2006 Marks & Spencer	7.7	2	7.4	2	8.0	2	7.5	2	7.0	3	7.1	3	7.3	3	6.3	3	7.0	3	65.21	2	572.30
2007 Marks & Spencer	8.3	1	8.8	2	8.5	2	8.3	1	8.8	1	8.0	1	9.2	1	8.0	1	8.3	1	76.33	1	554.57

QMan = Quality of management, FS = Financial soundness, QG&S = Quality of goods & services, AAT = Ability to attract, develop and retain top talent, VLTI = Value as a long-term investment, CI = Capacity to innovate, Mar = Quality of marketing, C&ER = Community and environmental responsibility, UCA = Use of corporate assets

3 Rentokil Initial, 1990–2007

ECONOMIST	QMan	Rank	FS	Rank	QG&S	Rank	AAT	Rank	VLTI	Rank	CI	Rank	QMar	Rank	C&ER	Rank	UCA	Rank	TOTAL	Rank	TOTAL
1990 Rentokil Group	6.86	2	7.45	2	7.18	4	6.23	3	6.86	2	6.00	4	7.50	1	6.65	2		1	54.73	2	487.96
1991 Rentokil Group	7.60	1	7.90	2	7.50	2	6.66	2	6.70	2	5.90	3	7.90	1	7.00	2		1	57.16	1	473.19
1992 Rentokil	9.17	1	8.50	1	8.33	1	7.50	1	7.17	1	8.17	1	8.50	1	6.17	1	7.83	1	71.33	1	456.38
MANAGEMENT TODAY																					
1994 Rentokil	8.63	1	8.63	2	7.75	2	8.13	1	8.88	1	7.88	1	8.25	1	7.75	1	8.25	1	74.13	1	497.51
1995 Rentokil	8.10	1	7.80	1	7.40	1	7.70	1	7.20	1	7.10	1	7.00	1	5.80	1	7.30	1	65.40	1	511.98
1996 Rentokil	8.00	1	6.83	2	6.92	2	7.33	1	7.25	2	6.75	1	7.08	1	5.92	1	6.42	2	62.50	1	510.76
1997 Rentokil Initial	8.50	1	7.15	2	7.46	3	7.46	1	7.31	2	6.62	4	8.08	1	6.67	1	7.81	1	67.05	2	567.88
1998 Rentokil Initial	7.14	1	7.00	2	7.00	1	7.43	1	7.29	1	6.71	3	6.57	2	6.00	1	6.43	2	61.57	1	537.48
1999 Rentokil Initial	6.67	2	7.33	2	7.33	2	7.33	1	6.67	2	5.67	4	6.33	3	5.50	4	6.00	4	58.83	2	528.77
2000 Rentokil Initial	5.4	9	7.1	1	6.4	5	6.4	2	5.4	9	5.0	8	5.4	8	5.1	2	5.9	6	52.0	4	527.36
2001 Rentokil Initial	5.6	7	5.5	7	6.8	4	6.4	6	4.6	9	5.1	10	6.5	4	5.4	8	5.8	5	51.6	7	543.85
2002 Rentokil Initial	6.8	4	8.0	1	7.2	2	6.6	3	6.6	3	6.6	2	6.6	1	6.6	1	8.0	1	63.0	2	566.08
2003 Rentokil Initial	7.0	5	7.8	3	7.5	2	6.7	6	7.3	4	6.7	4	7.2	1	6.0	2	7.2	4	63.3	4	584.65
2004 Rentokil Initial	4.9	10	5.7	9	6.3	9	5.3	10	5.4	9	5.9	7	6.6	6	6.3	5	6.0	8	52.3	9	588.22
2005 Rentokil Initial	3.7	10	4.9	9	5.4	10	4.4	9	3.7	10	4.5	10	4.6	10	4.6	10	4.2	10	40.1	10	521.59
2006 Rentokil Initial	4.1	10	3.7	10	4.3	10	4.1	10	4.2	10	4.1	10	4.3	10	6.3	2	4.2	10	39.4	10	525.47
2007 Rentokil Initial	4.5	10	4.3	10	4.6	10	4.8	10	4.1	10	3.4	10	4.7	10	6.3	3	4.3	10	40.9	10	570.28

QMan = Quality of management, FS = Financial soundness, QG&S = Quality of goods & services, AAT = Ability to attract, develop and retain top talent, VLTI = Value as a long-term investment, CI = Capacity to innovate, Mar = Quality of marketing, C&ER = Community and environmental responsibility, UCA = Use of corporate assets

4 Royal Bank of Scotland, 1990–2007

ECONOMIST	QMan	Rank	FS	Rank	QG&S	Rank	AAT	Rank	VLTI	Rank	CI	Rank	QMar	Rank	C&ER	Rank	UCA	Rank	TOTAL	Rank	TOTAL
1990 Royal Bank of Scotland	5.6	8	7.4	5	6.1	6	5.3	7	6.0	4	5.5	6	5.6	5	6.2	1		1	47.7	6	467.95
1991 Royal Bank of Scotland	6.1	4	6.9	6	6.1	4	6.1	3	6.4	5	6.1	3	6.1	4	4.9	6		1	48.6	4	437.18
1992 Royal Bank of Scotland	6.3	4	6.7	6	6.0	5	6.1	4	6.1	5	6.5	2	5.9	2	5.9	4	5.6	4	55.1	4	505.95
MANAGEMENT TODAY																					
1994 Royal Bank of Scotland	6.6	4	6.8	4	6.3	1	5.9	5	5.9	5	5.8	2	4.5	4	4.2	9	5.9	5	52.0	4	477.47
1995 Royal Bank of Scotland	6.5	3	6.8	8	6.7	1	5.7	6	6.3	4	6.8	1	6.7	7	5.3	5	6.2	2	57.0	3	530.39
1996 Royal Bank Of Scotland	6.4	8	7.5	8	6.8	3	6.4	5	6.6	4	6.8	2	6.3	3	5.9	3	6.4	7	59.1	4	581.07
1997 Royal Bank Of Scotland	5.8	8	6.4	9	6.6	3	5.8	5	5.8	7	6.1	3	5.5	5	5.4	3	5.7	7	53.0	7	549.12
1998 Royal Bank of Scotland	6.3	6	6.9	9	6.4	5	5.9	7	6.0	7	6.9	3	5.3	9	5.9	3	5.9	7	55.5	8	574.95
1999 Royal Bank Of Scotland	6.7	4	7.0	4	6.9	1	6.4	4	6.7	4	6.9	1	6.0	1	5.7	3	6.9	3	59.1	3	537.48
2000 Royal Bank of Scotland	6.8	4	7.6	5	6.3	5	6.7	5	7.2	2	6.7	4	6.2	3	4.8	6	6.8	2	59.1	3	552.83
2001 Royal Bank of Scotland	7.1	3	8.2	4	7.2	2	7.1	2	7.3	2	7.2	1	5.4	7	5.5	2	7.3	1	62.4	2	561.47
2002 Royal Bank of Scotland	7.7	1	8.2	2	6.5	6	7.7	1	7.6	2	6.6	3	5.8	6	5.8	4	7.7	1	63.3	3	549.45
2003 Royal Bank Of Scotland	7.8	1	7.7	2	6.7	4	7.4	2	7.8	1	6.7	2	6.3	2	5.6	3	7.5	1	63.4	2	543.73
2004 Royal Bank of Scotland	8.5	1	8.4	2	6.7	2	7.8	1	7.7	2	6.5	4	6.3	3	5.7	3	7.3	2	64.7	2	534.69
2005 Royal Bank of Scotland	7.8	1	8.5	2	6.0	3	7.6	2	7.6	1	6.5	4	6.1	4	5.8	5	7.3	2	63.3	2	550.05
2006 Royal Bank of Scotland	7.4	1	7.6	3	7.1	2	7.5	3	6.8	3	6.6	3	6.4	3	5.3	6	6.4	4	61.0	3	499.42
2007 Royal Bank of Scotland	8.3	1	8.1	1	6.3	2	7.5	1	7.4	1	6.8	1	6.4	3	6.3	5	6.7	4	63.48	1	549.80

QMan = Quality of management, FS = Financial soundness, QG&S = Quality of goods & services, AAT = Ability to attract, develop and retain top talent, VLTI = Value as a long-term investment, CI = Capacity to innovate, Mar = Quality of marketing, C&ER = Community and environmental responsibility, UCA = Use of corporate assets

Notes and references

Authors' note

1 Peters, T.J. and Waterman, R.H., *In search of excellence: Lessons from America's best run companies*, Harper and Row, New York, 1984.

1

1 Sir Clive Thompson's speech at the Savoy Hotel, London, 26 March 1997.
2 Fombrun, C.J. and Van Riel, C.B.M., *Fame and Fortune*, Prentice Hall, New York, 2004.
3 Fombrun, C.J. and Shanley, M., 'What's in a name? Reputation building and corporate strategy', *Academy of Management Journal*, Vol. 33, No. 2, 1990, pp. 233–58.
   Fombrun, C.J., *Reputation: realizing value from the corporate image*, Harvard Business School, Boston, MA, 1996.
   Fombrun, C., Gardberg, N. and Sever, J. M., 'The reputation quotient: a multi-stakeholder measure of corporate performance', *Journal of Brand Management*, Vol. 7, Issue 4, 2000, pp. 241–55.
   Pruzan, P., 'Corporate reputation: Image and identity', *Corporate Reputation Review*, Vol. 4, Issue 1, 2001, pp. 50–65.
4 Fombrun and Van Riel, op. cit.
5 Independent researchers including academic institutions and consultants have deconstructed and reconstructed the most admired surveys investigating their merits. Some of these studies are identified here. Separate studies have been undertaken in Britain's, America's and the world's most admired company surveys identifying the benefits of a positive reputation:
   Filbeck, G. and Preece, D., 'Fortune's best 100 companies to work for in America: Do they work for share holders', *Journal of Business Finance and Accounting*, Vol. 30, 2003, pp. 771–97.
   Filbeck, G., Gorman, R. and Preece, D., 'Fortune's Most Admired Firms: An investor's perspective', *Studies in Economics and Finance*, Vol. 18, Issue 1, 1997, pp. 74–94.
   Nanada, S., Schneeweis, T. and Eneroth, K., 'Corporate performance and firm perception: the British experience', *European Financial Management*, Vol. 2, No. 2, 1996, pp. 197–221.
   Filbeck, G. and Preece, D., 'Britain's Most Admired Firms: Are they worth it?', *Journal of Global Business*, Vol. 6, No. 11, 1995, pp. 23–30.

A good reputation correlates with superior returns:
Anderson, J. and Smith, G., 'A great company can be a great investment', *Financial Analysts Journal*, Vol. 62, Issue 4, 2006, pp. 86–93.

Antunovich, P., Laster, D. and Mitnick, S., 'Are high-quality firms also high-quality investments?', *Current Issues in Economics and Finance*, Federal Reserve Bank of New York, Vol. 6, No. 1, 2000, pp. 1–6.

Vergin, R.C. and Qoronfleh, M.W., 'Corporate reputation and the stock market', *Business Horizons*, Jan/Feb 1998, pp. 19–25.

A good reputation encourages shareholders to invest in a company:

Brown, D.M., 'The value of corporate reputation: Self perceptions, peer perceptions and market perceptions', PhD thesis, York University Library, 2006.

A good reputation attracts the best people:

Hamori, M., 'The impact of reputation capital on the career paths of departing employees', *Journal of Intellectual Capital*, Vol. 4, No. 3, 2003, pp. 304–15.

Filbeck, G. and Preece, D., 'Fortune's best 100 companies to work for in America: Do they work for shareholders?', *Journal of Business Finance and Accounting*, Vol. 30, 2003, pp. 771–97.

Hendry, C., Woodward, S., Harvey-Cook, J. and Gaved, M., 'Investors' views of people management', *Corporate Governance*, Vol. 7, No. 4, 1999, pp. 324–37.

A good reputation helps companies retain customers:

Luo, X. and Bhattacharys, C.B., 'Corporate social responsibility, customer satisfaction and market value', *Journal of Marketing*, Vol. 70, October 2006, pp. 1–18.

Luo, X. and Homburg, C., 'Neglected outcomes of customer satisfaction', *Journal of Marketing*, Vol. 71, April 2007, pp. 133–49.

Ittner, C.D. and Larcker, D.F., 'Are nonfinancial measures leading indicators of financial performance? An analysis of customer satisfaction', *Journal of Accounting Research*, Supplement, 1998, pp. 1–35.

Perhaps the most often undertaken research has been in terms of corporate and social responsibility and reputation:

Brammer, S.J. and Pavelin, S., 'Corporate Reputation: The importance of fit', *Journal of Management Studies*, Vol. 43, Issue 3, 2006, pp. 435–55.

Salama, A., 'A note on the impact of environmental performance on financial perspective', *Structural Change and Dynamic Economics*, Vol. 16, 2005, pp. 413–21.

Elsayed,K. and Paton, D., 'The impact of environmental performance on firm performance: static and dynamic panel data evidence', *Structural Change and Economic Dynamics*, Vol. 16, 2005, pp. 395–412.

Hasseldine, J., Salama, A.I. and Toms, J.S., 'Quantity versus quality: The impact of environmental disclosures on the reputations of UK Plcs', *British Accounting Review*, Vol. 37, 2005, pp. 231–48.

Toms, J.S., 'Firm resources, quality signals and the determinants of corporate environmental reputation: Some UK evidence', *British Accounting Review*, Vol. 34, 2002, pp. 257–82.

Waddock, S., 'The multiple bottom lines of corporate citizenship: Social investing, reputation, and responsibility audits', *Business and Society Review*, Vol. 105, Issue 3, 2000, pp. 323–45.

Herremans, I.M., Akathaporn, P. and McInnes, M., 'An investigation of corporate social responsibility reputation and economic performance', *Accounting Organizations and Society*, Vol. 18, No. 7/8, 1993, pp. 587–604.

Other research suggests that these positive relationships are not confined to the immediate period but also extend into the past and the future periods:

Brown, D.M., 'The value of corporate reputation; self perceptions, peer perceptions and market perceptions', PhD thesis, York University Library, 2006.

Roberts, P.W. and Dowling, G.R., 'Corporate reputation and sustained superior performance', *Strategic Management Journal*, Vol. 22, 2002, pp. 1077–93.

Fombrun, C.J. and Shanley, M., 'What's in a name? Reputation building and corporate strategy', *Academy of Management Journal*, Vol. 33, No. 2, 1990, pp. 233–58.

Lastly, there are several studies that indicate the strong relationship between management and corporate reputation:

Agarwal, V., Taffler, R. and Brown, D.M., 'Is management quality relevant?'. Paper presented at European Financial Management meeting, Basel, July 2004, and INQUIRE UK, Edinburgh, September 2004.

Epstein, M. J. and Roy, M-J., 'Evaluating and monitoring CEO performance: Evidence from US compensation committee reports', *Corporate Governance*, Vol. 5, No. 4, 2005, pp. 75–87.

Straw, B.M. and Epstein, M.J., 'What bandwagons bring: Effects of popular management techniques on corporate performance, reputation and CEO pay', *Administrative Science Quarterly*, Vol. 45, 2000, pp. 523–56.

The surveys are not without their critics, however. Some argue, for instance, that the financial characteristic, being the least intangible of the characteristics, has an abnormal weight among respondents, hence the term financial 'halo' effect:

Fryxell, G.F. and Wang, J., 'The Fortune corporate "reputation" index: Reputation for what?', *Journal of Management*, Vol. 20, No. 1, 1994, pp. 1–14.

Brown, B. and Perry, S., 'Removing the financial performance halo from Fortune's most admired companies', *Academy of Management Journal*, Vol. 37, 1994, pp. 1347–59.

6 Kaplan, R.S. and Norton, D.P., *Strategic maps: Converting intangible assets into tangible outcomes*, Harvard Business School, Boston, MA, 2004.

7 Fombrun and Van Riel, op. cit.

8 *Management Today*, December 1995.

9 Ibid.

2

1 Lustgarten, A., 'Dell beats Wal-Mart as Most Admired', *Fortune*, 22 February 2005.

2 *Fortune*, 9 January 1984.

3 Berkshire Hathaway, Owners Manual, 1996.

4 Kinder Morgan Energy Partners, Annual Report, 2006.

5 UPS, 'Social Responsibility', corporate website, 2007.

6 'Growing for Globalization: GE and Benetton's differing approach', *Strategic Direction*, Vol. 18, No. 8, 2002 (© MCB UP Ltd ISSN 0258–0543).

7 Henderson, K.M. and Evans, J.R., 'Successful implementation of Six Sigma: Benchmarking General Electric Company', *Benchmarking: An International Journal*, Vol. 7, No. 4, 2000 (© MCB UP Ltd ISSN 1463–5771C). Also on globalization and reputation, Miles, L. and Davies, G. 'The effect of globalization on reputation', *Strategic Communication Management*, Vol. 2, Issue 5, 1998, pp. 14–20.

8 Fishman, C., *The Wal-Mart Effect*, Penguin Books, 2007.

9 'The World's Largest Banks in 2006', *Euromoney*, August 2007.

10 Carrefour, 2006 Results Presentation.

11 BP, Annual Report and Accounts, 2006.

12 Edward de Bono and Robert Heller's 'Thinking Managers'. Heller, R., 'Business Reputations: How self-congratulation can destroy reputations and your business', 1 September 2004, www.thinkingmanagers.com/management/business-reputations.php

13 *Fortune*, 22 February 2006.

14 Corporate Executive Board, *Innovation and Agility*, Corporate Leadership Council, Washington, 2001.

15 The Disney Institute, *Quality Service*, The Disney Approach Series, 2007.

16 Hawn, C., 'If He's So Smart ... Steve Jobs, Apple, and the Limits of Innovation', *Fast Company*, Issue 78, January 2004. Hawn wrote:

> 'For most of its existence, Apple has devoted itself single-mindedly, religiously, to innovation.
>
> 'But wait. What can possibly be wrong with that? After all, we worship innovation as an absolute corporate good, along with such things as teamwork and leadership. Even more than these virtues, it has come to be seen as synonymous with growth. Political economists have assigned tremendous significance to it since at least the mid-20th century. Innovation is at the heart of Joseph Schumpeter's idea of creative destruction, for example: the process of "industrial mutation" that keeps markets healthy and progressive. Management theorists embraced the notion in the intervening decades, and a stream of academic papers and books promoting innovation as the critical element of business success issued forth from the likes of Peters and Drucker, Foster and Christensen. Innovate or die, we were told. It's the core of excellence and the root of entrepreneurship. It's the attacker's advantage, the new imperative, the explosion, the dilemma and the solution. (You can play this game at home, too, with any of the 49,529 titles that come up for "innovation" on Amazon.) And yet it's hard to look at Apple without wondering if innovation is really all it's cracked up to be.'

3

1 Speech at the American Chamber of Commerce – India/Confederation of Indian Industry, New Delhi, India, 18 December 2006.

2 Peter Jennings, 'One on One with Bill Gates', abc News, 16 February 2005.

3 Agarwal, V., Brown, D.M. and Taffler, R., 'Is management quality relevant?', unpublished article presented in Vienna, June 2007.

4 For notes on impression management see Leary, M.R. and Kowalski, R.M., 'Impression management: A literature review and two-component model', *Psychological Bulletin*, Vol. 107, Issue 1, 1990, pp. 34–47; Rosenfeld, P., Giacalone, R.A. and Riordan, C.A., *Impression Management in Organizations*, Routledge, London, 1995; Schlenker, B.R., *Impression Management: The self-concept, social identity, and interpersonal relations*, Brooks/Cole, Monterey, CA, 1980; Goffman, E., *The Presentation of Self in Everyday Life*, Doubleday Anchor, Garden City, NY, 1959.

5 Telegraph.co.uk, 28 April 2007.

6 BBC News, March 1999.

7 Bevan, J., *The Rise and Fall of Marks & Spencer ... and How It Rose Again*, Profile Books, London, 2001, p. xiv. Bevan's book provides an excellent account of how

the company evolved, declined and then pulled itself up by the bootstraps. See also Beaver, G., 'Competitive advantage, corporate governance and reputation management: The case of Marks & Spencer Plc', *Journal of Communication Management*, Vol. 4, Issue 2, 1999, pp. 185–96.

8 Marks & Spencer, press release, May 2007, and Bevan, op. cit, p. 287.

9 *Management Today*, December 2002.

10 Taylor, B., 'Shell shock: why do good companies do bad things', *Corporate Governance*, Vol. 14, No. 3, May 2006.

11 *Fortune*, 6 March 2006.

12 Toyota, Annual Report, 2006.

13 Spear, S.J., 'Learning to lead at Toyota', *Harvard Business Review*, May 2004.

14 Stewart, T.A. and Raman, P.A., 'Lessons from Toyota's Long Drive, Interview with Katsuaki Watanabe', *Harvard Business Review*, July/August 2007.

15 Kroll, M.J., Tooms, L.A. and Wright, P., 'Napoleon's tragic march home from Moscow: lessons in hubris', *Academy of Management Executive*, Vol. 14, No. 1, 2000, pp. 117–27; Hayward, M.L.A and Hambrick, D.C., 'Explaining the premiums paid for large acquisitions: Evidence of CEO hubris', *Administrative Science Quarterly*, Vol. 42, Issue 1, 1997, pp. 103–29; Roll, R., 'The hubris hypothesis of corporate takeovers', *Journal of Business*, Vol. 59, Issue 2, 1986, pp. 197–216.

4

1 *Fortune*, January 1990.

2 Graham, B., *The Intelligent Investor*, Collins Business Essentials, New York, 2006. Benjamin Graham knew his stuff when it came to investments. He entered Wall Street in June 1914 and was still commenting on financial soundness of stocks and shares in 1972. Warren Buffett is a fan.

3 *The Economist*, January 1991.

4 *Management Today*, December 2007.

5 Intel, Annual Report, 2006.

6 Collins, J., *Good to Great*, Harper Business, New York, 2001. Written in response to the question: Why don't any high technology companies appear in the study set?

7 Caulfield, B., 'Intel's Margin of Safety', Forbes.com, 16 October 2007.

8 Kobrick, F.R., *The Big Money*, Simon and Schuster Paperbacks, New York, 2007.

9 Land Securities, Group Fact Sheet, 2007.

10 Waples, J., 'Freeze puts City at tipping point', *Sunday Times*, 9 September 2007.

11 Siegel, J.G. and Shim, J.K., *Dictionary of Accounting Terms*, Barron's Business Guides, New York, 2005.

12 'Land Securities builds brand with Hat Trick', *Design Week*, 11 January 2007, p. 5.

13 J. Max Robins, 'Rupert's Gambit', Broadcasting and Cable, 6 August 2007.

14 News Corporation, Annual Report, 2007.

15 News Corporation, Annual Report, 2007.

16 Kobrick, op. cit.

5

1 *Fortune*, 3 March 2003.

2 Swinney, Z., 'Service is key to success', *iSixSigma* magazine, 2007.

3 Pande, P.S., Neuman, R.P. and Cavanagh, R., *The Six Sigma Way*, McGraw Hill, New York, 2000. Also on quality and perception, see Millson, F. and Kirk-

Smith, M., 'The effect of quality circles on perceived service quality in financial services', *Journal of Marketing Practice: Applied Marketing Science*, Vol. 2, No. 4, 1996, pp. 75–88.

4 Harry, M. and Schroeder, R., *Six Sigma*, Currency, New York, 2000.

5 Ibid.

6 Ibid.

7 Walton, M., *The Deming Method*, Management Books 2000 Ltd, 1994.

8 Pande *et al.*, op. cit.

9 Steinhauer, J., 'Are Nordstrom's Efforts Eroding Profits?', *New York Times*, 14 May 1997.

10 Nordstrom, Annual Report, 2006.

11 *Information Week*, 24 July 2000. There is some evidence that a variation of this happened way up in the north-west, where Nordstrom acquired a company that had once sold tyres but didn't any more, but some are still out to prove or disprove the story.

12 Steinhauer, op. cit.

13 Grewal, R. and Slotegraaf, R.J., 'Embeddedness of Organizational Capabilities', *Decision Sciences*, Vol. 38, No. 3, 2007.

14 Spector, R. and McCartney, P.D., *The Nordstrom Way: The Inside Story of America's No 1 Customer Service Company*, Wiley, New York, 2000.

15 *The Economist*, 26 January 1991.

16 Bevan, J., *The Rise and Fall of Marks & Spencer*, revised edition, Profile Books, London, 2007.

17 Rose, S., 'Back in Fashion', *Harvard Business Review*, Vol. 85, Issue 5, May 2007.

18 Genentech, Annual Report, *Where Science Meets Life*, 2006. Genentech is controlled by Roche Holding, a Switzerland-based 'research driven healthcare company that develops, manufactures and markets innovative, high-quality products and services'. Roche's pharmaceuticals divisions also include Chugai of Japan. 'Roche for Investors', Roche corporate website, 2008.

19 Genentech, corporate website, 2007.

20 Herper, M., 'Genentech's Next Act', Forbes.com, 26 January 2007.

21 Ibid.

22 Takenaka Corporation, *Datamonitor*, 13 January 2007.

23 Takenaka, corporate website, 2007.

24 Jido, J., *Quality management with TQM in Takenaka Corporation*, Proceedings of International Conference on Quality, Yokohama, 1996.

25 Wong, A. and Fung, P., 'Total quality management in the construction industry in Hong Kong: A supply chain management perspective', *Total Quality Management*, March 1999.

26 Takenaka, corporate website, 2007.

27 'Building a stronger alliance for the 21st century', special Japan advertising section, *Forbes*, 4 January 1993.

27 Stein, S., 'Steve Wynn', *Time* magazine, 30 April 2006. This was in response to Wynn's new development:

> For the Wynn Las Vegas, his $2.7 billion, 2,716-room hotel (an additional 2,054-room tower is on the way), he spent a year walking the 215-acre Strip property, jotting down ideas for the space and changing the rules he had created to make Vegas boom in the '90s. Instead of luring the suckers with beacon attractions right on the Strip – like his dancing waters at the Bellagio, pirate ship at Treasure Island and volcano at the Mirage – with Wynn Las Vegas, he hid the waterfalls, puppets

and giant screens behind man-made mountains, reserving them for his diners, gamblers and guests. The draw isn't glitz; it's buzz. He dropped the theme-hotel motif and made the hallways low and intimate. He broke the most basic rule of casinos by flooding the place with natural light. And he focused on small, calm spaces.

28 SEC filing number 1–06697, 30 September 1998.

6

1 Jagger, S., 'The hands-on approach that could mobilise the great and good at Davos', *The Times*, 21 January 2008.
2 CIPD, *Talent: Strategy, Management, Measurement*, Chartered Institute of Personnel and Development, London, 2007.
3 Gurchiek, K., 'Leadership Gap Poses Biggest Crisis, Executives Say', SHRM Online, 5 April 2007. This highlights a study by Bersin and Associates, *High Impact Talent Management*, 2007.
4 Chambers, E.G., Foulon, M., Jones, H.H., Hankin, S.M. and Michaels, E.G. III, 'The War for Talent', *McKinsey Quarterly*, 1998.
5 McGregor, J. and Hamm, S., 'Managing the Global Workforce', *Business Week*, 28 January 2008.
6 Bob Sutton, professor of management science and engineering at Stanford, Harvard Business Online, April 2007.
7 Unilever, 'Our Brands', corporate website, 2007.
8 Couwenbergh, P., 'Business Interview: Patrick Cescau, Chief Executive, Unilever', *Independent on Sunday*, 16 October 2005.
9 Collins, *Good to Great*, op. cit.
10 Ibid.
11 Vise, D.A., *The Google Story*, Pan Books, London, 2006.
12 Chartered Institute of Personnel and Development (CIPD), 'Developing Your Talent', HRD 2007, London, 17–19 April.
13 CIPD, 'Talent Management Update', Talent Management Conference, London, 19 June 2007.
14 CIPD, *Talent: Strategy, Management, Measurement*, op. cit.
15 CIPD, 'Talent Management Update', op. cit.
16 CIPD, 'Developing Your Talent', HRD 2007, London, 17–19 April.
17 Fisher, A., 'How admired companies find the best talent', *Fortune*, 23 February 2006.
18 Ready, D.A. and Conger, J.A., 'Make Your Company a Talent Factory: Stop losing out on lucrative business opportunities because you don't have the talent to develop them', *Harvard Business Review*, June 2007.
19 CIPD, *Talent: Strategy, Management, Measurement*, op. cit.
20 Friedmann, T., *The World is Flat: A Brief History of the Twenty-first Century*, Farrar, Straus and Giroux, New York, 2005.
21 'War for Talent II: Seven Ways to Win', *Fast Company*, December 2000.

7

1 Dow Theory Forecasts, Horizon Publishing Co., 27 August 2007.
2 Serco, 'Bringing Services to Life', corporate website, 2007.
3 Friedmann, *The World is Flat*, op. cit.
4 Dobbs, L., *Exporting America*, Warner Business Books, New York, 2004.

5 Rappaport, A., *Creating Shareholder Value*, The Free Press, New York, 1986.
6 Taggart, J.M., Kontes, P.W. and Mankins, M.C., *The Value Imperative*, The Free Press, New York, 1994.
7 Wolseley, 'The Name the World Builds On', corporate website, 2007.
8 Hamilton, S., 'The US Housing Slump Hits Wolseley Profits', *International Herald Tribune*, 25 September 2007.
9 Reece, D., 'Paul Walsh: The Smirnoff Ice man cometh to slate the drinks industry opposition', *Independent*, 17 September 2005.
10 'Walsh Says Diageo Brands Resilient to US Economic Downturn', Bloomberg. com, 30 August 2007.
11 Birkinshaw, J., 'Diageo's High Spirits', *Business Strategy Review*, Vol. 14, Issue 3, Autumn 2003.
12 Flexnews, Business News for the Food Industry, 27 September 2007.
13 ExxonMobil, *Taking on the World's Toughest Energy Challenges*, 2006 Summary Annual Report.
14 Stanford University, Global Climate and Energy Project (GCEP), 2007.
15 Birkinshaw, J., Van Batenburg, R. and Murray, G., 'Venturing to succeed', *Business Strategy Review*, Vol. 13, Issue 4, 2002.
16 'Verbund, BASF, The Chemical Company', corporate website, 2007.
17 Ibid.
18 Anderson, J. and Smith, G., 'A great company can be a great investment', *Financial Analysis Journal*, Vol. 62, Issue 4, July/Aug 2006, pp 86–93.
19 Antunovich, P., Laster, D. and Mitnick, S., 'Are high-quality firms also high-quality investments?', *Current Issues in Economics and Finance*, Vol. 6, No. 1, 2000.

8

1 Hawn, C., 'If He's So Smart ... Steve Jobs, Apple and the Limits of Innovation', *Fast Company*, January 2004.
2 Blessing White, *Leading Technical Professionals*, Princeton, 2006.
3 Colvin, G., '• and A: on the Hot Seat', *Fortune*, 27 November 2006.
4 'The Seed of Apple's Innovation', *Business Week*, 12 October 2004. Steve Job's said:

> But innovation comes from people meeting up in the hallways or calling each other at 10:30 at night with a new idea, or because they realized something that shoots holes in how we've been thinking about a problem. It's ad hoc meetings of six people called by someone who thinks he has figured out the coolest new thing ever and who wants to know what other people think of his idea.
>
> And it comes from saying no to 1,000 things to make sure we don't get on the wrong track or try to do too much. We're always thinking about new markets we could enter, but it's only by saying no that you can concentrate on the things that are really important.

5 Huston, L. and Sakkab, N., 'Connect and Develop: Inside Procter & Gamble's New Model for Innovation', *Harvard Business Review*, Vol. 84, No. 3, March 2006.
6 Ibid.
7 BSkyB Annual Report 2006
8 *The Guardian*, 13 July 2007.
9 Hawn, op. cit.
10 *Business Week*, op. cit.

11 Lafley, A.G. and Charan, R., *The Game Changer: How You Can Drive Revenue and Profit Growth with Innovation*, Crown Business, 2008.

12 Collins, *Good to Great*, op. cit.

13 Venkataraman, S., *PepsiCo: The Challenge of Growth Through Innovation*, Paper written with Summers, M., University of Virginia Darden School Foundation, Charlottesville, VA, 2002.

14 Collins, op. cit.

9

1 Kranhold, K., 'The Immelt Era, Five Years Old, Transforms GE', *Wall Street Journal*, 11 September 2006.

2 Kotler, P. and Armstrong, G., *Principles of Marketing*, Prentice Hall, London, 1989.

3 Macrae, C., *World Class Brands*, Addison Wesley Publishing, Wokingham, 1991.

4 De Chernatony, L. and Cottam, S., 'Internal brand factors driving successful financial services brands', *European Journal of Marketing*, Vol. 40, No. 5/6, 2006, pp. 611–33.

5 Ambler, T., 'Market metrics: what should we tell the shareholders?', *Balance Sheet*, Vol. 10, No. 1, 2002.

6 Aaker, D.A., *Managing Brand Equity*, The Free Press, New York, 1991.

7 Milmo, D., 'Another Blow to Image of World's Favourite Airline', *Guardian Unlimited*, 2 August 2007.

8 'Cadbury Schweppes Wins Britain's Most Admired Company Award', Press Release, 1 December 2004. CEO Todd Stitzer commented on the award (overall winner):

> Cadbury Schweppes is a company built on a foundation of strong values. It has been nurtured by generations of principled leaders passionate about performance and stewardship in the broadest sense, and driven for over 200 years by hundreds of thousands of loyal employees dedicated to compelling product quality, customer satisfaction and community well-being. I am honoured to accept this award on behalf of our 55,000 employees, without whose commitment and dedication this success would not be possible.

9 Cadbury Schweppes, 'Marketing Code of Practice', corporate website, 2007.

10 Cadbury Schweppes, *Marketing Code of Practice*, Issue 2, 14 September 2005, www.brandspeoplelove.com, 2007.

11 Rolls-Royce, corporate website, 2007.

12 Morrison, M., 'Product development of Rolls-Royce Aerospace Group', *Flight International*, 17 July 2007.

13 Thought Leadership, 'The Power of Access', FedEx, corporate website, 2007.

14 Louis, J.C. and Yazijian, H.Z., *The Cola Wars*, Everest House Publishers, New York, 1980; Allen, F.A., *Secret Formula*, HarperCollins, New York, 1994; Prendergast, M., *For God, Country and Coca-Cola*, Basic Books, New York, 2000.

10

1 Kotler, P. and Lee, N., *Corporate Social Responsibility: Doing the Most Good for Your Company and Your Cause*, John Wiley & Sons, New York, 2004. See also Matthews, M.R., 'Social and environmental accounting: A practical demonstration of ethical concern', *Journal of Business Ethics*, Vol. 14, Issue 8, 1995, pp. 663–73; McGuire, J., Sundgren, A. and Schneeweis, T., 'Corporate

social responsibility and firm performance', *Academy of Management Journal*, Vol. 31, No. 4, 1988, pp. 854–72; Verschoor, C.C., 'Corporate Responsibility: High priority for CEOs', *Strategic Finance*, Vol. 85, Issue 4, 2003, pp. 2–4.

2 Women in Technology website, 2007:

> Women in Technology (WIT) is a not-for-profit organization dedicated to offering women in all levels of the technology industry a wide range of professional development and networking opportunities. One of the organization's main goals is to create a forum where women in technology can be recognized and promoted as role models.

3 BT Group, *Changing World: Sustained Values, Sustainability Report*, 2007.
4 Linn, A., 'What's next for Whole Foods Market', MSNBC, 18 July 2007.
5 Whole Foods Market, 'Welcome to Whole Foods Market, The Whole Philosophy, Products', corporate website, 2007.
6 'Business, the Environment, the Bottom Line', GreenBiz.com, 19 January 2006.
7 UPS, corporate website, 2007. It was noted:

> UPS ranked as one of top 50 businesses for Hispanics. UPS was recognized by *Hispanic Business* magazine as one of the top companies in the world for Hispanics in the workforce. Overall, 50 companies were chosen based on their efforts to hire and retain those of Hispanic descent in their organization. Overall, more than 30 variables were used to measure each company's commitment to Hispanic hiring, promotion, marketing, philanthropy, and supplier diversity.

> UPS named among America's Top Corporations for Women Business Enterprises (WBEs). UPS was included in Women's Business Enterprise National Council (WBENC) list of 'America's Top Corporations for Women's Business Enterprises'. UPS was one of only three companies to be recognized each year since the award was created eight years ago. The award recognizes companies for their programs offering equal access for WBEs in competing for, and winning, corporate contracts for goods and services.

8 UPS, Annual Report, 2006.
9 *The Times*, 24 July 2007.
10 Luo, X. and Bhattacharya, C.B., 'Corporate Social Responsibility, Customer Satisfaction, and Market Value', *Journal of Marketing*, Vol. 70, October 2006.
11 *The Times*, op. cit.

11

1 Siegel and Shim, *Dictionary of Accounting Terms*, op. cit.
2 Cunningham, L.A., *The Essays of Warren Buffett*, John Wiley (Asia) Singapore, 2002.
3 Ibid.
4 'The Best Dividend Payers of the Past Decade', *Motley Fool Income Investor*, March 2007.
5 Pressman, A., 'What the Boss Didn't Get', *Business Week*, 19 March 2007.
6 Hosking, P., 'How Daniels steered clear of toxic waste', *The Times*, 23 February 2008.
7 BHP Billiton, corporate website, 2007.
8 Letter from outgoing CEO Chip Goodyear, BHP Billiton Annual Report, 2007.
9 Jagger, S., 'Less Bang for its Bucks', *The Times*, 17 November 2007.